WOMEN ON CORPORATE BOARDS OF DIRECTORS

Issues in Business Ethics

VOLUME 14

The titles published in this series are listed at the end of this volume.

Women on Corporate Boards of Directors

International Challenges and Opportunities

Edited by

RONALD J. BURKE

School of Business,
York University, Toronto, Canada

and

MARY C. MATTIS

Catalyst, New York City, U.S.A.

KLUWER ACADEMIC PUBLISHERS
DORDRECHT / BOSTON / LONDON

Library of Congress Cataloging-in-Publication Data

Women on corporate boards of directors : international challenges and opportunities /
edited by Ronald J. Burke, Mary C. Mattis.
        p. cm. -- (Issues in business ethics ; v. 14)
    Includes index.
    ISBN 0-7923-6162-8 (hb : alk. paper)
    1. Women executives. 2. Executives. 3. Directors of corporations. I. Burke, Ronald J.
II. Mattis, Mary C. III. Series.

    HD6054.3 .W67 2000
    658.4'22'082--dc21

                                                                    99-089697

    ISBN 0-7923-6162-8

Published by Kluwer Academic Publishers,
P.O. Box 17, 3300 AA Dordrecht, The Netherlands.

Sold and distributed in North, Central and South America
by Kluwer Academic Publishers,
101 Philip Drive, Norwell, MA 02061, U.S.A.

In all other countries, sold and distributed
by Kluwer Academic Publishers,
P.O. Box 322, 3300 AH Dordrecht, The Netherlands.

Printed on acid-free paper

Printed in the Netherlands.

DEDICATION

I dedicate this volume to the memory of my mother, Anne K. Burke. She combined work and family before it became fashionable. Her efforts contributed to a family environment that ultimately produced two writing sons. I also thank my friend and colleague Mary Mattis, along with her associates at Catalyst, for getting me interested in women's roles in corporate governance. Working with her has been a fruitful and rewarding collaboration. Finaly, a number of students have assisted in various projects. These included Rachel Burke, Graeme MacDermid, Elizabeth Kurucz and Cobi Wolpin. Their help is gratefully acknowledged.

Ronald J. Burke
Toronto, Canada

None of the research on which I have reported in this volume would have been possible without my co-workers at Catalyst, the staff of the Research and Advisory Services and Communications departments, and Catalyst's President, Sheila Wellington. Catalyst's annual censuses of women directors and corporate officers are funded by Sara Lee, whose Chairman and CEO, John Bryan, is a stalwart advocate for women's advancement in business. We are grateful for his generosity in funding this important research. In addition, I am indebted to my co-author, Ron Burke, who has been a major source of encouragement, inspiration and support over the years that we have worked together on projects of mutual interest. My husband, Richard Preston, cheers me on both in word and deed, and makes it all worthwhile.

Mary C. Mattis
New York, New York, USA

CONTENTS

CONTRIBUTORS

Ronald J. Burke, Editor, School of Business, York University, 4700 Keele Street, North York, Ontario, M3J 1P3, Canada.

Mary C. Mattis, Editor, Catalyst, 120 Wall Street, Fifth floor, New York, New York, 10005, USA.

Diana Billimoria, Department of Organizational Behavior, Weatherhead School of Management, Case Western Reserve University, 10900 Euclid Avenue, Cleveland, Ohio 44106-7234, USA.

Patricia Bradshaw, Schulich School of Business, York University, 4700 Keele Street, North York, Ontario, M3J 1P3, Canada.

Zena M. Burgess, Director, Student and Residential Services, Mail No. 22, Swinburne University of Technology, P.O. Box 218, Hawthorn, Victoria 3122, Australia.

Trevis S. Certo, Kelley School of Business, Indiana University, 1309 E. 10th Street, Management Department, Bloomington, Indiana, 47405-1701, USA.

Denise K. Conroy, School of Management, Queensland University of Technology, GPO Box 2434, Brisbane, Queensland 4001, Australia.

Catherine M. Daily, Kelley School of Business, Indiana University, 1309 E. 10th Street, Management Department, Bloomington, Indiana, 47405-1701, USA.

Dan R. Dalton, Kelley School of Business, Indiana University, 1309 E. 10th Street, Management Department, Bloomington, Indiana, 47405-1701, USA.

Nanette Fondas, 1345 Bentley Court, Southlake, Texas, 76092-9438, USA.

Vicki M. Holton, Ashbridge Management College, Ashbridge, Berkhamsted, Hertfordshire, HP4 1N5, England.

Dafna Izraeli, Department of Sociology, Bar Ilan University, Ramat Gan 52900, Israel.

David Leighton, RR3, Old River Road, Komoka, Ontario, N0L 1R0, Canada.

Judy McGregor, Department of Human Resource Management, Faculty of Business Studies, Massey University, Palmerston North, New Zealand.

Merle Pollak, Catalyst, 120 Wall Street, Fifth floor, New York, New York, 10005, USA.

Cecily Cannan Selby, 1 East 66th Street, Apartment 1F, New York, New York, 10021, USA.

Phyllis Tharenou, Department of Business Management, Monash University, P.O. Box 197, A Block, Caulfield East, Victoria 3145, Australia.

Susan Vinnicombe, Cranfield School of Management, Cranfield University, Cranfield, Bedford, MK 430AL, England.

David Wicks, Frank Sobey Faculty of Commerce, St. Mary's University, Robie Street, Halifax, Nova Scotia, B3H 3C3, Canada.

PART ONE

Women Corporate Directors:
A Research Appraisal

WOMEN ON CORPORATE BOARDS OF DIRECTORS: WHERE DO WE GO FROM HERE?[1]

RONALD J. BURKE
School of Business
York University

MARY C. MATTIS
Catalyst
New York, New York

1. Recent Research, Future Directions

Research on corporate board diversity, including gender diversity with which this volume is concerned, has to date largely taken the form of benchmarking – that is, comparing numbers and, to some extent, best practices – across companies and industries. Today, we have a great deal of this type of quantitative information for selected countries on the representation of women on corporate boards. Researchers have also compiled a large body of descriptive data on: (1) corporate boards' recruitment and selection processes; (2) individual women directors' expectations and actual experiences related to their participation on corporate boards; (3) background characteristics of women directors; and, (4) expectations and experiences of Chairmen and CEOs who have brought women onto their companies' boards or are considering doing so. In our experience, benchmarking the progress that companies operating out of different countries are making in increasing the representation of women in corporate governance is useful for:

- expanding our inventory of "best" and "worst" cases, along with the cultural and historical factors associated with women's progress (or lack thereof) in corporate governance
- providing the metrics needed to measure change over time, and to confirm or dispel public perceptions about the extent of progress for women in the arena of corporate governance generating healthy competition among corporate entities that draw on the same global markets and sources of labor

---
[1] Preparation of this manuscript was supported in part by the School o f Business, York University and Catalyst.

R.J. Burke and M.C. Mattis (eds.), Women on Corporate Boards of Directors, 3-10.

- surfacing best corporate practices that are effective in recruiting and effectively utilizing women in corporate governance
- creating change for women

1.1. NEED TO CONTINUE AND EXPAND BENCHMARKING EFFORTS

For these reasons, we need to (1) continue benchmarking activities in countries where research on women directors is well-established; (2) identify sources of data and generate research in geographical areas for which no data currently exist; (3) address barriers to cross-cultural benchmarking that prevent systematic comparisons.

These barriers include:
(1) lack of availability of data for many companies, especially privately-held firms; (2) lack of specific information on women directors' participation and contributions to corporate boards and on a variety of factors related to board dynamics, that cannot be surfaced through use of public documents; (3) lack of information for countries where there are, at present, no requirements for companies to report any information on corporate governance.

Where data is both available and accessible, lack of comparability of sources typically presents an additional barrier to systematic cross-cultural benchmarking of women's progress in advancing to the highest levels of corporate leadership. For example, a 1997 study of women directors in the UK, commissioned by Opportunity 2000, used the *Financial Times* list of top 200 firms, which includes a number of public-sector organizations. A 1998 census of Canadian companies, jointly sponsored by Catalyst and the Conference Board of Canada with assistance from the Schulich School of Business, used the *Financial Post* 500 list, which excludes major financial institutions such as banks and insurance companies, and Crown companies, and contains a much larger proportion of privately-held companies than the *Fortune* 500 list. (Financial and Crown companies were included as separate categories in the analysis.)

Historically, Catalyst used *Fortune* magazine's annual listing of top US companies to compile data on women directors. In 1994, *Fortune* magazine replaced the *Fortune* 500/Service 500 listing containing some 1300 companies with a combined list of industrial and services companies numbering only 500. As a consequence, Catalyst's pre-1994 statistics on women directors are no longer usable for benchmarking purposes within or outside of the US. While the total number of companies on *Fortune's* list is unchanged since 1994, each year 30-50 companies rotate on or off the list, resulting in variations from year to year in the percentage of private and public companies, and service and industrial companies, represented on the list.

Korn Ferry International has, for a number of years, conducted research on corporate boards of US companies using a mail survey of CEOs to determine the size of boards, the representation of women and minorities, and other board characteristics. With less than a 50% response rate, this survey consistently reports a higher representation of women on US corporate boards than does Catalyst's censuses.

1.2. NEED TO BUILD THEORY

At this point in time, we are long on numbers and short on theory relating to gender diversity in corporations. This is not so much a statement about the vitality and potential of the subject matter as it is about the relatively short time frame in which we have focused on this issue. Discussions among researchers at recent conferences points to a general consensus that we need to begin to develop a theoretical body of work about gender diversity on corporate boards that, in combination with benchmarking activities, will move both scholarly dialogue and the pace of change for women forward. Important questions that need to be addressed through rigorous hypothesis testing include:

- Why and for whom is diversity on corporate boards important?
- What difference does diversity make to a board's everyday functioning and to decisions that impact corporate responsibility and profitability?
- Does improving diversity performance in corporations impact corporate productivity and profitability and in what ways?
- What expectations do boards have of women and minority directors?
- Do women and minority directors share these expectations?
- In what ways, if any, does the participation and contributions of women and minority directors differ from those of white male directors?

These and a host of other questions, if addressed, would not only provide answers for scholars in the field, they would also assist practitioners in- and outside of corporations to identify and articulate the business case for diversity on corporate boards.

1.3. FUTURE DIRECTIONS FOR THEORY BUILDING

1.1.1. Predictive Value of Patterns in Countries With Well-Established Benchmarks

Theory building activities might also focus on whether or not patterns of gender representation and participation on US corporate boards, where there are comparatively more women directors, are predictive of outcomes for women in other countries where similar conditions are developing; e.g., is the increased representation of women in corporate professional, technical and management roles predictive of increased representation of women in corporate governance.

In the United States, increased representation of women in corporate management has been accompanied by increased representation of women on corporate boards. In fact these two time series have tracked very closely since 1996 when the Catalyst census of women corporate officers was created to provide data for comparisons with existing information on women directors. In 1998, women held 11.2 percent of corporate board seats compared to 11.1 percent of corporate officer positions in *Fortune* 500 companies; in 1997 the percentages were 10.6 percent and 10.6 percent respectively; and, in 1996 they were 10.3 percent and 10 percent.

Within individual companies, there also is a statistically significant positive correlation between the percentage of women corporate officers in a company and its percentage of women board directors. These data suggest that companies which are alert to women's talents manifest this awareness in multiple aspects of their operations.

Yet, the pace at which progress for women in US companies has occurred has been painfully slow. In 1998, women were 46 percent of the US labor force and 49% of managerial and professional specialty positions, yet their representation at the highest levels of corporate leadership was comparatively small: women held only 3.8% of the highest titles in *Fortune* 500 companies and constituted less than 3 percent of top-earning corporate officers. In 1999, as in 1998, there are only two women *Fortune* 500 CEOs.

Research on the glass ceiling undertaken by scholars in a number of countries point to the fact that women's advancement to top-level corporate executive and, ultimately, governance positions is dependent upon companies' success in providing high potential women with those key developmental opportunities traditionally given to high potential men. These opportunities include positions involving responsibility for profit and loss and revenue production – line and general management roles. Such opportunities need to be built into individual development plans to allow women, as well as men, to gain key competencies and to demonstrate leadership by occupying a series of increasingly challenging management positions historically associated with advancement to the highest leadership roles in their companies. Over the years, Catalyst censuses show only a slight increase in the representation of women corporate officers holding line positions. And, the minute representation of women among inside directors on *Fortune* 500 boards – less than two percent, with virtually no change over the past few years -- reinforces research from a number of sources suggesting that women are not getting the kind of experience they need to compete for the highest level leadership roles in corporate America.

Data from the US, then, suggest that while an increase in women's representation in corporate management is necessary for increased representation of women on corporate boards, it is not sufficient to bring about proportionate representation. That will require a qualitative change in the types and breadth of experience women obtain in corporate management positions.

1.1.2. Impact of Global Developments on National Trends

Another area of hypotheses testing might focus on whether events and trends within individual countries will be superceded by developments in the global business arena. The increasing globalization of corporations is creating a need for business leaders who can operate in a multi-cultural, constantly changing, and highly competitive business environment. Already, in some companies, the scarcity of qualified executives to fill international assignments has become a major constraint on the speed with which they can expand their global reach. Executives with global leadership capabilities will, in turn, constitute the pool from which corporate boards will recruit new board directors, given that international experience is becoming a key selection criterion.

Whether or not the emergence of a global economy will positively impact women's opportunities is yet to be seen and deserves the attention of researchers. Will historically insular corporate boards, for example, consider high level local nationals in their own or other companies as potential candidates for board seats as they seek to grow and compete in a global economy? This could constitute a positive outcome related to increasing women's representation corporate boards in that it would expand the pool of female candidates. However, a potential negative outcome would be exclusion of women executives from corporate board rooms due to their lack of experience with international assignments since, historically, women in US companies have not had equal access to international assignments due to stereotyping and assumptions about that their mobility is more restricted than that of men due to family responsibilities.

1.1.3. Impact of Changes in Board Structure and Dynamics

Finally, there has been considerable speculation that recent trends related to corporate board recruitment policies and practices and increased scrutiny of corporate boards' accountability to various stakeholders will have a positive impact on women's and minorities' representation. A common theme in recent studies of corporate boards is that, like the profile of the female director, corporate boards themselves are evolving in significant ways that will actually enhance board diversity, including,

- Corporate survival has become a central mandate of boards . Faced with an accelerating rate of competition from other countries and the need to develop strategies to compete in a global economy, US corporations have come to a critical juncture. Recent waves of corporate mergers, acquisitions and downsizing are indicative of the dramatic events that are shaping board dynamics. Observers have speculated that globalization of the economy is a positive trend for women, because companies are likely to be increasingly concerned about understanding diverse markets as well as leveraging the diversity in their labor force as a competitive advantage.
- Boards are encountering increasing pressure to protect the interests of non-shareholder constituents such as employees, communities and environmental groups. The increasing representation and influence of outside directors on corporate board boards could benefit women since most women directors come from outside of the companies on whose boards they serve.
- Directors will not automatically be reelected each year. The trend to limit terms of corporate directors will reduce the overall average length of service and free up seats for new candidates.
- Directors are serving on fewer boards due, in part, to increased concern about exposure to liability and the amount of time and work involved in

being a director today. Chairmen, CEOs and COOs – the traditional pool from which corporate directors have been recruited – are most likely to experience concerns in these areas. Conflict of interest is another concern that limits the availability of traditional board director candidates. This trend should positively impact opportunities for women with significant business experience not at the CEO/COO level to be considered for board directorships.

- Other positive indicators for increasing women's representation on boards include growing openness among CEOs, reported by a number of informed sources, for: restricting board tenure and the number of boards on which a director can serve; direct nominations of board members by shareholders; and, board nominating committees composed entirely of independent outside directors.

Whether or not these trends in corporate board organization and operating guidelines impact women's representation on corporate boards in the future is yet to be seen. These and other hypotheses raised by contributors to this volume suggest future directions for research on women directors that would include hypothesis-testing and theory construction.

Interest in corporate governance, and the role of boards of directors in corporate governance, continues to increase. Most of the leading schools of business offer elective courses dealing with boards of directors. An increasing number of executive seminars on corporate governance and the role of directors are being offered by executive development institutions. And more surveys are being conducted by international consulting organizations of corporate board governance which highlight trends and permit comparisons of company practices.

There is a need for more case study research. What happens to board dynamics and process when one women is added - if anything? What happens to board dynamics and process when a second women is added - if anything? What happens to board dynamics and process when half its board members are women - if anything? The National Bank of Canada would like half of its board members to be women. How will they get there?

There is a need to replicate the census-type study in new countries to develop bench-mark data. There is also a need to tie research on women on corporate boards more directly to board process and board effectiveness indicators.

When an organization comes to Catalyst, or another board director placement firm, what happens? What are they looking for? How does the placement firm go about identifying potential appropriate women candidates?

What do consultants who work with boards of directors do to the increase board effectiveness?

We need more intensive understanding of the board experiences of women and men, best obtained through in-depth interviews. How were they identified? How were they nominated and selected? How were they oriented to the board? What are their backgrounds and credentials? What are their roles?

Does board size matter? Does the proportion of women on a board matter as Kanter (1977) suggests? Does it matter if women serve as internal versus external directors?

A major challenge in addressing these critical questions is gaining access to corporate boards so that issues of board dynamics and process may be studied. A cloak of secrecy has traditionally existed in these bodies. Considerable ingenuity will be required here.

2. Specific Research Questions for Consideration

1. What theoretical frameworks have been useful to you in your research on representation of women in high-level management and governance roles?
2. How could we begin to document the impact of women at the top? That is, what empirical outcomes for organizations would we expect to be associated with increased representation of women at the top?
3. What assumptions about women undergird the existing research? Should we challenge those assumptions – how would we go about that?
4. What motivates organizations to address the issue of representation of women at the top? What assumptions about diversity are they operating with?
5. In what ways can academics and applied researchers work together to develop a theory-based approach to research on women at the top? What are the advantages of such collaborations? What are the limitations?
6. What relationships would we hypothesize exist between the representation of women in corporate governance and at senior levels of corporate management?
7. Does the proportionate number of women at the top change the dynamics or outcomes of women's participation in decision-making roles?
8. What empirical differences in the culture, work environment, productivity, retention, opportunities, job satisfaction, etc., would we expect to see in organizations where women have achieved a critical mass in professional and management ranks?
9. Why is the proportion of board members that are women higher in the US than in any other country?

3. The Present Volume

This is the first volume, to our knowledge, devoted exclusively to the subject of women on corporate boards of directors. The overall aim of this book is to present a comprehensive overview of the current international findings on the subject. This volume brings together an international group of eminent contributors who provide censuses of women directors in a number of countries, present research findings important to understandings the small percentage of board members that are women and women's experiences on corporate boards, and suggestions for increasing the number of qualified women now serving on corporate boards.

In keeping with the notion of international opportunities and challenges, authors and research findings represent six countries: Australia, Canada, England, Israel, New Zealand and the United States. Invitations were extended to potential contributors from six other countries as well (France, Mexico, Norway, The Netherlands, Columbia and Malaysia), but given the preliminary state of research in these countries these authors were not yet ready to contribute. The next volume in this area will likely include these countries as well as others.

The contributions are also varied in methods. These include both empirical and conceptual chapters, quantitative and qualitative methodologies, a description of Catalyst's program for assisting corporations identify qualified women candidate for board appointments, and experiences of individuals who have served on corporate boards of directors.

4. Research and Practice

We believe the subject of women on corporate boards of directors has both research and practical relevance. Because this area has only gained research attention within the past decade, many research questions remain unanswered or have been only partially addressed. In addition, increasing the numbers of qualified women serving on corporate boards has practical implications for women, men, corporate boards, and organizations.

We hope this book will serve to interest more organizational researchers to consider the issues of women serving (or aspiring to serve) on corporate boards of directors. We also hope that it will encourage some organizations to make greater efforts to identify potentially qualified women directors.

References

Kanter, R.M. (1977) Men and women of the corporation. New York: Basic Books

THE FUTURE OF CORPORATE WOMEN:

PROGRESS TOWARD THE EXECUTIVE SUITE AND THE BOARDROOM?

CATHERINE M. DAILY
Kelley School of Business
Indiana University
Bloomington, IN 47405-1701

S. TREVIS CERTO
Kelley School of Business
Indiana University
Bloomington, IN 47405-1701

DAN R. DALTON
Kelley School of Business
Indiana University
Bloomington, IN 47405-1701

Abstract

The past two decades have given rise to considerable discussion and debate regarding the extent to which women have made progress in breaking the glass ceiling. This debate is especially salient when considering women's ascension to the boardroom and executive suite. Some organizational observers suggest that considerable progress is evident, while others provide a more pessimistic view of progress. We develop this issue by providing an overview of the rationale offered on both ends of the continuum—that women have made progress in breaking the glass ceiling and that women have made little progress in breaking the glass ceiling. We also summarize two recent studies which examine the extent to which women are better represented among corporate directors and in the executive suite. We conclude with extensions to these studies which empirically examine changes in the profile of female directors, as compared to their male counterparts, over a ten year period.

R.J. Burke and M.C. Mattis (eds.), Women on Corporate Boards of Directors, 11-23.
© 2000 *Kluwer Academic Publishers. Printed in the Netherlands.*

1. Introduction

Both the practitioner and academic communities have voiced strong opinions regarding the progress of women in reaching the executive suite and the corporate boardroom. Proponents on each side of the current debate offer evidence suggesting the accuracy of their respective positions. One view holds: "The fight is over. The battle is won. Women are now accepted as outside directors in the preponderance of corporate boardrooms" (Lear, 1994: 10). An alternative perspective, however, suggests there is much progress left. An illustration of the type of remaining barriers is provided by T. J. Rodgers, chief executive officer (CEO) of Cypress Semiconductor Corp., who has commented that "a 'woman's view' on how to run our semiconductor company does not help us" (Rodgers, 1996: 14).

Regardless of where one falls along the spectrum anchored at one end by the view that women have made substantial progress in reaching the upper echelons of corporations and anchored at the other end by the view that women have barely begun to penetrate the "inner sanctum" of corporations, the central issue is the extent to which women have succeeded in cracking the proverbial "glass ceiling." The glass ceiling is a metaphorical barrier which prevents women from attaining the upper-most organizational positions (e.g., Karr, 1991; Morrison, White, Van Velsor, and the Center for Creative Leadership, 1992; Powell & Butterfield, 1994; U. S. Department of Labor, 1991). While the exact level at which the glass ceiling exists across organizations is subject to some debate, our focus is on the executive suite and boardroom. We believe that admission to these ranks would provide some evidence that the glass ceiling has been permeated, if not removed.

We focus on both directors and CEOs because we see these positions as intertwined with regard to addressing progress in breaking the glass ceiling. As will be developed, service as a corporate CEO may be an essential criteria for being selected for service on other firms' boards of directors (e.g., Lorsch & MacIver, 1989). Also, service as an inside director is a common prerequisite for eventual service as CEO (e.g., Vancil, 1987).

The following sections provide an overview of the rationale offered in support of the progress view, as well as rationale which suggests that progress is still largely elusive at the executive and director levels. These sections are followed by empirical evidence from two recent studies which provide some perspective on these respective views. Importantly, we provide overviews and extensions of these two studies which examine the extent of progress in both the traditional, large firm and entrepreneurial environments. Consideration of both domains may be important, as the traditional, large firm environment may provide an overly conservative view of progress. It may be that the entrepreneurial corporate environment provides greater opportunities for women to ascend to prominent corporate positions such as CEO and director. By considering both contexts—the traditional, large firm (i.e., *Fortune* 500) and entrepreneurial (i.e., *Inc.* 100) corporate environments—we believe we will be able to broadly assess the state of progress of female CEOs and directors.

2. In Search of Progress

2.1. THE AFFIRMATIVE VIEW

There are several factors which support the view that women have made substantial progress in breaking into the executive suite and boardroom. One such factor is the extent to which organizations have made a conscious effort to develop and promote female employees. Women have, for example, made substantial progress in securing mid and lower-level management positions. According to the U. S. Department of Labor (1992), 42 percent of managerial positions are now held by women (see also Pipes, 1996). We would anticipate that over time these positions would lead to advancement to the upper-most levels in organizations. Given women's participation at various managerial levels and the influx of women into graduate schools of business beginning in the 1970s, there would appear to be little reason why women would not have ascended to executive and director positions. As noted by Ann Fudge of General Foods: "The bubble has now risen up through the business schools and the corporate arena, so the pool of women with broader experience is greatly expanded" (Schonfeld, 1994: 15).

This position is supported by Harrigan's (1981) finding that the likelihood of a firm appointing a woman to serve on the board of directors is a function of the ratio of female middle managers to total managers. This finding suggests that as women's representation at the lower and middle management levels increases, this progress will filter up through the executive and director ranks. Consistent with this view, the participation of women on corporate boards has steadily grown in recent years, with women now holding just under 11 percent of large firm director positions (*Business Week*, 1997b).

Progress may be self-reinforcing. As more women move into high-ranking corporate positions, the presence of role models may further encourage other women to seek similar positions. Moreover, greater numbers of women in positions of authority may lead to an increase in the general acceptance of women in positions of authority (e.g., Morrison et al., 1992).

Lastly, the increased exposure which the glass ceiling phenomenon has generated in the past decade, in particular, may encourage organizations to more aggressively develop and/or search for women to fill executive and director positions (e.g., Scherer, 1997). As noted by John H. Bryan, CEO/chair of Sara Lee Corporation, the "pool of women with the capability and experience to serve on boards is larger than generally believed. Availability is no longer an excuse" (Sweetman, 1996: 13).

2.2. THE NEGATIVE VIEW

There are also several factors which might lead one to be relatively pessimistic with regard to the progress women have made in reaching the executive and director levels in corporations. While women have clearly made some progress, less than 10 percent of executive-level positions in large corporations are held by women (Barr, 1996; Fisher, 1992; Himelstein & Forest, 1997; Morrison et al., 1992; *Industry Week*, 1997). Moreover, when this focus is narrowed to board chair, CEO, president and vice-president positions, women's representation is a modest 2.4 percent (Himelstein & Forest, 1997).

Another barrier to women's progress is the general perception that women are appointed for affirmative action reasons or to appease special interest groups. Consistent with this view, Karla Scherer, chair of The Karla Scherer Foundation, has criticized female directors as follows: "Too often they are mere sops to appease public opinion" (Scherer, 1996: 4).

A further factor impacting women's progress is the limited exposure to appropriate developmental opportunities (Van Velsor & Hughes, 1990). Job experiences may be fundamental to the management development process (Feldman, 1988; Heisler & Benham, 1992; McCall, Lombardo, & Morrison, 1988; McCauley, 1986; McCauley, Ruderman, Ohlott, & Morrow, 1994; Morrison & Hock, 1986). To the extent to which women have less exposure to visible job opportunities and those opportunities which might prepare them for executive-level responsibilities, they may find themselves less prepared for advancement than their male colleagues (e.g., Bray, Campbell, & Grant, 1974; Davies & Easterby-Smith, 1984; Dipboye, 1987; Hall, 1976; Kelleher, Finestone, & Lowy, 1986; McCall et al., 1988; Morrison et al., 1992; Van Velsor & Hughes, 1990). Ohlott, Ruderman, and McCauley (1994), for example, found that women were equally exposed to new organizational experiences and challenges as their male colleagues, but that the men's job experiences were more critical, more visible, and provided greater external exposure.

More limited job opportunities may also negatively impact women's progress toward the executive suite and boardroom by limiting their ability to effectively fulfill key director roles. These roles include monitoring/control, resource dependence, and service/expertise (Johnson, Daily, & Ellstrand, 1996; Lorsch & MacIver, 1989; Zahra & Pearce, 1989). While we are unaware of any compelling reason why women could not effectively fulfill the monitoring/control role, the resource dependence and service/expertise roles may present problems. The resource dependence role requires directors to serve as linkages between the firm and its environment (Pfeffer, 1972, 1973; Pfeffer & Salancik, 1978; Provan, 1980; Selznick, 1949; Zald, 1967). In this role, directors not only provide access to critical resources in the firm's environment, but they also provide legitimacy to the firm as a function of their reputations. Should women not currently be positioned to serve in this role, we would expect their likelihood of being invited to serve on a corporate board or as CEO to be diminished. This view is also consistent with class hegemony theory which suggests that the corporate elite are chosen as a function of their professional and social connections (D'Aveni, 1990; Ratcliff, 1980; Useem, 1984).

The service/expertise role may also be problematic. This role requires directors to serve as sounding boards and sources of advice and counsel to the CEO. Lorsch and MacIver (1989: 174) suggest that other firms' CEOs may best fill this role since they "have the most relevant experience and expertise to be effective directors." To the extent to which women have not successfully risen to executive-level positions, if not CEO, they might be unlikely to be invited for service on other firms' boards of directors. Earlier we noted T. J. Rodgers' position on female directors. He further commented that "...unless that woman has an advanced degree *and experience as a CEO*" she need not express an interest in a board position at Cypress Semiconductor (Rodgers, 1996: 14; emphasis added). Mr. Rodgers' view would seem to underscore the importance of experience in the executive suite as a precursor for board positions.

A final reason for pessimism with regard to women's progression to the executive suite and boardroom is that women may not remain in positions which expose them to necessary job experiences long enough to be invited to serve on boards or be promoted to the executive suite. This tendency has been noted among women in public accounting. Dalton, Hill, and Ramsey (1997a, 1997b), for example, found that women were more likely than men to leave public accounting partner and manager positions. Additionally, when women leave these positions they tend to leave the accounting profession altogether; whereas their male colleagues tend to simply move to another accounting firm.

3. Empirical Evidence: Which View Is Right?

Two recent studies may help illuminate the extent of progress women have made in advancing to the executive suite and boardroom. Each of these studies has examined women's progress toward the executive suite and boardroom over a ten year period. One study focuses on traditional, large firms (i.e., *Fortune* 500 firms), while the other focuses on smaller, high-growth firms (i.e., *Inc.* 100 firms). These studies are valuable because they provide a relatively comprehensive picture of the state of progress by including both large and entrepreneurial corporations.

The study focusing on traditional, large corporations examined all firms included on the 1988 and 1997 *Fortune* 500 lists (Daily, Certo, & Dalton, in press). The authors empirically examined the extent to which women's representation on corporate boards and in the executive suite has improved over the ten year study period. They found that women had, indeed, made progress in being appointed to corporate boards of directors, but this same progress was not apparent in the executive suite.

Specifically, Daily et al. (in press) found that the presence of women in corporate boardrooms had significantly increased from 1987 to 1996. In 1987 women were represented on 42.6 percent of *Fortune* 500 boards; this number had increased by a significant amount to 81.2 percent by 1996. The authors note, however, that the typical *Fortune* 500 board in 1996 still had, on average, only one female director.

Another finding of note in their study was that the increase in women directors was accompanied by an increase in the proportion of female directors with corporate backgrounds and women employed at organizations which either do, or might do, business with the firm (affiliated directors, e.g., bankers, legal counsel). Daily et al. (in press) suggested that this finding indicated that female directors were not simply appointed to appease special interest groups or demonstrate a commitment to board diversity initiatives. These directors are those which have the requisite skills to be effective at the resource dependence and service/expertise director roles.

Daily et al. (in press) also examined progress toward the executive suite. Contrary to the progress noted in the boardroom, they found no increase in the number of female CEOs from 1987 to 1996. Importantly, they also noted little promise for a significant change in this status. A common progression to CEO involves service as an inside director on the company's board (Vancil, 1987; see also, Bilimoria & Piderit, 1994; Dobrzynski, 1996; Greene & Greene, 1997; Kesner, 1988). Vancil (1987: 139) has noted the value of this succession process: "...if there are two or three candidates to succeed the incumbent CEO, putting them on the board two or three years ahead of the event is an excellent way for the outside directors to get acquainted with them." Consequently, an increase in the number of female CEOs post-1996 would likely be a function of some increase in the number of female inside directors during the study time period. Daily et al. (in press), however, note a decline, not an increase, in both the numbers and proportions of female inside directors from 1987 to 1996.

While these findings are encouraging for women seeking outside directors positions, the findings provide little optimism for women seeking inside director or CEO positions. It may be, however, that the large firm (i.e., *Fortune* 500) environment provides a rather stringent test of women's progress in breaking the glass ceiling. As Dobrzynski (1996: 108) noted of the state of progress: "The score is a little better at smaller, less hierarchical companies..." Consistent with this view, Daily, Certo, and Dalton (1998) examined women's progress among high-growth, entrepreneurial firms. Specifically, they relied on all firms included on the 1987 and 1996 *Inc.* 100 lists. Progress in this domain may, in part, explain the exodus of women from traditional, large firms to entrepreneurial settings (e.g., Brush, 1992; *The Economist*, 1996; Hymowitz, 1997; Ragins, Townsend, & Mattis, 1998; Smith & Smits, 1994).

Daily et al. (1998) found no evidence of progress in women's representation on *Inc.* 100 boards during the study period. In fact, over the ten year period the number of *Inc.* 100 firms with women on the board dropped from 16.9 percent to 16.7 percent. The average *Inc.* 100 board in 1995 had a mere .17 female directors. The level of representation is clearly well below that found for *Fortune* 500 firms during the same time period.

Despite no appreciable change in the representation of women on *Inc.* 100 corporate boards, the profile of the typical female outside director did change significantly. Female directors with corporate backgrounds increased from 12.5 percent to 72.7 percent during the study period. A similar change was not, however, noted for female directors affiliated with firms which either do, or might do, business with the focal firm. In fact, Daily et al. (1998) noted a significant decline in affiliated female directors from 50 percent in 1986 to 18.1 percent in 1995.

Daily et al. (1998) also considered progress toward the executive suite. Here, too, the results are not encouraging. In 1995 there was only one women serving as CEO of an *Inc.* 100 firm, as compared to no women serving in that role in 1986. Consistent with the findings for *Fortune* 500 firms, the authors found a decrease in the number of female inside directors from six to five over the study period. Clearly, the entrepreneurial environment does not afford women greater opportunities to serve as board members or CEOs.

4. Extensions and Discussion

The Daily et al. (in press, 1998) studies provide a mixed view of the state of women's progress in assuming board member and CEO positions. As noted, these studies demonstrate progress in women's representation on boards only for traditional, large corporations. Both the *Fortune* 500 and *Inc.* 100 firms, however, increased the proportion of female directors with corporate experience. Only the *Fortune* 500 firms also increased the proportion of female directors with professional affiliations. No progress was noted in either domain with regard to women assuming the CEO position or being positioned to ascend to CEO through service as inside board members.

We extend the Daily et al. (in press, 1998) studies by investigating two additional aspects of any change in women's representation on corporate boards. Firstly, we consider the extent to which any changes in directors' profiles differ between male and female directors over the 10 year study period. It may be, for instance, that both the proportion of male and female inside directors declined over the study period. We examine this possibility for both inside directors and directors with corporate vs. non-corporate backgrounds. Secondly, we examine the extent to which the "progress" noted for these firms may be overstated as a function of these women holding multiple *Fortune* 500 or *Inc.* 100 directorships respectively.

We consider the extent to which any changes in the representation of female inside directors during the study period are similar to changes in male inside director representation. By comparing the change for both groups we can assess the extent to which the noted decrease in female inside directors for both the *Fortune* 500 and *Inc.* 100 firms may have been a function of a trend toward fewer inside directors among both female and male directors. It may be unreasonable to expect a significant increase in female inside directors if the proportion of male inside directors is also declining over the study period. In 1987, 5.5 percent of all *Fortune* 500 female directors were insiders. This percentage had declined to 1.4 percent of all *Fortune* 500 female directors by 1996. Importantly, this decline is statistically significant ($Z = -3.38$; $p < .01$). During this same period the percentage of all *Fortune* 500 male directors that were insiders was 29.4

percent in 1987. By 1996 this percentage had also declined, to 23.7 percent of all *Fortune* 500 male directors serving as insiders. This decline, too, is statistically significant ($Z = -6.46$; $p < .001$).

We considered the same data for the *Inc.* 100 firms. In 1986, 42.9 percent of all *Inc.* 100 female directors served as insiders. By 1995, this percentage had dropped to 31.3 percent. This difference is not statistically significant ($Z = -.66$); however, the lack of significance is a function of the small total number of female directors in the *Inc.* 100 during these time periods (14 and 16 respectively). As with the *Fortune* 500, there was also a drop in the percentage of male inside directors for the *Inc.* 100. In 1986, 36.7 percent of all male directors in the *Inc.* 100 were insiders. By 1995, this number had dropped to 33.7 percent. We would note that, unlike the *Fortune* 500, this decline was not statistically significant ($Z = -.98$) and the lack of statistical significance was not a function of a small numbers problem.

By placing the decline of female inside directors within the context of the decline in male inside directors during the same time period, we might begin to better appreciate the lack of progress for women on this dimension. Any decline for female inside directors, however, is notable given the low base rate of female directors in 1987 for the *Fortune* 500 firms and in 1986 for the *Inc.* 100 firms.

Another factor in better appreciating the context of progress for female directors is to assess the noted increase in female directors with corporate backgrounds, as compared to any change in the percentage of male directors with corporate backgrounds over the same period. As we previously noted, corporate experience may be essential for subsequent board service (e.g., Lear, 1994). Those individuals with the credentials to effectively discharge the resource dependence and service/expertise director roles would be most likely to be invited for corporate board service. As Lear (1994) has noted, too many women have traditionally lacked the necessary business and executive experience to advance to director positions (see also Bowen & Hisrich, 1986 for related discussion).

Daily et al. (in press) noted a significant increase in female directors with corporate backgrounds from 1987 to 1996. Specifically, 24.3 percent of *Fortune* 500 female directors had corporate backgrounds in 1987. This number increased to 31.2 percent by 1996. This increase was statistically significant ($Z = 2.02$; $p < .05$). During this same time period the percentage of *Fortune* 500 male directors with corporate experience declined from 72.5 percent in 1987 to 67.8 percent in 1996. This difference, too, was statistically significant ($Z = -5.15$; $p < .001$). In comparing the trends for female and male directors in the *Fortune* 500, these findings indicate that corporate experience may have been more critical for women seeking board seats than for their male counterparts.

The findings for the *Inc.* 100 firms differed slightly from those of the *Fortune* 500. The representation of directors with corporate experience increased for both groups, but these increases were not statistically significant. In 1986, 50 percent of female directors in the *Inc.* 100 had corporate profiles. By 1995, this number had increased to 81.3 percent. This increase is statistically significant ($Z = 1.81$); however, as with the female inside directors, the lack of statistical significance is a function of the small number of female directors in the *Inc.* 100 for both years. In 1986, 63.3 percent of the male *Inc.* directors had corporate backgrounds. By 1995, 65.1 percent of male directors had this profile.

These findings, in concert, indicate that not only is corporate experience essential for women's appointment to corporate boards, but that the women appointed to these boards have a profile which enables them to effectively contribute in their various director roles (see also, Bilimoria & Piderit, 1994; Kesner, 1988).

Lastly, we examined the extent to which the overall increase in *Fortune* 500 directorships held by women is a function of the same women holding multiple directorships. Any enthusiasm for the increase in women's representation on corporate boards might be tempered should we find that the same core set of women account for this increase. We do not conduct the same analysis for the *Inc.* 100 firms, as there were no female directors holding multiple *Inc.* 100 directorships in 1986 and there were only two female directors holding multiple *Inc.* 100 directorships in 1995. Both of these women held two *Inc.* 100 directorships.

In 1987, the average female director served on 1.28 *Fortune* 500 boards. By 1996, this number had increased to 1.48. This difference is statistically significant ($Z = 2.99$; $p < .05$). This finding suggests that, on average, a given female director holds .20 more directorships; however, the average number of female directors per board increased from .54 to 1.2 from 1987 to 1996 (Daily et al., in press). Examination of the descriptive statistics reveals the extent of multiple directorships. In 1987, there were 48 female directors holding multiple *Fortune* 500 board seats. Thirty-nine of these women sat on two *Fortune* 500 boards and nine of these women sat on three *Fortune* 500 boards. By 1996, 154 female directors sat on multiple *Fortune* 500 boards. One hundred and twenty-nine of these women sat on two *Fortune* 500 boards, 19 sat on three *Fortune* 500 boards, four women held seats on four *Fortune* 500 boards, and two of these women held boards seats at five *Fortune* 500 firms.

The reliance on a core set of women for *Fortune* 500 directorships may reflect a bias for "name-brand" directors (Dobrzynski, 1993: 50). These multiple directorships may also indicate the presence of a Catch-22 for women seeking board seats (Dobrzynski, 1993). The most direct route to being appointed to a *Fortune* 500 board may be through service on another *Fortune* 500 firm's board. This, too, may create another interesting Catch-22, however, as pressure to limit the number of directorships a given director holds continues to increase (Browning, 1997; Lesly, 1995; Lublin, 1996). Such pressure may constrain continued gains in women's representation on *Fortune* 500 boards unless the perceived qualifications for board service are expanded.

5. Conclusion

We began our review and analysis with the question: Have women made progress in assuming corporate board seats and ascending to the executive suite? The answer is largely no. Even that progress noted, while admirable, does not leave corporate women well-positioned to assume director and executive positions in proportion to their participation in the workforce. We find this unfortunate given that our analysis of female directors' backgrounds and affiliations indicates that women have clearly accumulated the types of skills and experiences which prepare them for such positions.

Importantly, while women have made progress in being appointed to an increasing number of corporate board seats among *Fortune* 500 firms, such progress is not noted among the *Inc.* 100. Moreover, we question whether the proportion of female directors is commensurate with the presence and contributions of women in corporate America. The central issue for us is that effective utilization of the totality of an organization's human resources is ultimately an issue of the organization's ability to achieve sustained competitive advantage in an increasingly complex and rivalrous business environment. Most organizations simply do not have the slack resources to ignore the talents of, on average, 50 percent of their workforce. Inclusion of women's expertise and perspective at all levels of the organization is especially critical for those firms which largely rely on female customers.

James Preston, former CEO of Avon Products Inc., for example, noted that "60% of all purchases in this country are made by women, having women on the board just makes good business sense" (Sweetman, 1996: 13; see also Lublin, 1995). Mary Mattis, co-editor of this volume, has also noted that too many corporations have failed "to recognize the competitive advantage in the recruitment of women" (Bilimoria, 1995: 10). Consistent with these views, a study by Catalyst found "that 41 of the 50 most profitable *Fortune* 500 companies had at least one female director" (Sharpe, 1993: B5). Sheila Wellington, Catalyst President, noted that "[w]omen may help a company's profitability because they bring a different viewpoint to the boardroom. With more diverse points of view boards can make better, more informed decisions" (Sharpe, 1993: B5).

In 1988 Williams noted that "...women are advancing through the corporation on schedule..." (p. 129). Our review suggests that Williams' view may have been overly optimistic; much progress remains. Even those firms making great strides in developing and promoting women have considerable room for improvement. Avon Products Inc., one of the more progressive companies, provides an excellent example. Forty-four percent of senior-level positions at Avon are held by women (*Business Week*, 1997a). Yet, when Avon's board recently selected a CEO, the board chose Charles Perrin, a male outside director at Avon, over two high-ranking female officers of the company (Dugan, 1998; Parker-Pope, 1997). This event poignantly captures the situation senior-level corporate women find themselves facing in the near-term. As noted by Bilimoria (1995: 13): "...even when women do all the right things and have all the right stuff, they continue to be blocked from the inner most circles of power."

References

Barr, S. (1996) Up against the glass, *Management Review* **85 (9)**, 12-18.
Bilimoria, D. (1995) Women directors: The quiet discrimination, *Corporate Board* **July/August**, 10-14.

Bilimoria, D. and Piderit, S. K. (1994) Board committee membership: Effects of sex-based bias, *Academy of Management Journal* **37**, 1453-1477.

Bowen, D. D. and Hisrich, R. D. (1986) The female entrepreneur: A career development perspective. *Academy of Management Review* **11**, 393-407.

Bray, D. W., Campbell, R. J., and Grant, D. L. (1974) *Formative years in business: A long-term AT&T study of managerial lives*, Wiley, New York.

Browning, E. S. (1997) Wharton study connects strengths and flaws of directors to companies' financial returns, *The Wall Street Journal* **April 25**, C2.

Brush, C. G. (1992) Research on women business owners: Past trends, a new perspective and future directions, *Entrepreneurship Theory and Practice* **16 (4)**, 5-30.

Business Week, 1997a, Women must have a champion at the top, **February 17**, 110.

Business Week, 1997b, In business this week: Et cetera, **October 13**, 44.

Daily, C. M., Certo, S. T., and Dalton, D. R. (In Press) A decade of corporate women: Some progress in the boardroom, *none* in the executive suite, *Strategic Management Journal*.

Daily, C. M., Certo, S. T., and Dalton, D. R. (1998) Entrepreneurial ventures as an avenue to the top?: Assessing the advancement of female CEOs and directors in the *Inc.* 100, Manuscript under review.

Dalton, D. R., Hill, J. W., and Ramsey, R. R. (1997a) Women as managers and partners: Context specific predictors of turnover in international public accounting firms, *Auditing Practice & Theory* **16**, 29-50.

Dalton, D. R., Hill, J. W., and Ramsey, R. R. (1997b) The threat of litigation and voluntary partner/manager turnover in big six firms, *Journal of Accounting and Public Policy* **16**, 379-413.

D'Aveni, R. A. (1990) Top managerial prestige and organizational bankruptcy, *Organization Science* **1**, 121-142.

Davies, J. and Easterby-Smith, M. (1984) Learning and developing from managerial work experiences, *Journal of Management Studies* **21**, 169-183.

Dipboye, R. L. (1987) Problems and progress of women in management, in K. S. Doziara, N. H. Moskow and L. D. Turner (eds.), *Working women: Past, present, future*, Bureau of National Affairs, Washington, DC, pp. 116-153.

Dobrzynski, J. H. (1993) The 'glass ceiling': A barrier to the boardroom, too, *Business Week* November **22**, 50.

Dobrzynski, J. H. (1996) Linda Wachner, *Working Woman* **November/December**, 106-108.

Dugan, I. J. (1998) Why Avon called a 'nonwoman', *Business Week* **March** 16, 57-60.

The Economist. (1996) Breaking the glass ceiling **August 10**, 15.

Feldman, D. C. (1988) *Managing careers in organizations*, Scott, Foresman, Glenview, IL.

Fisher, A. B. (1992) When will women get to the top? *Fortune* **September 21**, 44-56.

Greene, K. and Greene, R. (1997) The 20 best-paid women in corporate America: Executive privilege, *Working Woman* **January**, 26-30.

Hall, D. T. (1976) *Careers in organizations*, Goodyear, Pacific Palisades, CA.

Harrigan, K. R. (1981) Numbers and positions of women elected to corporate boards, *Academy of Management Journal* **24**, 619-625.

Heisler, W. J. and Benham, P. O. (1992) The challenge of management development in North America in the 1990s, *Journal of Management Development* **11 (2)**, 16-31.

Himelstein, L. and Forest, S. A. (1997) Breaking through, *Business Week* **February 17**, 64.

Hymowitz, C. (1997) Colleagues often have the wrong ideas about why women quit, *The Wall Street Journal* **November 11**, B1.

Industry Week (1997) Glass ceiling still intact, **November 3**, 11.

Johnson, J. L., Daily, C. M., and Ellstrand, A. E. (1996) Boards of directors: A review and research agenda, *Journal of Management* **22**, 409-438.

Karr, A. R. (1991) Labor's Martin is out to break "glass ceiling", *The Wall Street Journal* **August 9**, B6.

Kelleher, D., Finestone, P., and Lowy, A. (1986) Managerial learning: First notes from an unstudied frontier, *Group and Organization Studies* **11**, 169-202.

Kesner, I. F. (1988) Directors' characteristics and committee membership: An investigation of type, occupation, tenure, and gender, *Academy of Management Journal* **31**, 66-84.

Lear, R. W. (1994) Here come the women directors, *Chief Executive* **April**, 10.

Levy, L. (1995) Are these 10 stretched too thin?, *Business Week* **November 13**, 78-80.

Lorsch, J. W. and MacIver, E. I. (1989) *Pawns or potentates: The reality of America's corporate boards*, Harvard Business School Press, Boston, MA.

Lublin, J. S. (1995) Survey finds more *Fortune* 500 firms have at least two female directors, *The Wall Street Journal* **September 28**, A5.

Lublin, J. S. (1996) Report urges curb on number of directorships, *The Wall Street Journal* **November 12**, B1-B2.

McCall, M. W., Lombardo, M. M., and Morrison, A. M. (1988) *The lessons of experience: How successful executives develop on the job*, Lexington Books, Lexington, MA.

McCauley, C. D. (1986) *Developmental experiences in managerial work: A literature review*, Technical report no. 26, Center for Creative Leadership, Greensboro, NC.

McCauley, C. D., Ruderman, M. R.,..Ohlott, P. J., and Morrow, J. E. (1994) Assessing the developmental components of managerial jobs, *Journal of Applied Psychology* **79 (4)**, 544-560.

Morrison, A. M., White, R. P., Van Velsor, E., and the Center for Creative Leadership (1992) *Breaking the glass ceiling: Can women reach the top of America's largest corporations?*, Addison-Wesley, Reading, MA.

Morrison, R. F. and Hock, R. R. (1986) Career building: Learning from cumulative work experiences, in D. T. Hall & Associates (Eds.), *Career development in organizations*, Jossey-Bass, San Francisco, pp. 236-273.

Ohlott, P. J., Ruderman, M. N., and McCauley, C. D. (1994) Gender differences in managers' developmental job experiences, *Academy of Management Journal* **37**, 46-67.

Parker-Pope, T. (1997) Avon isn't calling on a female CEO yet, *The Wall Street Journal* **December 12**, B1, B6.

Pfeffer, J. (1972) Size and composition of corporate boards of directors: The organizational and its environment, *Administrative Science Quarterly* **17**, 218-228.

Pfeffer, J. (1973) Size, composition, and function of hospital boards of directors: A study of organization-environment linkage, *Administrative Science Quarterly* **18**, 349-364.

Pfeffer, J. and Salancik, G. R. (1978) *The external control of organizations: A resource dependence perspective*, Harper & Row, New York.

Pipes, S. (1996) Glass ceiling? So what?, *Chief Executive* **April**, 16.

Powell, G. N. and Butterfield, D. A. (1994) Investigating the "glass ceiling" phenomenon: An empirical study of actual promotions to top management, *Academy of Management Journal* **37**, 68-86.

Provan, K. G. (1980) Board power and organizational effectiveness among human service agencies, *Academy of Management Journal* **23**, 221-236.

Ragins, B. R., Townsend, B., and Mattis, M. (1998) Gender gap in the executive suite: CEOs and female executives report on breaking the glass ceiling, *Academy of Management Executive* **12**, 28-42.

Ratcliff, R. E. (1980) Banks and corporate lending: An analysis of the impact of internal structure of the capitalist class on the lending behavior of banks, *American Sociological Review* **45**, 553-570.

Rodgers, T. J. (1996) A letter to a shareholder, *Directors & Boards* **20 (4)**, 13-17.

Schrer, K. (1997) Women directors: Talent before gender, *The Corporate Board* **May/June**, 1-5.

Schonfeld, E. (1994) A fissure in the glass ceiling, *Fortune* **September 5**, 15.

Selznick, A. (1949) *TVA and the grass roots*, University of California Press, Berkeley.

Sharpe, R. (1993) Number of women on firms' boards rose 1% in year, *The Wall Street Journal* **November 10**, B5.

Smith, P. L. and Smits, S. J. (1994) The feminization of leadership?, *Training & Development* **48 (2)**, 43-46.

Sweetman, K. J. (1996) Women in boardrooms: Increasing numbers qualify to serve, *Harvard Business Review* **January/February**, 13.

U. S. Department of Labor (1991) *A report on the glass ceiling initiative*, U. S. Department of Labor, Washington, DC.

U. S. Department of Labor (1992) *Employment and earnings*, Washington, DC, **39 (5)**, Table A-22.

Useem, M. (1984) *The inner circle: Large corporations and the rise of business political activity in the U.S. and U.K.* Oxford University Press, Oxford.

Van Velsor, E. and Hughes, M. W. (1990) *Gender differences in the development of managers: How women managers learn from experience*, Technical report no. 145, Center for Creative Leadership, Greensboro, NC.

Vancil, R. F. (1987) *Passing the baton: Managing the process of CEO succession*, Harvard Business School Press, Boston, MA.

Zahra, S. A. and Pearce, J. A. (1989) Boards of directors and corporate financial performance: A review and integrative model, *Journal of Management* **15**, 291-334.

Zald, M. N. (1967) Urban differentiation, characteristics of boards of directors, and organizational effectiveness, *American Journal of Sociology* **73**, 261-272.

BUILDING THE BUSINESS CASE FOR WOMEN CORPORATE DIRECTORS

DIANA BILIMORIA
Case Western Reserve University
Department of Organizational Behavior
Weatherhead School of Management
Cleveland, OH 44106-7235
(216) 368-2115
(216) 368-4785 (Fax)
dxb12@po.cwru.edu

This chapter addresses the need for research that builds a convincing business case for the presence and effective utilization of women corporate directors. What needs to be done to establish the value of women at the corporate governance apex? On what topics should organizational research be conducted so as to generate the knowledge and insights that can compel positive change in the representation and status of women on corporate boards? What should such research look like? What research methods are most likely to yield evidence of women's contributions in the governance of firms? These and similar questions are addressed in this chapter, with the intent of further spurring the growth of theory-driven empirical research on this topic.

1. The Current State

In recent years, there has been an increase in the number of women serving on the corporate boards of the largest industrials. For the first time ever, women occupied more than 10% of corporate board seats at <u>Fortune</u> 500 board tables in 1996 (Catalyst, 1996). In 1997, 84% of these industrials had a woman director, up from 69% just four years ago (Catalyst, 1997, 1993). The number of women being appointed to these seats has slowly increased; the total number of individual women holding board seats was 444 in 1997, close to a hundred women more than a mere three years before (Catalyst, 1997, 1994). Even the popular media rhetoric suggests that "the fight is over. The battle is won. Women are now accepted as outside directors in the preponderance of American corporate boardrooms" (Lear, 1994: 10; see also Romano, 1993).

Despite these advances, research has failed to establish a convincing case for the presence of women on corporate boards of directors. There has been limited analytic

R.J. Burke and M.C. Mattis (eds.), Women on Corporate Boards of Directors, 25-40.
© 2000 *Kluwer Academic Publishers. Printed in the Netherlands.*

effort to determine the importance of and value provided by women directors. CEOs and members of nominating committees of large corporations continue to recruit only a few women for openings in directorships, partly to quell pressure from activist shareholder groups and the general public (Browder, 1995; Dogar, 1997) and partly as a mimicking response to the actions of comparable other organizations. Evidence of the lack of a convincing business case for women corporate directors abounds: the percentage of women corporate directors has stabilized after a period of rapid growth, hovering merely at a little over 10% in the largest corporations. More than 80 Fortune 500 companies do not have even one woman on their boards (Catalyst, 1997). Most of the firms with women directors have only a single woman, furthering the suspicion that image, not strategic value, is being serviced by women's inclusion. Only one Fortune 500 company has achieved parity on its board with 5 women and 5 men directors (Catalyst, 1997). And only 1% of inside directors on Fortune 500 boards (12 out of the 1,199 individuals drawn from a firm's top management) are women (Catalyst, 1997), signaling that the internal corporate board pipeline for qualified women top managers is still a fairly hollow conduit.

Further, only 444 women occupy the 643 of the 6,081 total seats on Fortune 500 boards (Catalyst, 1997) thereby continuing the conventional spread of a few prominent women over multiple corporate boards. CEOs continue to believe that the available pool of qualified women candidates is extremely limited (Mattis, 1997, 1993). In a recent survey, one third of the Canadian chief executives studied estimated the current size of the pool of potential women directors available to them at 50 or fewer women, and 80% thought the pool was less than 250 women (Burke, 1994a). In another study, nearly half the U.S. CEOs studied believed that the pool consisted of less than 250 women (Catalyst, 1993).

Additionally, even those few women who reach the corporate governance apex tend to be utilized in sex-biased and stereotypical ways; for example, women corporate directors overproportionately serve on public affairs committees and underproportionately serve on executive, compensation, and finance committees (Bilimoria & Piderit, 1994). Another study found that committees having women were generally larger than committees not having women; these authors concluded that committees were made larger by adding a woman rather than by replacing a man (Sethi, Swanson and Harrigan, 1981).

On most corporate boards, women continue to face the additional burden of tokenism: being the only woman or one of a very small minority. Only 36% (181 companies) of Fortune 500 companies had two or more women directors in 1997, up from 177 (35%) in 1996 (Catalyst, 1997). Of the Fortune 1000 corporations, only 198 (19.8%) had more than one woman (Catalyst, 1994). A 1995 survey of major corporations (in the manufacturing, service, high tech, financial, and utilities sectors) in nine countries indicated that 29% of the responding firms had one woman director, 11% had two women directors, and 2% had three or more women on their boards (National Association of Corporate Directors, 1995). As Juanita Kreps, an early woman director who has served on numerous corporate boards notes, one woman on a board is not likely to change corporate policy (in her speech entitled, 'Help! There's a woman in the boardroom', cited in Mattis, 1993). Additionally, interviews of women directors reveal the loneliness and difficulties experienced as the only woman on a board (Sethi, Swanson and Harrigan, 1981; see also Tifft, 1994).

Clearly, these more detailed statistics and findings are in contrast to the popular media rhetoric. However, research has been slow in advancing insights about the antecedents, dynamics, and consequences of women's representation and status as corporate directors. Although several years of empirical work have yielded a slew of demographic statistics, board composition surveys, descriptions of personal experience, and profiles of successful women, cumulatively these have resulted in few substantive insights about the behaviors, treatment, and contributions of women at the corporate governance apex (Bilimoria & Wheeler, in press).

Instead of systematic and rigorous empirical documentation of women's boardroom contributions, the extant literature generally addresses the benefits proffered to corporations by women directors through prescriptive writings and anecdotal illustrations. For example, writers have hypothesized that positive business and political impact accrues from an increase in women in corporate governance positions (Bilimoria, 1995; Fernandez, 1993; Mattis, 1993; Morrison, 1992; Schwartz, 1980). Others have suggested that women directors help corporations gain competitive advantage by dealing more effectively with diversity in their product and labor markets (Morrison, 1992; Fernandez, 1993). Another perceived benefit has been that women directors function as champions for change on women's issues by keeping issues of recruitment, retention and advancement of women high on the board's agenda; women directors serve as role models, mentors and champions of high-performing women in the organization (Tifft, 1994; Mattis, 1993; Schwartz, 1980; Burke, 1994a, 1994b; Catalyst, 1993; 1995). However, there is limited research evidence indicating support for these conjectures; a substantive case for women corporate directors has yet to materialize. A recent comprehensive survey of the empirical literature on the representation and status of women corporate directors concluded that "overall, there are simply too few theoretically rigorous studies to yield cumulatively powerful patterns and conclusions. At this time, women corporate directors remain an undertheorized and understudied domain of corporate governance and policy" (Bilimoria and Wheeler, in press).

The few empirical studies that address the question of women's added value on corporate boards generally have relied on survey and interview methodologies to descriptively report the views of CEOs (e.g., Catalyst, 1995) and current women directors (e.g., Burke, 1997). For example, a recent set of 25 indepth interviews with <u>Fortune</u> 500 CEOs indicated that many of these individuals believed that women directors bring strategic input to the boards on which they serve, generate a more productive discourse around the board table, and have a positive effect on employee morale by serving as role models and mentors (Catalyst, 1995). Similarly, other writings speculate that because the average female board member is younger than her male counterpart (Ibrahim & Angelides, 1994; Mattis, 1993), boards may benefit from the infusion of new ideas and approaches into business deliberations (Burke, 1993, 1994b; Ibrahim & Angelides, 1994; Schwartz & Harrison, 1986).

This chapter augments the existing literature by highlighting the most critical research areas in which theoretical arguments favoring the presence women corporate directors need to be developed and tested. To establish a compelling business case for women at the governance apex, future empirical research should focus on the distinct contributions of women corporate directors in four major areas of corporate leadership and governance: overall corporate financial status and reputation, strategic input on women's product/market issues and corporate direction, effective boardroom behaviors, and contributions to other women employees.

2. Future Research Topics

Given the highly competitive nature of the global marketplace, economic necessity dictates that women's voices be heard in the general corporate arena (Business Week, 1992). This is becoming ever so much more important as women's presence in the corporate world reaches critical mass (Business Week, 1992). In large numbers, women are obtaining the experience and expertise perceived as necessary for board membership (i.e., senior leadership positions involving line experience in corporations). However, in order to establish a convincing business case for the inclusion and effective use of women in the topmost corridors of corporate power, research in the following areas needs to be conducted, showing positive impacts from the contributions of women corporate directors.

2.1. OVERALL CORPORATE FINANCIAL STATUS AND REPUTATION

The overall corporate bottom-line impact of women directors needs to be investigated specifically. Are firms with women directors indeed more profitable than firms without women on their boards? Do companies with multiple women directors show a healthier return than companies with only one woman director? Two recent studies have begun to provide preliminary evidence of a compelling business bottom-line case for women corporate directors. An analysis of the 50 most profitable Fortune 500 companies indicated that 41 (82%) had at least one woman director as compared to 48.6% of the companies in the overall list having at least one woman director (Catalyst, 1993). In another study, the top 100 Fortune 500 firms by revenue were found to be more than twice as likely to have multiple women directors as the bottom 100 (Catalyst, 1997). Other rigorous empirical research, controlling for appropriate other direct and intermediary effects, needs to be conducted to identify and establish the financial benefits from women on corporate boards.

Additionally, the relationship between the presence of women in the boardroom and a firm's reputation needs to be investigated. In recent years, corporations have begun to face organized external pressures to recruit and retain corporate women directors.

Although there is at present no penalty for excluding women from corporate boards (Burke, 1994b), increasingly, institutional investors and other shareholder associations have begun to pressure corporate boards to increase their representation and use of women directors (Investor Responsibility Research Center, 1993). Investors such as the Teachers Insurance and Annuity Association/ College Retirement Equities Fund (TIAA/CREF), U.S. Trust Co., and church groups affiliated with the Interfaith Center on Corporate Responsibility, targeting specific companies, have indicated their intention to offer shareholder proposals aimed at increasing board diversity. In October 1993, TIAA/CREF issued a Policy Statement on Corporate Governance that for the first time endorsed the concept of board inclusiveness. The Investor Responsibility Research Center's (1993) survey, Voting by Institutional Investors on Corporate Governance Issues, indicated that 39% of respondents, up from 26% in 1992, said that the lack of women and/or minority members on a board may affect their voting decisions, and 4% of respondents noted that their guidelines require them to withhold their votes in such cases. Thus, the absence of women directors appears to have certain negative influences on perceptions of the corporation among large stockholders.

Concurrently, the visible presence of women corporate directors appears to influence opinions held by the media and the general public about corporate effectiveness. For example, in determining the top 25 public companies for executive women, Working Woman magazine narrowed the pool first to those publicly held companies that have at least two women on the board of directors. Only after this cut-off, the list employed a number of other criteria to determine if a company made it into the list (cf. Cleaver, 1998). Additionally, the number one criterion used was female directors (other criteria were women in senior management positions, women at the level of corporate vice president and above, and the ratio of female managers to female employees).

Thus, future research needs to rigorously investigate the influence of corporate women directors on stockholder and media/public images of corporate reputation. For example, are companies with women directors held in higher esteem by large stockholders and the general public? Do firms with multiple women directors have better business reputations than those with one or no women corporate directors? What is the nature of the influence large shareholders exert in the recruitment and appointment of women corporate directors? What is the relationship between a company's Fortune annual reputational ranking score and the number of women on its board of directors?

2.2. STRATEGIC INPUT ON WOMEN'S PRODUCT/MARKET ISSUES AND CORPORATE DIRECTION

Anecdotal descriptions of the strategic importance of the inclusion of women on corporate boards of directors point to their direct contributions with regard to services or products aimed at women. For example, Nike Corporation's first woman director is credited with urging the board and top management to invest in developing and marketing sports shoes made exclusively for women, a forward-thinking decision which now generates almost a third of Nike's total revenues.

Specifically, women directors have been thought to help corporations gain a competitive advantage to more effectively deal with diversity in their product markets (Morrison, 1992; Fernandez, 1993). Women directors have a variety of backgrounds which result in different perspectives (Burke, 1994b), adding fresh views on strategic issues to augment the traditional men's "cozy club" decision making that permeates most corporate boardrooms (Dobrzynski, 1993:50).

Empirical research is needed to identify examples of the added value provided by women directors through women-specific strategic product/market input, together with evidence of the impact of their ideas. Empirical research needs to answer questions such as: Do firms with women corporate directors generate more business from women customers? Do firms with women corporate directors move successfully into new women-specific markets? Do firms with women corporate directors innovate more with more women-oriented products? Is intrapreneurship more likely in firms with women corporate directors?

Additionally, more rigorous research needs to be conducted to explore the stakeholder sensitivity that is thought to be provided by women corporate directors in board deliberations and decision making about corporate direction and policy. For example, the impact of women corporate directors' contributions regarding issues of the corporation's environmental impact, corporate ethical actions, and support for community development need to be documented. Are boards with women directors more likely to adopt a multiple stakeholder interests view of the firm than are other boards? Are companies with women directors more environmentally-friendly than are other companies? Does the presence of women directors influence a company's community relations, and if so, how? Are companies with women directors considered more socially responsible than are other firms? These are some beginning questions, the answers to which will contribute to building the business case for women corporate directors.

2.3. EFFECTIVE BOARDROOM BEHAVIORS

The literature on the impact of women corporate directors on board room processes and activities highlights the confusion spurred by the introduction of women, particularly if more than one, to a traditional all-male setting. CEOs report fears that gender diversity may complicate or slow down board processes (Burke, 1994b). Because men are not used to women at the table, they are not sure what to expect, causing concern that the new and different perspectives likely to result from the increased diversity may be too new and different. CEOs and male directors remain concerned that uncomfortable issues, normally ignored or held for private conversations, will become part of the general discussion (Dobrzynski, 1993); CEOs fear that women will not play by conventional rules. Additionally, men may be uncomfortable with socializing with women, many of whom may be single (Adams, 1993). Perhaps for some of these reasons, women directors feel constrained in their boardroom influence; a recent survey conducted by the executive search firm Korn/Ferry International indicated that women directors do not feel as if they have as much influence on critical decisions as do their male counterparts, particularly on important boardroom issues such as management succession and executive compensation (Briggins, 1998; Koretz, 1997).

On the other hand, other writings and anecdotal evidence suggest that women corporate directors play an extremely constructive role in board processes and deliberations. First, women's presence on the board may positively influence men's behavior. In a recent poll conducted by <u>Across the Board</u> (1994) male directors agreed ten to one to being more careful about what they said or did when women were present. Second, women are speculated to enhance boardroom discussions on account of their superior listening skills and enhanced sensitivity toward others. Third, because of their unique interactive leadership qualities (characterized by preferences for collaboration, sharing of power and resources, and flexibility), women are speculated to readily provide the transformational leadership necessary for the new business realities facing corporations today (<u>Fortune</u>, 1990; Rosener, 1990). As newer forms of organizing through teamwork, alliances, and networks increasingly become the order of the day, women are thought to proffer an underutilized talent pool for corporations seeking to rejuvenate their executive and boardroom suites. In support of the notion that women are capable corporate leaders, a recent study, examining 164 line and staff executives, suggested that significantly more women executives display leadership potential than do their male counterparts (Enslow, 1991). Thus, in contrast to the conventional argument that women may prove to be more disruptive than constructive influences in boardroom deliberations, more recent theory suggests that women, in fact, may have the capabilities to effectively lead and participate in board decision making.

Empirical research needs to be undertaken to sort out and examine these alternative scenarios describing women's boardroom activities and influence. What examples do we have of how women corporate directors generate more productive boardroom discourse? Do companies having women directors engage in different patterns of corporate alliancing and networking than do companies with no women directors? Is board decision making more effective when women directors are fully engaged in discussions? What institutional and structural arrangements cause women directors to contribute effectively and feel influential during the board's critical decision making processes? Again, these are some beginning questions, the answers to which can contribute to a compelling case for women corporate directors.

2.4. CONTRIBUTIONS TO CORPORATE WOMEN EMPLOYEES

By virtue of their position at the top of the corporate hierarchy, female directors are speculated to serve other corporate women in unique ways: as role models, mentors, and champions for high-performing women in the organization, and to keep issues of recruitment, retention, development, and advancement of women high on the board's agenda (Mattis, 1993; Nation's Business, 1990; Schwartz, 1980). The visible presence of women directors in positions of power and authority is perceived to help break down the stereotypes that frequently hold other corporate women from performing and advancing. In a recent study of chief executives, the most frequently mentioned effect of women on boards was making female employees more positive (Burke, 1994a). Not surprisingly, women's presence impresses women employees and stockholders (Burke, 1994b).

A survey of women corporate directors indicated that they recognize their responsibility to address issues relating to women employees, and see their concerns as appropriate business issues for board discussion (Mattis, 1993). A 1990-1991 Catalyst survey of women directors found that 81% of respondents felt that their presence makes female employees feel more positive about working at the company, 73% felt that their presence increases board sensitivity to issues affecting female employees, and about 33% felt that their presence had positive impact on the recruitment of women or the representation of senior women in management (Mattis, 1993).

Yet, women directors appear to experience considerable role confusion and anxiety about their role and identity in the corporation. While many women directors view themselves as directors, and not women directors (Burson-Marsteller, 1977; Catalyst, 1993; Collins, 1978; Sethi, Swanson & Harrigan, 1981;), they believe that an important reason they were recruited is because they are women (Mitchell, 1984; Sethi, Swanson & Harrigan, 1981). Women directors acknowledge that CEOs frequently cite the fear that women will disrupt an otherwise cooperative boardroom climate by adversarially raising difficult "women's issues" (such as family care and health benefits) as a reason for not hiring women directors (cf. Burke, 1994a; Dobrzynski, 1993; Lear, 1994). They also continue to be aware of the dangers of being perceived as having a "women's agenda", being a "single-issue woman", or being a "constituent director" (Burson-Marsteller, 1977; Catalyst, 1993; Investor Responsibility Research Center, 1993; Mattis, 1993). Burke (1993: 12) captures the role ambiguity felt by many women corporate directors as follows, "whether women serving on corporate boards have, as part of their implicit mandate, responsibilities for leveling the playing field for women in these organizations ... is not routinely specified in the job description of women directors. Some organizations would look on these initiatives favorably; others would not. Some women directors would feel comfortable with these activities; others would not".

Concurrently, polls reveal women employees' increasingly pessimistic view of Corporate America's record in hiring and promoting women: 70% of 400 female managers, up from 60%, felt that the male-dominated corporate culture is an obstacle to their success, 56% noted the impediment of the glass ceiling, and more than one-third thought that in five years' time, the number of senior women executives at their companies will have remained the same or fallen (Business Week, 1992). Increasingly, enterprising and qualified women are opting out of the corporate world. The number of women applying to MBA programs nationwide has been flat at 29% since 1994 (Wall Street Journal, 1998). The National Foundation of Women Business Owners (NFWBO) indicates that the number of women-owned businesses in the U.S. increased by an average of 9.1% per year between 1991 and 1994 to a total of 7.7 million. Employment in women-owned businesses increased by an average of 11.6% per year during this same period, or more than twice the 5.3% rate for all firms. Women-owned businesses now represent 36% of all firms in the U.S., providing employment for 26% of the nation's workers, and generating 16% of the nation's business sales (National Foundation of Women Business Owners, 1996). In a publication entitled "Women-Owned Businesses: Breaking the Boundaries", the NFWBO has pointed out that in contrast to the advancement difficulties faced by women in the corporate sector, women are starting new businesses at four times the rate of men, employing in the U.S. more people than all the Fortune 500 companies employ worldwide (National Foundation of Women Business Owners, 1995).

Thus, particularly in these times of increasing pessimism about the state of the corporate world for women employees, women corporate directors appear to have the potential for tremendous positive impact on other corporate women. Previous research has begun to shed some light on these relationships. For example, Harrigan's (1981) research indicated a positive association between the ratio of female to total managers and the likelihood of a woman director being elected. A recent study of women partners and associates of law firms indicated that sex roles were more stereotypical and more problematic in firms with relatively low proportions of women partners (Ely, 1995). Another study, generated by the Interfaith Center on Corporate Responsibility, found a correlation between the lack of diversity on the board and a lack of diversity in the company's employment practices (Investor Responsibility Research Center, 1993). These empirical findings serve to empirically confirm the intuition that women directors have a positive role to play as mentors, champions and role models for other corporate women.

Future research should more specifically address the relationship between corporate women directors and women in the corporate hierarchy. How do women directors facilitate the recruitment, retention, development and advancement of women in corporate management? In what ways are senior women managers benefited by the presence of corporate women directors? What are the overt and covert mandates for women directors with regard to other women in the organization, and how are these played out in boardroom dealings? Do companies with women directors have more women in senior management than organizations that have no women directors? Do companies with more women directors have lower turnover among women in top management positions?

3. The Conduct of Future Research

Clearly there is need for a compelling body of evidence that cumulatively establishes the business case for women corporate directors. Such a body of research can have important organizational consequences (cf. Dunnette, 1992; Lawler, Mohrman, Mohrman, Ledford, Cummings & Associates, 1985). Organizational science and organizational practice construct each other in a dynamic interplay of scholarship and practical interests (Benson, 1977, 1983). The organizational concerns of both participants and scholars provide the impetus for research. At the same time, knowledge generated through research guides organizational participants in better understanding and dealing with organizational phenomena. In this sense, organizational research "constructs" organizations as much as it studies them (Calas & Smircich, 1992).

3.1. THE PARAMETERS OF IMPACTFUL RESEARCH

For research to have the greatest potential to build a convincing business case for women corporate directors and to spur positive organizational change in their representation and status, three requirements need to be fulfilled. First, a critical mass of empirical research must draw attention to women's issues and contributions as important organizational and boardroom concerns, providing the parameters for policy discussion at the highest corporate levels, and framing boardroom conversation in gender-specific ways. Empirical research of sufficient quantity and rigor must generate a coherent and forceful framing of ideas, language, and insights useful to board members in constructing their collective reality. Research must generate the plausible hypotheses and the generalizable conceptual knowledge that helps practitioners order their thinking about the multifold benefits arising from the presence and effective use of women corporate directors.

Researchers undertaking work on women corporate directors must recognize the inherent responsibility of their work to spur organizational and board change. To be impactful, researchers must pay choiceful attention to the assumptions underlying their work, as well as the content domains and the methodological conduct of their research. Researchers must realize that the mere asking of research questions can be an organizational intervention, creating curiosity, raising expectations, and engaging affect in boardrooms. Researchers must recognize that the ways by which they approach the conduct of their inquiries about women directors influence how their results are received. They must engage in choiceful selection of organizations and participants, the methods used, and the feedback given.

Second, future research on women corporate directors must question and critically evaluate extant institutional conditions, exposing the hidden dynamics of boardrooms, and bringing to light the systemic structures that underlie organizational arrangements affecting women. Research must reveal the often indiscernible and seemingly random patterns, flows, and trends that influence board composition, structure, procedures, and operations. Research must explicate the causes and consequences of board actions regarding organizational women including board members, spotlighting both the embeddedness of institutional phenomena and the discreteness of leadership choices. And research must link society's treatment of women in general to institutional practices of women's boardroom representation and status.

Researchers should dare to ask difficult questions about existing configurations of power and control in the boardroom. They should pay attention to the underlying dimensions of the board's institutional arrangements and artifacts, such as its composition, internal organization, procedures, and the formal and informal distributions of power, work, and information, particularly as these impact women directors. Researchers must examine their own roles in perpetuating and legitimizing existing structures of power, control, opportunity, and legitimacy through the character and conduct of their research and through their presence as researchers.

Third, future research must provide alternatives to limiting organizational arrangements. Research must produce both the generalizable and board-specific conclusions to spur generative organizational action about women directors. It must signal the pathways to positive action that board members may be otherwise blind to, or incapable of accessing. Research must proffer the knowledge structures, linguistic constructions, and paradigmatic framing within which new boardroom actions regarding women directors are encouraged and justified. Presented as knowledge, research findings must be directed toward legitimizing the creation of new and vital boardroom structures and practices conducive to improved representation and status of women. In short, research must contribute to the impetus for organizational change in this area.

Researchers must take on the challenge of allowing their findings to speak positively about change. Based on insights generated from their studies of women directors, researchers must detail the precise individual and organizational actions necessary for improvement in women's' boardroom representation and status. Researchers must study positive exemplars of organizations and boards employing innovative practices regarding women, so as to engender encouragement and hope in other organizations that change is possible and effective. Researchers must find ways to creatively publicize their insights, collectively organizing research colloquia and conferences on this topic, employing multiple other forums (such as consulting and teaching appointments) to share these learnings, and making creative use of the general and business media.

3.2. METHODS OF CONDUCTING IMPACTFUL RESEARCH

Research on women corporate directors must be conducted in ways that are likely to maximize its impact on organizational practice. Following Lawler's (1985) recommendation that many practical questions concerning organizational behavior require large scale, multivariable, complex research because of the complex, interactive, ever-changing realities of organizations, more sophisticated research on women corporate directors needs to be undertaken to build a compelling business case for their presence and effective use.

Since the topic of women directors has been undertheorized and underresearched to date (Bilimoria & Wheeler, in press), there is need for the conduct of both broad-brush studies and fine-grained studies in this area. Researchers undertaking broad-brush studies utilize few variables and many cases, and analyze organizations from a distance, frequently through questionnaires or secondary data. The advantage of such studies are the clarity and generalizability of the results and the replicability of the methods; their major drawback is that they capture only a small segment of organizational complexity, thereby lacking, in the eyes of practitioners, a comprehensive understanding of the phenomenon under study (Lawler, 1985). For example, a recent broad-brush analysis, referring to the underlying patterns of sex-typing in committee memberships, summarized in the business section of the New York Times (Bilimoria & Piderit, 1995) received a response from a woman director that decried the "easy-to-research questions" of the study (Pinsdorf, 1995).

Despite this drawback, however, broad-brush studies are critical to the advancement of theoretical knowledge that impacts practice because they often produce counterintuitive insights that are otherwise undiscoverable by practitioners through their everyday experience. As Seashore (1985: 47) argues, "The varieties of knowledge we work with and need exceed the capacity of research methods that are constrained by the unique case, by direct involvement in the phenomena under study, and by "experience" accessible to participants in such approaches to knowledge generation. Some kinds of knowledge and theory can be generated only by comparative study of populations of persons, groups, and organizations rather than a single case; some require distancing from and abstractions from the phenomenon under study." Particularly in exposing the underlying patterns, causes, and consequences of institutional arrangements that limit women directors' representation and status, broad-brush analyses are vitally important.

However, fine-grained analyses are also likely to be useful for impacting practice (Lawler, 1985). Researchers undertaking fine-grained studies are intensely involved in the study of a small part of individual or group behavior in organizations through methods of observation, action, and consultation. The biggest advantage of fine-grained studies is that they provide complex insights into real organizational phenomena to which practitioners can quickly identify; their challenge is to extract general conclusions, insights, and frames that contribute to a larger body of knowledge (Lawler, 1985). A recent example is provided by Gallese (1991) whose five-month intensive study of 24 corporate women yielded the theory that women are held back in part by the way they and their male peers perceive women's capacity for attaining and exercising power. Similarly, Bilimoria and Huse's (1997) comparison of the personal stories of 2 U.S. and 2 Norwegian women directors yielded the conjecture that gender-related board structures and processes differ by country.

Clearly more of this sort of fine-grained analysis is required, particularly in the form of site-specific analyses (case studies) that are comparative in nature (cf. Hackman, 1985; Lundberg, 1985). In particular, following Pondy and Olson's (1977) exhortation that extreme cases provide more understanding of a phenomenon than empirically common cases, researchers should search out the unique corporate exemplars of women directors' representation and status for in-depth analyses of their boardroom and organizational dynamics. Even more specifically, if researchers are truly committed to engendering organizational reflection on existing policies and practices, they should focus on the study of positive exemplars that point in the desired directions of change and give persuasive evidence of effectiveness.

To build a compelling case for women corporate directors, researchers may need to use innovative methods of conducting their inquiries beyond the constraints imposed by the traditional scientific paradigm. For instance, researchers in this field must expand the categories to which the parties of interest to and potential help in conducting the research belong. Following Hackman's (1985) suggestion for forming active partnerships between academics and practitioners to undertake research that makes a difference, CEOs, board chairs, and male and female board members should be invited to join in as co-inquirers, and the views of other corporate governance constituencies (e.g., board consultants, senior executives, and women employees) should be incorporated within the research if it is to have systemic and long term corporate impact. As Seashore (1985: 54) puts it, "Suppose that we came to regard organizational practitioners (that is, managers) as potential researchers, consultants as potential subjects or informants, informants as clients, subjects as colleagues, action researchers as teachers, disciplinary colleagues as consultants to us, and so on. Suppose also that we came to regard the advancement of theory, knowledge, and practice not as a task for organizational behavior specialists with academic roots or connections but rather as a task that, by its intrinsic nature, requires a joint effort by the full community of interested parties. Would (could) we then organize ourselves for the task in new ways - ways that...salvage more of the information that gets generated and lost, that connect research and practice more closely or more often, that make our product more widely public for evaluation and potential application, that make our choice of issues for research and intended impact more attuned to "reality" as defined by the community of parties at interest?"

    Because current women directors on corporate boards are often the only woman in the group of directors, or one of a very small minority, their support is crucial for the conduct of research that makes a difference in their boardrooms. Using feasible research resources, the inputs of women directors should be innovatively included in all stages of research: design, implementation, documenting, feedback, and dissemination for action.

3.3. THE DISSEMINATION OF RESEARCH

Up to this point, I have argued that researchers must alter the content and conduct of future research to both advance the body of knowledge about the contributions/benefits of women corporate directors and generate increased corporate awareness and positive action. However, certain system-wide factors other than the nature of the research itself also influence the impact engendered on organizational practice. Two such institutional factors pertaining to the dissemination of research findings by the academy of management scholars are discussed below: the pressures to separate research and consulting, and exposure of research findings through the general and business media.

    First, institutional forces in academia separate the conduct of research and consulting/management development projects. The results of consulting-based inquiries are not often published in mainstream research journals. Similarly, research findings are frequently either considered too specialized and narrow for general usability or too broad and simplistic for application to complex organizational issues. This disjuncture of research and consulting is detrimental to conducting impactful research since the entry to and influence on organizational practice readily provided by such projects is lost to research.

    It is increasingly apparent, however, that through consulting and mangement development relationships research can have impact on organizational and individual realities and "organizations can actually try new ideas and breakthroughs in practice" (Lawler, 1985: 14). When such projects consist of learning activities with written outputs such as consulting reports, case studies, and problem-focussed articles, and are included in the evolutionary sequence of knowledge creation, research serves the dual purposes of contributing to extant knowledge and generating useful implications for practice (Walton, 1985).

Second, for broad research impact, the dissemination of research findings through media exposure must be improved. Measures must be taken at the level of the academy of management scholars to innovatively gain the media exposure necessary for impact in the information age. The organizational machineries of academic research, particularly associations of researchers such as the Academy of Management, top level research journals, as well as universities themselves, must engage in creative and consistent circulation of research findings to the general and business media. With sufficient positive press on the topic of the contributions of women corporate directors (that highlights the complex insights and understandings unavailable simply through practitioners' everyday experiences), theory driven academic research is likely to yield a compelling business case for women corporate directors and to have a constructive influence on organizational and boardroom structures and practices.

References

Across the Board. (1994) Gender chill?, **September**, 1.
Adams, B. (1993) Glass ceiling: Are women and minorities blocked from the executive suite, *CQ Researcher*, October 29, **3**, 40, 939-948.
Benson, J.K. (1977) Organizations: A dialectical view. *Administrative Science Quarterly*, **22**, 1-21.
Benson, J.K. (1983) Paradigm and praxis in organizational analysis, *Research in Organizational Behaviour*, **5**, 33-56.
Bilimoria, D. (1995) Women directors: The quiet discrimination, *Corporate Board*, **July/August**, 10-14.
Bilimoria, D. and Huse, M. (1997) A qualitative comparison of the boardroom experiences of U.S. and Norwegian women corporate directors, *International Review of Women and Leadership*, **3**, 2, 63-76.
Bilimoria, D. and Piderit, S.K. (1995) Sexism on high: Corporate boards, *New York Times*, **February 5**, Section 3, p. 11.
Bilimoria, D. and Piderit, S.K. (1994) Board committee membership: Effects of sex-based bias, *Academy of Management Journal*, **37**, 6, 1453-1477.
Bilimoria, D. and Wheeler, J.V. (In Press) Women Corporate Directors: Current Research and Future Directions, in M. Davidson, and R.J. Burke (eds.), *Women in Management: Current Research Issues, Volume II*, London: Paul Chapman Publishers, Chapter 10.
Briggins, A. (1998). Equity lacking in the boardroom, *Management Review*, **87**, 2: 6-
Browder, D. (1995) Shareholders are valuing diversity, *Directors & Boards*, **19**, 3, 12-15.
Burke, R.J. (1993) Women on corporate boards of directors, *Equal Opportunities International*, **12**, 6, 5-13.
Burke, R.J. (1994a) Benefits of women on corporate boards of directors as reported by male CEOs, *Psychological Reports*, **75**, 1, 329-330.
Burke, R.J. (1994b) Women on corporate boards of directors: Views of Canadian Chief Executive Officers, *Women in Management Review*, **9**, 5, 3-10.
Burke, R.J. (1997) Women directors' activism on corporate boards of directors: Thriving or surviving? *International Review of Women and Leadership*, **3**, 2, 77-84.
Burson-Marsteller, (1977) *Study of Women Directors*. Burson-Marsteller, New York.
Business Week. (1992) Corporate women: How much progress? **June 8**, 74-83.

Calas, M.B. and Smircich, L. (1992) Using the 'F' word: Feminist Theories and the Social Consequences of Organizational Research, in A.J. Mills and P. Tancred (eds.), *Gendering Organizational Analysis*, Sage, Newbury Park, CA, pp. 222-234.

Catalyst. (1993) *Women on Corporate Boards: The Challenge of Change*, Catalyst, New York.

Catalyst. (1994) *1994 Census of Female Board Directors Fact Sheet*, Catalyst, New York.

Catalyst. (1995) *CEO View: Women on Corporate Boards*, Catalyst, New York.

Catalyst, (1996) *1996 Catalyst Census of Women Board Directors of the Fortune 500*, Catalyst, New York.

Catalyst, (1997) *1997 Catalyst Census of Women Board Directors of the Fortune 500*, Catalyst, New York.

Cleaver, J. (1998) 25 top leading companies for women, Working Woman, **23**, 8: 50-64.

Collins, E.G.C. (1978) A woman in the boardroom: An interview with Joan Ganz Cooney, *Harvard Business Review*, January-February, **56**, 77-86

Dobrzynski, J.H. (1993) The 'glass ceiling': A barrier to the boardroom, too, *Business Week*, **November 22**, 50.

Dogar, R. (1997) Crony baloney, *Working Woman*, **22**, 1, 34-37.

Dunnette, M.D. (1992) Blending the Science and Practice of Industrial and Organizational Psychology: Where Are We and Where Are We Going? in M.D. Dunnette and L. Hough (eds.), *Handbook of Industrial and Organizational Psychology*, Consulting Psychologists Press Inc., Palo Alto, CA.

Ely, R.J. (1995) The power in demography: Women's social constructions of gender identity at work, *Academy of Management Journal*, **38**, 3, 589-634.

Enslow, B. (1991) Why women follow, *Across the Board*, June, 28, 6, 21.

Fernandez, J.P. (1993) *The Diversity Advantage: How American Business Can Outperform Japanese and European Companies in the Global Marketplace*, Lexington Books, New York.

Fortune. (1990) Do women manage differently? **Decemeber 17**, 115-117.

Gallese, L.R. (1991) Why women aren't making it to the top, *Across the Board*, April, **28**, 4, 18-22.

Hackman, J.R. (1985) Doing research that makes a difference. In Lawler, E. E., Mohrman, A. M., Mohrman, S. A., Ledford, G. E., Cummings, T. G. & Associates (Eds.), *Doing research that is useful for theory and practice*, San Francisco: Jossey-Bass, pp. 126-149.

Harrigan, K.R. (1981) Numbers and positions of women elected to corporate boards, *Academy of Management Journal*, **24**, 3, 619-625.

Ibrahim, N.A. and Angelides, J.P. (1994) Effect of board members' gender on corporate social responsiveness orientation, *Journal of Applied Business Research*, **10**, 1, 35-40.

Investor Responsibility Research Center. (1993) Institutions campaign for greater board diversity, *Corporate Governance Bulletin*, **10**, 6: 8-12.

Koretz, G. (1997) A boardroom gender gap, *Business Week*, **November 24**, 32.

Lawler E.E. (1985) Challenging Traditional Research Assumptions, in E.E. Lawler, A.M. Mohrman, S.A. Mohrman, G.E. Ledford, T.G. Cummings, and Associates (eds.), *Doing Research That Is Useful For Theory and Practice*, Jossey-Bass, San Francisco, pp. 1-17.

Lawler, E.E., Mohrman, A.M., Mohrman, S.A., Ledford, G.E., Cummings, T.G. and Associates. (1985) *Doing Research That Is Useful For Theory and Practice*, Jossey-Bass, San Francisco.

Lear, R.W. (1994) Here come the women directors, *Chief Executive*, April, **93**, 10.

Lundberg, C.C. (1985) Response and commentary. , in E.E. Lawler, A.M. Mohrman, S.A. Mohrman, G.E. Ledford, T.G. Cummings, and Associates (eds.), *Doing research that is useful for theory and practice*, San Francisco: Jossey-Bass, pp. 60-66.

Mattis, M.C. (1993) Women directors: Progress and opportunities for the future, *Business & the Contemporary World*, **Summer**, 140-156.

Mattis, M.C. (1997) Women on corporate boards: Two decades of research, *International Review of Women and Leadership*, **3**, 2, 11-25.

Mitchell, M. (1984) A profile of the Canadian woman director, *Business Quarterly*, **49**, 1, 121-127.

Morrison, A.M. (1992) *The New Leaders: Guidelines on Leadership Diversity in America*, Jossey-Bass, San Francisco.

National Association of Corporate Directors. (1995) *The 1995 Corporate Governance Survey*, National Association of Corporate Directors, Washington, DC.

National Foundation of Women Business Owners. (1995) *Women-owned businesses: Breaking the boundaries: A report on the progress and achievement of women-owned enterprises*.

National Foundation of Women Business Owners. (1996) *Women-owned businesses in the United States: 1996 Fact Sheet.*

Nation's Business. (1990) Companies court women for boards, January, **78**, 52.

Pinsdorf, M.K. (1995) The dynamics of board room politics. *New York Times*, **March 5**.

Pondy, L.R. and Olson, M.L. (1977) Theories of extreme cases. Paper presented at the American Psychological Association Meeting, San Francisco, August.

Romano, C. (1993) All a-board! The composition of the boardroom is changing - albeit slowly, *Management Review*, **82**, 10, 5.

Rosener, J.B. (1990) Ways Women Lead, *Harvard Business Review*, **November-December**, 119-125.

Schwartz, F. (1980) Invisible resource: Women for boards, *Harvard Business Review*, **58**, 2, 6-18.

Schwartz, F. and Harrison, P. (1986) Beyond the first generation of women directors: On the other side of the roadblock, *Directors & Boards*, **11**, 1, 39-41.

Seashore, S.E. (1985) Institutional and organizational issues in doing useful research, in E.E. Lawler, A.M. Mohrman, S.A. Mohrman, G.E. Ledford, T.G. Cummings, and Associates (eds.), *Doing research that is useful for theory and practice*, San Francisco: Jossey-Bass, pp. 45-59.

Sethi, S.P., Swanson, C.L. and Harrigan, K.R. (1981) Women directors on corporate boards, Working Paper No. 81-01, Center for Research in Business and Social Policy, The University of Texas at Dallas.

Tifft, S.E. (1994) Board gains, *Working Woman*, **19**, 2, 36-39, 70, 74-75.

Wall Street Journal. (1998) Career matters: Business schools are still facing a gender gap, **November 10**, B1.

Walton, R.E. (1985) Strategies with dual relevance, in E.E. Lawler, A.M. Mohrman, S.A. Mohrman, G.E. Ledford, T.G. Cummings, and Associates (eds.), *Doing research that is useful for theory and practice*, San Francisco: Jossey-Bass, pp. 176-204.

PART TWO

International Research Findings

WOMEN CORPORATE DIRECTORS IN THE UNITED STATES

MARY C. MATTIS, Ph.D.
Catalyst
New York, New York

1. Introduction

Catalyst measures the number of women directors on the boards of major U.S. companies because we know that in business, what gets measured gets done. The *Catalyst Census of Women Board Directors of the Fortune* 500 was created in 1993 to encourage the leaders of *Fortune* 500 companies to increase the number of women serving on their boards. Since successful, large public companies are the standard against which businesses in the United States measures themselves, we also hoped to encourage smaller corporations to add women to their boards.

Prior to 1993 Catalyst tracked the representation of women on the boards of companies, reporting the findings in aggregate form only. In 1993, a decision was made to publish the census findings in a report to be broadly circulated, including a mailing to all of the CEOs of the *Fortune* 500 companies. Today, the census report outlines (Catalyst, 1998) quantitative findings related to the number of women board directors, the number of seats they hold, and the number of companies with women directors. An industry, regional and state-by-state listing is also provided. More importantly, the report provides a company-by-company listing along with the number of women, including none, that serve on each company's board. The purpose of this publication is to promote corporate accountability,create competition, and assist companies in benchmarking their progress against industry peers and other leading American corporations.

2. Why focus on women directors?

Catalyst focuses on women directors because: (1) directors of leading American corporations, as elsewhere in the world, have exceptional power and influence; (2) board directors are a highly visible group; (3) board directors are selected largely from among the highest ranking officers in corporate America. By tracking women's representation on corporate boards we can ascertain the extent to which women are attaining power, influence and visibility in corporate American. The findings are also suggestive of the

R.J. Burke and M.C. Mattis (eds.), Women on Corporate Boards of Directors, 43-56.

extent to women have risen to the highest ranks of corporate management, the pool from which corporate directors are recruited. (In 1996, Catalyst initiated a census of corporate officers to systematically track the representation of women at the highest levels of corporate management and among top-earning officers).

Corporate directors impact the lives of untold employees and consumers in the United States, and patterns of economic opportunity on both a domestic and global scale. Women directors play an additional critical role, serving as beacons of hope for other women climbing the corporate ladder. They serve as role models and frequently mentor senior women in the companies on whose boards they serve and, in some cases, advocate for increasing women's participation and advancement in the company. Therefore, it is critical that women are represented in the highest reaches of corporate governance. By holding up to public scrutiny the progress of individual companies, we are seeking to make change for women while reminding corporate America that the representation of women is a continuing concern.

3. Methodology

In June of 1998, Catalyst sent a letter to the Corporate Secretary of each of the *Fortune* 500 companies (as published in the April 27, 1998, issue of *Fortune* magazine). The letter requested verification of the company's total number of board members as of the cut-off date of March 31; confirmation of the numbers and names of any inside (directors who come from within the company's management ranks) or outside women board members; and, for the first time in 1998, information regarding the membership and leadership of board committees by gender.

The information sent to companies for verification is derived from Catalyst's proprietary database, created from the previous year's census and updated throughout the year, along with public data sources such as corporate annual reports and proxy statements. Companies may verify or correct the information by letter, fax, or telephone. Repeated follow-up faxes and phone calls are made to obtain verification from as many of the 500 companies as possible. Private companies present a special challenge to obtaining information since they are not required by law to report this information.

4. Findings: Increased Numbers, Small Incremental Change

4.1. NUMBER OF BOARD SEATS HELD BY WOMEN

The number of board seats held by women has continued to increase over the years during which Catalyst has conducted a census, although the incremental change from year to year is small. As of March 31, 1998, women held 11/1 percent of the seats on the boards of *Fortune* 500 companies, up from 10.6 percent in 1997. Of the total of 6,064 directorships in *Fortune* 500 companies in 1998, women occupied 671, an increase of 28 board seats held by women since 1997. The increase between 1997 and 1998 was 4.4 percent. Since 1994, there has been an increase of 126 seats held by women, or 23 percent.

Since 1997, there has been no change in the number of board seats per individual woman director, putting to rest the perception held by some that a few women hold many seats on corporate boards. In 1998, 471 individual women held a total of 671 board seats, for an average of 1.4 board seats per woman, similar to the average for male directors. Seventy-five percent of women directors serve on only one *Fortune* company board. Only 18 women directors hold seats on four or more corporate boards.

4.2. NUMBER OF INDIVIDUAL WOMEN BOARD DIRECTORS

1998 also saw a net increase of 27 women who serve on the boards of *Fortune* 500 companies. The total number of individual women on boards in 1998 was 471, up from 444 in 1997. Since 1994, a 34 percent increase in the total number of individual women board directors has been observed.

Sixty-four women serving on *Fortune* 500 boards in 1998 (14 percent of all women directors) did not do so during the previous year. Of these, 25 percent are on the boards of some of the 35 companies new to the *Fortune* 500 in 1998. A test of statistical significance comparing companies new to the *Fortune* list with companies remaining on the list from 1997 shows that companies that were established on the list were more likely to have women on their boards than were companies coming onto the list in 1998. Thirty-four percent of the companies new to the list had no women directors, compared to 13 percent of companies that were on the list in 1997. In addition, of the new companies on the list, only 11 percent have two or more women board members; while 40 percent of companies who were on the list in 1997 have two or more women directors.

4.3. NUMBER OF COMPANIES WITH WOMEN DIRECTORS

Eighty-six percent of *Fortune* 500 companies (429) now have one or more women directors as of March 31, 1998. Since the inception of the *Catalyst Census of Women Board Directors of Fortune* 500 *Companies,* there has been a 24 percent increase in the number of boards with women directors, leaving only 71 companies in 1998 without female board representation

4.3.1. *Number of Companies with Multiple Women Directors*
Of the *Fortune* 500, 38 percent (188) have more than one woman on their boards, an increase of four percent from 1997 and of 29 percent since 1994. The fact that the percentage of *Fortune* 500 companies with multiple women directors keeps growing (albeit it, slowly), suggests that, each year, more companies are recognizing the business case for board gender diversity on their boards. Though it may not be reality, when a corporate board has only one woman director, she is frequently perceived to be a token. And, because women are not a monolithic group, adding more than one woman to a

board brings more than gender diversity.

4.3.2. *Characteristics of companies with multiple women directors*

In 1998, for the first time, there were two companies with more than five women directors -- Avon with six and TIAA-CREF with nine (due in part to a merger of TIAA and CREF producing an unusually large board of 35 members). Thirty-four companies (7 percent of the *Fortune* 500 companies) had three or more women directors as of March 31, 1998:

- Twenty-three *Fortune* 500 companies had three women on their boards (Aid Association for Lutherans, Ameritech, Baxter International, Chase Manhattan Group, Dayton Hudson, Eastman Kodak, General Motors, Johnson & Johnson, Kellogg, Kroger, Maytag, Metropolitan Life Insurance, Nationsbank Corporation, Northeast Utilities, Northwestern Mutual Life Insurance, Pacific Life Insurance, Pacific Power and Light (PP&L) Resources, Phoenix Home Life Mutual Insurance, Principal Financial, Prudential Insurance Company of America, Travelers Corporation, Wellpoint Health Networks, Xerox).

- Seven companies had four women directors (Aetna, Bell Atlantic, Beverly Enterprises, Consolidated Edison, Gannett, Hasbro, SLM Holding).

- Two companies had five women (Fannie Mae, and Golden West Financial, with one of the *Fortune* 500's two female CEOs).

- One company had six women (Avon Company).

- One company had nine women (TIAA-CREF)

In 1994 there were only 19 boards with three or more women directors, representing a 79 percent gain in this category.

In 1998, just three percent, or 17, *Fortune* 500 companies reported that women held one-quarter or more of their board seats, but that is double the number of such companies (eight) recorded in 1997. One company -- Golden West Financial, with a female CEO -- has moved beyond gender parity to a female majority of its board. A second company -- Avon Products, Inc. -- is nearing parity, with six women directors out 13 seats. Two other companies achieved percentages of 40 percent or above: Beverly Enterprises at 44 percent and Gannett Company at 40 percent. Since the number of companies with multiple women directors continues to be so small, the question of what will bring about greater change in this arena is inevitable.

5. Key Role of the CEO

Catalyst's research shows that a developed business case is necessary but not sufficient to guaranteeing women's advancement. Top-down support is also necessary to champion initiatives and hold managers accountable for diversity results. The Chairmen and CEOs of companies that are successful in retaining and advancing women have committed their time and their companies' resources to driving diversity through the organization. Avon is a case in point. The business case for women's representation on Avon's corporate board seems obvious and, therefore, may also appear to have been inevitable. However, other companies with largely female consumer bases such as Borden, Smithfield Foods, Food 4 Less, and Safeway, do not have any women directors. In fact, an industry analysis comparing companies that market primarily to women, e.g., apparel, food and drugstores, and food services, with others, shows that only one of these industries -- soaps and cosmetics -- has a comparatively greater representation of women corporate directors -- 24 percent vs. the 11.1 percent average for the *Fortune* 500 as a whole.

Nonetheless, it would seem that when a company has a largely female employee, and/or consumer-client base it increases the likelihood that women will be represented in leadership roles. Among the companies with three or more women directors, about one-fifth market primarily to women -- Dayton Hudson, Johnson & Johnson, Kellogg, Kroger, Maytag. Among the remainder, more than half are companies where the majority of employees are women - banks, insurance companies, health care providers. Several others are utilities companies -- an industry that historically has been highly regulated and subject to intense scrutiny relating to social responsibility. However, there are companies on the list that do not fall into these categories including Baxter International, Eastman Kodak, Gannett, General Motors and Xerox. Interesting, and similar to Avon, each of these companies has a history of executive leadership committed to diversity. And along with Avon, three of these companies -- Baxter, Eastman Kodak, and Gannett -- have been recognized by Catalyst for initiatives to recruit, retain and advance women.

These findings suggest that when a company has a large percentage of female consumers and employees the business case for board diversity is more obvious. However, a large representation of women among a company's employees and/or consumers is not sufficient to ensure representation of women in leadership roles. Above all else, top-down support is critical to the success of such initiatives.

Catalyst's 1995 survey of CEOs shows that diversifying a board, or for that matter any corporate entity, requires a powerful champion/sponsor to make the business case and to provide ongoing support for "non-traditional" directors. One thousand CEOs of *Fortune* companies were contacted for this study with a mail survey, with a corresponding response rate of 33 percent. Fifty of the responding CEOs indicated a willingness to be interviewed. Subsequently, 20 CEOs were interviewed by telephone. In the interviews, CEOs who had personally recruited female board members, or those who had taken over the leadership of a board with a female director indicated that the decision to recruit the first female director is almost always deliberate. The search either specifies gender as a key criterion or as a strong preference in the recruiting profile. Still, the arrival of the first female director in the board room is frequently championed by a committed CEO.

Almost all CEOs interviewed acknowledged the pressure of being a pioneer in seeking the first woman to sit on their board. CEO commitment to place the first woman is matched by caution and a commitment to find the "right" woman with the appropriate skills and demeanor. One CEO observed that his success or failure in integrating the first woman into his board would influence his ability to continue to bring on more women and minorities:

> "I didn't want to make a mistake, for her or for me, or for that matter, the company. This is a ninety-plus-year old company taking its first woman director. If you want to get the second and the third and you want some minorities, the first one is going to represent all the people who come after. So, I wanted to be sure that I got the right person to match."

Another reported:

> "I was specifically pursuing a woman for our board. I wanted someone who could sit down and make a contribution of significance in 60 seconds later. Indeed, that's exactly what happened. We chose a person who was truly qualified. So I was very happy with that choice."

6. Why Still So Few Women Corporate Directors?

There are at least two obvious reasons why a company might not have a women as a member of its board, even if a woman director was desired. One reason would be that a woman formerly on the board had left and the company was in the process of replacing her when the census was completed. Since turnover on corporate boards is slow, another reason would be a lack of vacancies on a board that preventing companies from bringing on new members. A recent report by an executive search firm that specializes in recruiting women directors cited these reasons for the paucity of women directors: (1) relatively few women meet the specifications for directors outlined by companies -- i.e., few women have reached the level of former or current CEO, COO or Chairman of a major U.S. company -- the pool from which most boards select their directors; (2) the relatively small number of women whose skills and experience conform to the typical director pick and choose the board invitations they accept very carefully; (3) a recent trend is for executives to hold fewer directorships due to liability issues and directives from their own company's boards is impacting the availability of qualified female candidates; (4) since serving on a corporate board can be a major distraction from one's own career, especially for women candidates who are more likely than their male counterparts to be in the middle of their careers and in line for the next promotion, qualified women decline to accept invitations to join boards (Daum, 1999).

6.1. CEOS' VIEWS

A majority of the CEOs responding to Catalyst's 1995 Catalyst survey reported that they want female representation in their board rooms. Almost three-fourths (72%) indicated that recruiting a female director to their board was either a 'top priority' or a 'priority' and only five percent ranked it as a 'very low priority.' A majority of CEOs (86%) also agreed that it is important for corporations to increase the representation of women on boards as a general principle. Only 14 percent of CEOs responding to the survey said that gender was *not* a relevant recruitment criterion. If this is the case, why are there still so few women serving on the boards of large, public companies in the US?

Approximately half of the CEOs surveyed reported that female candidates for corporate boards were 'difficult to find.' This was the third most frequently cited reason by CEOs for the low representation of women on corporate boards. The most frequently cited reason was the 'small number of women with appropriate business experience'(87% CEOs in manufacturing; 78% CEOs in services) followed by 'women have not been in the pipeline long enough.' In comparison, less than five percent of CEOs cited 'opposition of male board members.'

What "appropriate" business experience are these CEOs talking about? In the interviews, CEOs were able to be more specific about this citing 'operational experience' 'industrial experience in a top-drawer manufacturing company with a global presence,' 'significant general management experience,' and 'line' experience.

International experience was also ranked as a 'high priority' qualification by 20 percent of the survey. In an earlier (1993) Catalyst study of CEOs, international ranked far below other types of experience desired in candidates for corporate baords. The fact that this type of experience was elevated in importance in just a few years points to the growing phenomenon of globalization in American companies. It also suggests that, even as corporate boards are seeking female directors, they are "raising the bar" on their specifications for the kinds of experiences candidates need to have. Another key reason given by CEO respondents for why there aren't more women on corporate boards was the belief that women have not been in the corporate pipeline long enough suggesting that the passing of time will solve this problem. One CEO homed in on what is perhaps the heart of the pipeline issue for women noting that "it's not how long women have been in the pipeline, it's what they've been doing there." His reference was to the difficulty of finding women candidates for boards who have meaningful corporate line and general management experience.

Catalyst's 1998 census showed that only about one-third of women directors held corporate positions. The remainder were recruited from academic (17%), entrepreneurial (12%), nonprofit (12%) or other pursuits (9%), and 9% were retired. Looking at the employment history of the newest women on *Fortune* 500 boards, closer to half are in corporate jobs, suggesting that the profile of women directors is changing.

In 1998, Catalyst also carried out a census of women corporate officers and top-earners The unit of analysis for that census was the same *Fortune* companies contacted for the census of women directors. One finding from this census was that women hold only 6.2 percent of line positions held by corporate officers in *Fortune* 500 companies. Male corporate officers in line positions total 4,546, compared to 301 women officers. With men holding 94 percent of line positions, we have clear evidence of just how narrow the pipeline still is.

Similarly, women corporate officers hold only 3.8 percent of the positions that yield the greatest influence and authority in corporations, defined by Catalyst for this census as Chairmen, CEO, Vice Chairman, President, COO, SEVP, and EVP. Eighty-three women and 2,184 men hold such positions. As reported earlier, only 2 women hold the title of CEO in a *Fortune* 500 companies along with 4 female Vice Chairmen, 3 female Presidents, and no female Chairmen or COOs. The majority of women -- 73 out of 83 -- are EVPs, at the bottom of the "clout title" pecking order.

6.2. WOMEN DIRECTORS'S VIEWS

In 1993 Catalyst surveyed by mail all women (approx. 400) serving as directors on the *Fortune* 500/*Service* 500 companies for whom an address could be located, with a resulting 41% response rate. Among the questions put to women directors was: "In your opinion, why aren't there more female directors of *Fortune 500/Service 500* companies?" Women directors gave the following reasons why they believe there are so few women serving on corporate boards:

- Fear of appointing women who are not current board members (51%)
- Companies don't know where to look for qualified women (46%)
- Concern that women will have a "women's issues agenda" (44%)
- Belief that women are unqualified for board service (38%)
- Lack of desire for more female members (where there is one) (37%)
- Too few qualified women   (24%)
- Qualified women fail to communicate their interest   (22%)

In contrasting the responses of women directors with those of the CEOs outlined above, there are some areas of agreement and some areas of disagreement. CEOs reported that qualified women were difficult to identify. Women directors believe companies don't know where to look for qualified women. The top reason given by women directors for why they are still so few in number was, 'fear of appointing a woman without prior board experience.' Prior board experience was specified as a 'top priority' or 'priority' by 58% of the CEOs surveyed.

Women directors' responses also echo those of CEOs regarding the critical role of the CEO champion/sponsor, especially around the appointment of the first woman to his board: 54% of women directors were recommended by the CEO of the company for their first appointment compared to 32% who were recommended by a board member or recruited by the nominating committee. However, the responses of women directors who have served on more than one board suggest that the direct involvement of the CEO may be less important once they have proved themselves on another corporate board: only 32% said they were recommended by the CEO of the company for subsequent corporate board appointments.

In keeping with this finding, 77% of women directors said that gender was a factor contributing to their recruitment to their first corporate board, compared to 39% who cited it as a factor in subsequent appointments. Beyond this perceived reason for their recruitment, a majority also mentioned 'appropriate job title or leadership position,' 'possessed desired area of expertise or responsibility,' and, 'had high visibility,' compared to much smaller percentages who identified other factors as significant. This response mirrors the importance CEOs attach to appropriate business experience and time in the pipeline (if time equals greater visibility).

7. The Business Case for Increasing Women's Representation on Corporate Boards

In working with prestigious American corporations for close to four decades, Catalyst has found that the companies that succeed in retaining and advancing women have developed and articulated the business case for doing so, i.e., the connection between their business strategies and diversity goals/outcomes. In the United States, it is increasingly easy to make what might be called the general business case for diversity -- the changing demographics of both the labor and consumer markets due to immigration and the differential birth rates of Caucasians and other racial/ethnic groups. In 1998, women made up 46% of the U.S. labor force and 49% of managerial and professional specialty positions (Department of Labor, 1998). Companies cannot ignore this important source of talent. As women have come to comprise an ever larger percentage of the professional and managerial ranks of American companies the cost of turnover of women has become more obvious, leading companies to think about what they are doing to develop these women and to advance them to top management and governance roles.

In some industries, it is also possible to advance a specific business case for increasing women's representation in leadership roles, most notably companies that employ large numbers of women or market their products primarily to women.

In contrast, only a small number of companies have gone so far as to develop a business case for diversity that is unique to their particular products, services and business operating environment.

7.1. FINANCIAL INCENTIVES FOR DIVERSITY ON CORPORATE BOARDS

As women's representation in the labor force has increased, so has their buying power. Today, women influence decisions about the purchase of cars, trucks, computers and financial services, along with more traditionally "female" purchases such as groceries, cosmetics and clothing. And, today businesses understand that targeting women's business means recognizing the diverse roles they occupy in the US economy. Not only do women buy for themselves as individuals and for their families, they make up a growing percentage of small business owners who buy goods and services from larger companies and women who work in sales and purchasing in larger business organizations.

Women entrepreneurs are flourishing in the United States. In 1998, more than 8.8 million American women owned their own businesses employing 35 percent more workers than all the *Fortune* 500 companies combined worldwide and generating in excess of $2.2 trillion annually. It is projected that by the year 2000, nearly one-third of all small businesses will be owned by women. Women entrepreneurs want to work with companies where they are represented in senior management and governance.

"The fact that we even have to ask about having women directors is odd," says The New York Times Company chairman, Arthur Sulzberger, Jr. 'Fifty percent of our customer base is women and our senior-, middle- and junior-management levels are well-populated with women. The question is, "Why wouldn't you want your board to reflect the diversity of your staff and customer base?" Another corporate chairman who was until recently CEO of Avon Products, Inc., cited the business case for women on boards when it was observed that Avon has had women on its board since the early 1970s, "If the company is to understand the market and position products and communications to women, then women must be represented at all levels, starting with the board. This is a business issue."

Catalyst's 1995 census of women board directors shows that of the top 100 companies by revenue, 97 have at least one woman on their board. Dividing the *Fortune* 500 into quintiles according to revenue shows that the higher the quintile in which a company is found, the greater the likelihood of the company's having at least one woman director. Companies in the first quintile are twice as likely to have multiple women directors as those in the fifth quintile. The top ten companies by profit all have at least one woman director; the top eight each have two or more women directors. General Motors, the number one ranked company has three.

There could be several explanations for this association between financial success and board diversity. Clearly, there is no way to demonstrate that gender diversity is causally related to financial success. An alternative explanation could be that because the top 100 companies, and especially the top 10, are highly visible, they may feel more external pressure to demonstrate social responsibility.

7.2. OTHER FORMS OF VALUE ADDED BY WOMEN DIRECTORS

Both CEOs and women directors studied by Catalyst mentioned other contributions made by women on corporate boards that are valued though not easy to measure.

7.2.1. *CEOs Views*

Some CEOs recognize that lack of diversity on a board can contribute to lack of critical thinking and innovation. As one CEO observed:

"It's easy for boards to get club-like and ingrown. The notion of a bunch of old men who grew up in the same environment governing a company -- it's the best formula I know of for getting out of step in a changing world."

Nearly two-thirds (62%) of the CEOs surveyed reported that they 'expect the contributions of female directors to be no different from those of male directors, which they explained in statements like the following:

"I think a good smart person is a good smart person, no matter who they are."

"My personal experience does not suggest that women impact boards any differently than men do."

"In terms of our own company, at least from what I've been able to notice, there's absolutely no difference. They're just all board members."

However, in response to this 'check all that apply' question, 60% of CEOs also expect female board members to 'exemplify their company's commitment to diversity to shareholders;' 59% expect women directors to 'exemplify the company's commitment to advancing women':

"It is a view, a perception of goodness...that a company beginning at the board level, is not discriminatory in terms of making qualified directors or executives of any race or persuasion, male or female."

"It's a question of perception of course. It sends a good signal, a positive signal that we don't discriminate."

"I think that it lends a sense of credibility or integrity to what we have been saying and doing around diversity issues, around fairness to the employee base. If we don't manage to have success a the senior officer ranks and at the board ranks and openness to differences, then it rings very hollow. So, it validates our commitment to what we've been preaching across the organization."

In addition, 49% of CEOs said they expect women directors to 'contribute a perspective different from those of male directors;' 46% believe women directors will 'enhance the company's ability to recruit and retain women.' Interestingly, far fewer CEOs expect women board members to: 'initiate discussions about issues that affect female employees' (29%); or, 'reflect female consumers' perspectives' (26%).

7.2.2. *Women Directors' Expectations and Experiences*

Women directors must walk a fine line between representing the concerns of women and being viewed as having a 'single-issue agenda' as exemplified in the comments of two women who participated in Catalyst's study:

"Women are not on boards to represent women. Why not ask a man what he's contributed as a man. The business of a director is to be a good director. Women and men should both be part of that and not merely representatives of their sexes. Constituency directorship leads to chaos. The group has to decide, and for a decision to be reached, goals have to be similar. If I said I wanted to see X women on a board, I would isolate myself as a director."

> "I have a personal goal of constantly reminding a largely masculine world that there are competent women to be brought in and promoted and liked...I try to learn about women on the staff and what they perceive to be barriers to their promotions. I would like to see mor women in the executive offices -- if they merit it, not just because they're women."

The fact is that both men and women have certain expectations of women directors which women directors may or may not feel are their responsibility to fulfill solely because of their gender. However, while women directors may be ambivalent around this issue, many reported that they brought to their boards a sensitivity to the concerns of marginalized and minority persons: 58% said they had 'initiated discussions on equal opportunity for women in the company;' 46% had 'raised the issue of bringing more women onto the board;' 39% had 'discussed equal opportunities for minorities;' 36% had 'initiated discussions about policies that enable employees to balance work and family;' and, 43% had 'raised other issues related to the company's social responsibility.' Comments recorded from interviews with a sample of women directors indicate that these women did not see initiating such discussions solely an extension of their personal agenda, but rather, they see them as business issues that are appropriate to bring before a corporate board.

8. Recommendations for Corporations

Catalyst has found that several barriers continue to work against increasing women's representation on corporate boards. These center around the director selection process and risk aversion on the part of corporate board leaders. The following recommendations are intended to help corporate leaders who want to recruit and use the talents of female directors:

8.1. BROADEN THE DIRECTOR CANDIDATE POOL

Board chairmen and nominating committees need to consider the pool of women with significant experience who have attained senior-level positions in both operations and general management. Though these women do not hold the title of Chairman, CEO or COO, they are qualified, ready and desirous of serving on corporate boards.

Catalyst's research shows that boards frequently seek to recruit women with proven experience on another corporate board. Established directors appear, on the surface, to represent less risk for the board. However, in taking this 'safer' approach, boards are actually less likely to get a woman with solid business experience relevant to their industry. This is because earlier generations of women directors, i.e., those who are serving on one or more corporate boards, are more likely to have been recruited from academic or nonprofit careers than from business organizations. Furthermore, in selecting a woman who is serving on more than one board, it is likely that the company will get less than her full attention to its business.

8.2. DEVELOP WOMEN IN THE COMPANY'S SENIOR LEADERSHIP RANKS

By developing and promoting women in their own management ranks, corporate leaders can expand the pool of female candidates for their own boards and for other boards as well. By providing women with opportunities to gain core business experience, CEOs will increase the number of women qualified for board service.

8.3. MODIFY THE DIRECTOR SELECTION PROCESS

Selection criteria for corporate directors were developed decades ago, before the globalization of American business. In recent years, the vast changes that have taken place in the way companies do business and the concerns of shareholders, employees and customers have led to increasing scrutiny related to the composition of boards and the way directors are selected. This activism, according to recent studies, has led to modification of the recruitment process in some companies where there is now broader involvement of nominating committees and shareholder groups with director selection.

8.4. SUPPORT THE APPOINTMENT OF WOMEN TO KEY BOARD COMMITTEES

Corporate leaders should examine the extent to which women are represented on key board committees such as compensation, executive, and nominating committees. Women are often placed on committees dealing with issues that are perceived as 'soft,' such as public affairs and corporate social responsibility. Adding women to committees dealing with 'hard' governance issues will enhance the visibility, status, and impact of women directors.

8.5. POSITION DIVERSITY ISSUES AS BUSINESS ISSUES

Corporate board chairmen who recognize women as a critical business resource and are concerned about the advancement of women in their companies' management ranks must take the lead in initiating diversity discussions with the board. Female directors are concerned about being perceived as having a single-issue agenda, especially when they are new to a board. By taking the leadership for these discussions, CEOs and board chairmen position them as business issues for which the board has key responsibility.

References

Catalyst, (1993) Women on Corporate Boards: The Challenge of Change, Catalyst, New York.
Catalyst, (1995) The CEO View: Women on Corporate Boards, Catalyst, New York.
Catalyst, (1998) Catalyst Census of Women Board Directors of *Fortune* 500 Companies, Catalyst, New York,
Daum, J. (1998) Women on Board! *Chief Executive*, October, pp. 40-43.

Daum, J.(1999) Why CEOs Have a Tough Time Recruiting Women Directors, Spencer Stuart Board Index
      1998, New York.
U.S. Department of Labor, Bureau of Labor Statistics, (1998) Employment and Earnings, No.98-2, May, 1998,
      Table 1. Washington DC.

MAKING IT TO THE TOP IN BRITAIN

S. VINNICOMBE, V. SINGH AND J. STURGES
Centre for Developing Women Business Leaders
Cranfield School of Management, Cranfield University, UK

1. Introduction

This chapter examines the career development of six female directors and six male directors within a leading British telecommunications company. The aim is to highlight the key factors in their career development which, in their view, have contributed to their later success. We compare the experiences of the men and women for differences and similarities.

While there is no evidence to suggest that women are less suited to managerial careers than men (Powell, 1990), the women in management literature suggests that the process of career development may be different for males and females. Women managers tend to occupy different types of managerial jobs than male managers. They tend to hold "specialist" support roles, such as personnel and marketing, rather than "generalist" line management roles which generally have higher status than support roles. Furthermore, women managers in the UK are clustered in certain business areas, such as the public sector, which is featured by lower pay than the private sector, and service organisations, such as retailing (Davidson and Cooper, 1992). Some major initiatives have been taken to address these issues. A Hansard Society Commission was set up in 1989, which reported on what it saw as "formidable barriers" for women at the top in 1990 and again five years later (McRae, 1995). Good progress had been made in some areas, and some progress in most areas, towards getting more women into positions of power and influence. But at board level, only 1% of British executive directors were women in 1995. One of the Commission's outcomes was Opportunity 2000, launched in 1991 under the direction of Britain's top business leaders, and organisations which joined showed a doubling of women directors from 8% to 16% by 1995 (McRae, 1995). In 1996, women made up a third of all British managers, and 13% of senior and middle managers were women, but only 3.3% of directors. Where women were board members, they tended to be non-executive directors (EOC, 1997). Thus it can be seen that British women managers still have a long way to go to reach top management in numbers similar to their male peers. Yet this study will show that some women have succeeded to a remarkable level, and we

R.J. Burke and M.C. Mattis (eds.), Women on Corporate Boards of Directors, 57-73.
© 2000 *Kluwer Academic Publishers. Printed in the Netherlands.*

will try to understand how they have done so.

2. Career Development Theory

Career theorists such as Super (1957) and Schein (1971) assume that a career is a life-long, uninterrupted experience of work, which can be divided up into neat stages of development, starting with initial ideas about working and ending with retirement. These stages echo the chronological stages identified by researchers on the process of (male) adult development such as Erikson (1963) and Levinson (1978). There is no allowance for any variation or aberration from the norms they establish. However, the patterns of women's career development are frequently constrained by family as well as workplace commitments and responsibilities, unlike those of men (although this may well be changing in the late 1990s). Therefore, Astin (1984) proposed that career development theory should describe women's careers separately from men's. Her model of career development is based upon four constructs, which she believes shape women's career development: work motivation, work expectations, sex-role socialisation and structure of opportunity, which includes factors such as sex-role stereotyping, distribution of jobs and discrimination.

Larwood and Gutek (1987) concluded that any theory of women's career development must take account of five factors. The first is career preparation, or how females are brought up to view the idea of a career and whether they believe they will have one or not. Availability of opportunities should be taken into consideration, and whether they are limited for women, compared with men. Marriage is the next factor, viewed as neutral for men, but harmful to the careers of women. Similarly, pregnancy and having children inevitably cause women to take some kind of career break. The final factor is timing and age, as career breaks and family relocations often mean that women's careers do not follow the same chronological patterns as those of men.

Powell and Mainiero (1992) claimed that women have two overriding concerns in their lives, for their career and for others (e.g. family and friends). Their model therefore incorporates the influence of personal, organisational and societal factors to describe the balance between work and non-work aspects of life which most women strive to achieve. They develop the concept of "emphasis on career" versus "emphasis on relationships with others", which they claim dominates the choices women make about their careers. A woman may change to emphasise one or the other at various points in her life. The model portrays these as opposite banks of "the river of time". Powell and Mainiero's model differs further from classic models of career development in that it does not assume straightforward, linear progression throughout the career.

3.   The Process of Career Development

Hence, from such career models, it can be seen that women's careers are influenced by several factors which do not affect men's careers to anywhere near the same extent. In particular, the process of career development appears to be very different for female managers, compared with male managers. In a study of the influences which lead to women and men's managerial advancement, Tharenou, Latimer and Conroy (1994) tested situational and individual influence models, and found that whilst training was of advantage to both men and women, it actually had a greater influence for men than women, and that women had less encouragement from their seniors to undertake training. Women's advancement was hindered by having dependants at home, whilst for men, having a spouse at home was a contributory factor to career progression. Career encouragement, on the other hand, had a greater effect on women's advancement, and organisations were advised of the benefits of fast-tracking women's careers, encouraging female managers, and providing opportunities for training and development.

Women have to learn to manage themselves as well as others. They have to develop strategies to deal with being different to male managers, being different to many of the women around them, having few same-gender role models to emulate, and being treated differently to men in the organisation. Shapiro, Haseltine and Rowe (1978) defined role models as "individuals whose behaviors, personal styles and specific attributes are emulated by others". They said: "In a professional setting, such emulation or modelling is a contributory factor in the construction of professional identity." Shapiro et al came to the conclusion that role models were not sufficient for attaining leadership positions, and that patrons and peer pals offered a better model for career success. The patron had the paternal power and could take a parental role, whilst the peer pals approach was more democratic, had two-way benefits, and could be more easily structured to meet the needs of women. These findings were echoed by Kram and Isabella's (1985) research on the value of peer relationships in career development.

The patron's role can also be described as mentoring, "a developmental relationship between an individual (*protégé*) and a more senior and influential manager or professional (*mentor*)" (Dreher and Cox, 1996). Women with mentors do better, because the mentors provide reflected power, feedback, resources and access to the power structure (Ragins and Sundstrom, 1989; Turban and Dougherty, 1994; Vinnicombe and Colwill, 1995). The mentoring relationship can provide training in corporate politics, and access to information sources which might not be otherwise available. However, as there are so few senior women, female managers usually have to seek male/female mentor relationships, which bring fear of exploitation and gossip. Women may not want to approach males for mentorship in case the approach is construed as a sexual come-on (Ragins and Cotton, 1991). Senior males may not consider women to be appropriate as protégés for future senior management. Schein's "think manager, think male" survey of corporate managers, which she undertook fifteen years previously and repeated recently, still elicited the same stereotypical attitudes to women in management (Schein, Mueller et al., 1996). They found that male managers still thought of "men as being more qualified than women to be managers". Women may seek out female mentors, but they are often less powerful and may not be able to deliver many of the benefits of being mentored in a male-dominated organisation.

Tepper (1995) categorised mentorships into formal and informal categories, and found that women had to monitor their behaviour carefully in dealing with upward male relationships, whereas they could be more friendly with women
mentors. According to Hoschette (1995), "the right kind of mentor will sponsor you, watch out for you, polish your act, and help you get the more testing (hence more rewarding) job assignments. Tough assignments are a chance to prove you are ready for promotion." He felt that a good male mentor should give women the same advice he would give a man, "to take bold strides forward". He warned that mentor partners should be wary that the relationship did not start to cause problems with wives (what about the women's husbands?), and to watch out for any unwelcome sexual involvement.

There is evidence that women are less adept than men at handling informal networks to manage their careers and, as a result, respond better than men to formal organisational career management. Pazy (1987) reported that the more women managers perceived that the organisation had formal mechanisms to develop their careers, the less willing they were to use informal mechanisms. This fits in with Mainiero's claim (1994a) that "political seasoning", or being aware of the informal, as well as the formal networks within organisations, is an important stage in the development of women managers who later achieve success.

4.   The Distinguishing Features of Successful Careers

So what are the distinguishing features of the careers of successful women managers? Some of the key ones appear to be early challenge, a chance to prove oneself and gain confidence early on, a wide range of experience and finding a mentor (Stamp, 1986, Ragins and Sundstrom, 1989).

Early challenge is thought to be a key factor for later success for managers (Hall, 1976). When examining the work histories of their sample of "successful" women, White, Cox and Cooper (1992) found that they generally included early challenge, success generating success. Yet challenge may be different for men and women. Ohlott, Ruderman and McCauley (1994) concluded that men got challenge from their jobs, whereas women obtained challenge from the obstacles which they faced at work. They stated that "there is cause for concern because women face greater challenges deriving from lack of personal support. Women continue to feel left out of important networks, have difficulty in finding supportive people to talk to, and feel they must continually fight to be recognised for the work they do". Their findings are substantiated by Ragins and Sundstrom, who said: "For women, the path to power contains many impediments and can be best described as an obstacle course. In contrast...the path for men contains few obstacles that derive from their gender.... therefore strategies for advancement that work effectively for men might not work for women and vice versa". The importance of a chance to prove oneself early on was highlighted by Stamp, who found that a majority of her sample of women managers and military officers mentioned an occasion in their career "that had served as a turning point for establishing their confidence".

Mainiero (1994b) proposed four key stages through which women managers must pass en route to becoming senior executives. *Political naiveté* leads to awareness that outspokenness and honesty must be tempered with an understanding and awareness of the corporate culture. She must *build credibility* with her superiors, peers and subordinates, and begin to form alliances and interpersonal networks. *Refining a style* means learning to be tough as well as direct, and finally, *shouldering responsibilities,* as the sole woman at the top, means taking responsibility for mentoring others.

Likewise, Morrison, White and van Velsor (1992) pointed to four paradoxes, which they claimed women managers must contend with, if they wished to have successful organisational careers. They must take risks but remain consistently outstanding, be tough but not macho, be ambitious but not expect equal treatment, and take responsibility but follow others' advice.

TABLE 1: Some models of career development

Astin (1984)	Larwood & Gutek (1987)	Mainiero (1994b)	Ragins, Townsend & Mattis (1998)
Work motivation Work expectations Sex-role socialisation Structured opportunities	Career preparation Available opportunities Marriage & Pregnancy Timing & Age	Assignment to high visibility projects Demonstration of critical skills Top level support Entrepreneurial initiative Accurately identifying what company values	Consistently exceeding performance Developing style with which males were comfortable Seeking challenging assignments Having influential mentors

Despite the difficulties, there are indications that the glass ceiling is being broken, by some women in some US organisations, but progress is slow, according to Ragins, Townsend and Mattis (1998). They reported a study by Catalyst of senior women executives and CEOs of *Fortune* 1000 companies. Through a survey and interviews, Ragins et al explored the advancement of women from their own perspective, as well as seeking answers from their CEOs, by asking them to rate the importance of each of 13 career strategies. Four items were particularly significant: exceptional performance; development of a style with which their male peers were comfortable; seeking challenging assignments, and having influential mentors. Almost all the women reported the existence of mentors in their careers. The women saw the "exclusionary corporate culture" as their biggest barrier, whilst the CEOs reported that the barrier was that women tended not to have the appropriate kind of experience for further advancement, although this did not appear to be the case for the surveyed women.

This review of the literature has highlighted several models of career development processes for women. Table 1 sets these out by date. It can be seen that the later studies include factors of political awareness and active career self-management. We now turn to the British study of the telecommunications directors, which sought their views of the key facilitators to their success.

5.   The Research Project

The sample of twelve directors was selected on the basis that there were six women at this level in the company, so a similar group of males would provide useful comparisons.

The Personnel Department assisted in identifying the matching male peers. Given the glass ceiling phenomenon, this organisation's relatively large number of women at director level is still unusual in British companies. All the directors were aged between 40 and 50, and most had a broad range of experience both in line and support management roles.
    The aim of the research was to examine the career development experiences of the directors in depth to get a rich picture of their explanations for their career achievements, and to see if there were gender differences in those experiences. Individual semi-structured interviews were held at the company offices. These lasted 1½ hours and were taped and transcribed. Analysis proceeded initially through review of the transcripts by the researchers to gain an in-depth understanding of the individual experiences of the directors, and then by identifying concepts and themes which allowed a more structured approach for the next stage of analysis. The transcripts were imported into the qualitative software package QSR NUD.IST (Version 4), and hierarchical coding was undertaken using the themes and concepts identified on the hard copy transcripts (Lofland and Lofland, 1995; Kelle, 1995). The data were interrogated iteratively through the software's document and index search systems. Reports were made of segments of text coded at the nodes of interest, then patterns of similarities and differences were identified by gender (Miles and Huberman, 1994), and discussed between the researchers for reliability checks. The emphasis has been on keeping coding close to the original data, so that the respondents' own views may emerge in the report, rather than being imposed by the researchers.

6.   The Key Facilitators to Success

Three key factors influencing career development emerged from the interviews, and as we will see from the evidence, they were all inter-linked. These were finding a mentor; taking on challenge; and becoming visible. These factors appear crucial to the career development of the sample, and equally so for both the men and the women. What is significant, however, is that they seem to have operated differently for the male and female directors.

The twelve directors were asked what was the key factor in their success, and some of them mentioned several features. Almost all of them talked about the impact of a champion or mentor, particularly during the early stages of their careers, and similar new relationships as they developed as managers. Five also talked of their own personal qualities and strategies. The most significant factor overall was the mentor, who facilitated opportunity and visibility, which together with personal strengths such as drive and brainpower, led to growth for the young aspiring manager. We will now examine these influences in more detail.

6.1. THE IMPORTANCE OF GETTING A MENTOR

Most of the sample, including all the women directors, mentioned the importance of at least one person who had taken on a mentor role for them, especially in the early stages of their career. Formal mentoring schemes were not then in operation, although they have since been introduced in this organisation as elsewhere in Britain in the 1990s. Half of both the male and female directors reported that they had several informal mentors, rather than just one or two. Ragins and Cotton (1991) had reported that there were more barriers for women than men to gaining a mentor where there were cross-gender relationships to be negotiated. In this telecommunications company, there was a very male-dominated management, so these mentoring relationships were almost all cross-gender, although one male had a significant mentorship with a senior female in his previous organisation. The women said that earlier in their careers, senior managers had taken it on themselves to help them.

> "I found that there were a whole load of people who wanted to help me, and I just had to make it clear to them that I wanted to be helped, and they helped me tremendously."
> (Female director)

In contrast, most of the male directors said that they were the ones who started the mentoring relationship. They were far more likely than the women to regard a mentor as a "useful" superior whom they cultivated. They identified those whom they saw as influencers, and engineered opportunities to socialise and interact with them.

> "Usually I've cultivated my boss. I don't think I've ever had a mentor directly outside the line. I do tend to cultivate people, certainly my bosses and any key influencers I can find about the place. I do it now. I find out who is important and who is worth influencing."
> (Male director)

> "You can't wander along to people and say 'Hey, let me tell you what I stand for', so you need to engineer ways of talking to people." (Male director)

So it seems that these male directors were being more active and more selective in their mentoring relationships than the women, as Ibarra (1992, 1995) had found in her study of male and female usage of networks. She identified homophily in organisational networks as a significant feature of senior males; they preferred to have same gender relationships, which they used instrumentally, putting less effort into social relationships than the females once the benefits had been exploited and the network tie was no longer seen to be of high future value.

Mentors as fatherly sponsors appear to have been significant for the women in the sample. Many of the women were "adopted" at a crucial stage in their organisational career by a more senior manager, who had a powerful influence on their future career development. Some of the women talked about the protection offered by the male mentors, during which they were able to grow and carve out a managerial identity for themselves.

> "He did everything he could to help you progress, learn .... He steered me quite heavily towards creating a bit of the company I could make my own...with his help I started to understand it better and found that actually there weren't many other people who understood it at that level and, I suppose, I singled myself out with his help." (Female director)

> "It was that protection, that giving you of space, that protecting you to grow." (Female director)

Again, the same kind of help was acknowledged by male directors, but presented in a more ego-enhancing style, as one said that the senior mentor "had a tremendous respect for me", and others indicated that they had found the mentor rather than the mentor finding them.

> "What was even more fortunate was that there was a senior manager within the team at that time who had a tremendous respect for me and who personally steered my career over those first few years. He took a genuine personal interest in what I was doing." (Male director)

> "What has helped me in my career...is finding the useful people who have taken an interest in the things I've done and in me." (Male director)

The roles played by the mentors included giving career advice, counselling, coaching on management techniques and acting as an advocate on their behalf. One of the benefits for some of the women was "executive mirroring" – giving the women a view of the appropriate managerial identity for success in the organisation. Wahl (1998) said that men receive confirmation of their identity as leaders, through their shared maleness, whilst unless there are female leaders, women managers do not. Turban and Dougherty (1994) talked of mentors providing role models of behaviours that are important for the protégé's success. The mentor played an important role in this respect for the women directors in this study.

> "I remember one person who was quite a senior manager, and I was only on Level 1. He happened to be on one of the selection boards that I'd gone to, and he kept in touch, and kept counselling me on things, styles, behaviours, management techniques etc, which I found very useful." (Female director)

Sometimes this mirroring was more impersonal. Her silent observation of her superiors, according to one woman director, had helped develop her management style and career, as she learned what was and was not effective, and she learnt about organisational politics.

> "You learn an awful lot. I used to shadow the board, so I got an awful lot of experience in terms of board etiquette, board decisions and their debate. I watched all the ramifications." (Female director)

> "Through watching him, watching people's reactions around him, that really gave me the sort of understanding, 'Well, OK, that's not the way we do it." (Female director)

One woman reported that she had been a senior male manager's protégé without realising it. He had been acting as her sponsor because he wanted to see a woman on the board, and she was not happy about this.

> "When he left, he wrote me a letter and said, 'Well, I apologise. ... I wanted to help you as the first female director of XXX and I was mentoring you that way." (Female director)

Although she did not like being mentored without knowing, she had her own informal "silent mentors" who did not know they were mentoring her.

> "They don't know they are mentoring me, but I am watching them and saying, how do they operate on that, and how would I have done it, how could I improve on that. I am always reflecting." (Female director)

Most of these directors reported good relationships with their mentors, "an absolutely wonderful man", "a real friend", and "old and wise, like a father". Male directors also reported learning from their mentors, and the words below indicate a "locker-room" camaraderie between the two male parties, which would be difficult for a female/male pairing to achieve.

> "I learnt an enormous amount of him, he was wonderful. He'd say things that were true, he'd hit me over the head, and I'd say, I haven't done anything. But he'd reply, it's important to hit you over the head once a week." (Male director)

Both male and female directors talked of continued use of mentors over a long period, especially to discuss major career moves. They sought advice about where the senior individual thought the organisation was moving strategically, and where they would be best positioned for further advancement. They valued the kind of help where they formed their own decision, rather than having guidance foisted upon them.

> "He made me think it through, which I think is all you need. You need somebody to give you that opportunity to talk yourself through what you want to do." (Female director)

6.2.   GETTING THE OPPORTUNITY FOR CHALLENGE

Like mentors, supportive bosses played an important role in the careers of most of the directors, again particularly the women's careers. Male mentors might not wish to mentor women because of the visibility if things were to go wrong, as this would reflect back on the mentor, according to Ragins and Scandura (1994), but these directors had found bosses who were prepared to take the risk.

> "There have been some people that have been very critical to my career. There have been people who have been prepared to put their necks on the block for me - the person who gave me the job as X, was the first person in the company who had ever taken that risk."
> (Female director)

These quotations epitomise the key way in which supportive bosses had helped all these directors' careers to develop, that is by taking a risk on them when they were relatively inexperienced and giving them a chance to prove themselves in a job or situation which stretched their abilities to the full.

> "Absolutely no question he was taking a big risk...of all my other colleagues on the senior team' I don't think there was one of them under 50. And I was under 30...it was just a great job; I was learning and it was a job of influence. This chap was the person who set me on my senior management career." (Male director)

> "X was a very important person in my career because he was the one who gave me the opportunity to set up Y. I know it was a risk. He was told it was a terrible risk by a number of people; he told me that himself. That (job) was a big step up for me and I think that surprised a lot of people at the time. (Female director)

Taking a risk on an unproved manager commonly was the result of earlier outstanding performance. Sometimes, however it simply reflected a boss's intuition about an employee's potential ability.

> "That's what they needed, someone with a fresh approach and I had shown ability in my previous roles. Therefore they gave me the chance; my career has been littered with people who gave me the chance." (Female director)

> "X is very special in so far as he is prepared to take a chance on people (who have) got the right feel in his eyes and put them into a job which on the face of it they have absolutely no qualifications or experience at all." (Female director)

Interestingly, there appeared to be differences as to how men and women reacted to being offered a challenging job opportunity. Men seemed to accept unquestioningly such chances to prove themselves. They expressed no doubts about their ability to fulfil the roles offered to them. In contrast, some of the women reported having strong doubts about their ability in the same situation. This suggests that even though the women had been given the same development opportunities as their male counterparts, there was still an issue of lack of confidence.

"I was not at all happy about making this move, although it was a promotion, I didn't want to do it; I didn't know how to do it: I didn't know what it would entail. More of the classic female insecurity issues, confidence issues emerged. I was really distressed at that point but X in the end made it clear to me that I didn't have too much choice. If I didn't offer to do it, he was going to instruct me to do it. So that point I gave in." (Female director)

"X said 'I want you to do the job. I really want you to do the job. I said 'I can't do it' and he said 'You can, you know'. I thought he must know better than I did." (Female director)

The chances given to the directors to prove themselves, at a stage in their career when they were relatively inexperienced, all posed a challenge of some kind, and success in meeting these challenges was clearly crucial to their career development, particularly in terms of building their confidence and beginning to heighten their visibility.

Yet despite indications in the literature that women obtain challenge from the obstacles they face at work, rather than from their jobs because women tend to be given less challenging positions than their male peers (Ohlott, Ruderman and McCauley 1994), this was not the case for these directors. All the women directors were given the same kind of on-the-job challenges as their male colleagues. Every director interviewed had powerful stories of challenges which they had successfully undertaken and overcome throughout their career, but particularly challenges early on in their career.

"I was offered a line manager job managing six hundred telephonists.... I found when I started to do the job that I was completely and utterly hooked...That was the most sensational thing that had ever happened to me in terms of my career...I was 23." (Female director)

"The marketing people didn't know what to do with me, so they did something which I have always regarded as the most brilliant thing the company has done for me. (They gave me) 95,000 Intercom phones to flog - inside two years, I had taken a 25% share of the market from a standing start. They gave me a complete insight into how to run a business." (Male director)

The kind of challenging work experiences enjoyed by the directors included taking sole charge of a project or even a business, being the pioneer in a green-field area, breaking new ground, handling a crisis or a turnaround situation, and taking on new responsibilities far beyond their previous experience. This evidence fits well with

Mainiero's (1994b) findings of entrepreneurial initiative, as reported in Table 1.

"They set up a network to run the Y business...within three months I became the London manager. I ran it as a standalone area, with profit and loss accounts. It was a step change from the world I was in." (Male director)

"My second job was to create a graduate recruitment scheme for the Midlands from scratch. This job started a trend for me, because a lot of my jobs have been green-field jobs, starting things from scratch." (Female director)

"She let me loose on the Cabinet Office and I found myself dealing with permanent
secretaries and so on...the important part was not so much that it was successful but that it
took me onto a different plane of the Civil Service." (Male director)

Taking on challenges and succeeding clearly had an important effect on the
directors' confidence in themselves and the impression they created in the organisation.

"Well, I just thought it was a turning point in my life...I had done a very good job...I had
turned the place over." (Female director)

"Suddenly they had a success on their hands. And because of the way I did it, it went down
quite well. There was the marketing department wanting to show what marketing was and
here was a marked example of it succeeding." (Male director)

6.3.   THE IMPORTANCE OF VISIBILITY

Several of the directors obtained jobs early on in their career as personal assistants to
senior managers. This gave their visibility a boost by bringing them into contact with a
range of senior staff whom they would not normally have got the chance to meet at that
stage in their career. Not only did this increase their visibility; it also gave them access to
an important network of influential contacts and an overview of how the organisation
worked.

"I joined the (managing director's) team as a young PA...my job was to handle all the
customer complaints that came through either to his office or to the chairman's
office...that was a turning point because I learnt about the company and I learnt about the
industry.... I was exposed to all the directors." (Female director)

"They borrowed me to be secretary of a committee on internal communication -
everybody who was sitting round the table was either a director or a senior director. I
learnt a lot by just watching senior management at play." (Male director)

Taking on and succeeding at challenging tasks made these future directors
visible within the organisation. Becoming known in this way was something all the
directors had experienced. It clearly affected peoples' attitudes to them and therefore
ensured that they continued to be given challenging and high profile jobs. Their visibility
had contributed to their ultimate success.

"I made a stand on the issue and I ended up pushing it nationally. There was a big court
case and I was the lead expert for the company.... At that stage I was beginning to be
noticed." (Female director)

"I became very well known cross departmentally. I became something of a figure. It
made a difference to my own view of myself and my colleagues' perception of me."
(Male director)

"I suppose I singled myself out, with his help, as somebody who could talk with a degree
of sense and in a fairly articulate way about this Cinderella subject in the company. And
that helped me to get noticed in a way that wouldn't otherwise have happened." (Female
director)

But it was not just visibility that was important to the directors' careers. It was being visible to the people who mattered, the senior managers and those with most influence within the organisation. This emphasis on visibility fits with the evidence from another study where the visibility to senior managers of commitment through taking on challenge was seen as a key factor for promotion (Singh and Vinnicombe, 1999). Many of these directors had jobs early on in their careers, which brought them into contact with or to the notice of influential people high up in the company.

> "And that job, more than my previous jobs, started to bring me into contact with our headquarters' people and our regional people, and I was then invited into various working groups and started to become known, I suppose." (Male director)

> "The job with networks meant I had to travel to London a lot, which meant I got involved with group headquarters. I suppose that created openings and got you noticed." (Female director)

> "It was obvious I'd made it by then...I was known the right people." (Male director)

Becoming visible was equally important for the male and female directors, and the circumstances in which they achieved it were generally similar. However, many of the women felt that being female actually helped increase their visibility within the company. The majority of them did not feel that their gender had inhibited their career development. Their view is in contrast to much of the literature on women managers, which has traditionally emphasised the pressures women managers face when in token positions in organisations.

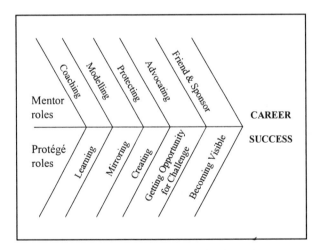

Figure 1: The Mentor/Protégé Relationship

"I would say a very strong bit of why I got the job was X's positive discrimination. He wanted a woman general manager." (Female director)

Interestingly, this view that the women's gender had helped their career development was not shared by any of the male directors, who all suggested that it was much harder for women managers to reach the top, because of discrimination and prejudice, and that those who made it were "truly exceptional".

Figure 1 shows the roles played by mentors and protégés, as reported by these directors. The early roles of coach and role model developed gradually into friend and sponsor, and some of these relationships were maintained over many years, particularly by the women.

7. Conclusion

The pattern of career development appeared to be very similar for the men and women. While this appears to contradict some of the literature in this area, this may be because the research only considered the most senior women in a very large company. Their careers might have had to be similar to those of their male colleagues for them to reach director level positions in the organisation.

Most of this group of directors talked about their own personal qualities, such as drive, determination and energy, which together with brainpower, intelligence and education led to them being visible early in their career. Other visible factors were their enjoyment of what they were doing, their flexibility when opportunities arose, and their active role in steering their careers once under way. Some of these women may have started under the wing of a mentor, but soon started driving their careers forward in a similar way to the men.

In addition to identifying this overall similarity in the male and female directors' descriptions, this study highlights three key factors in their career development process. As well as the personal strengths, which got them noticed in the first place, these factors were as follows:

- *Mentor(s)*: Sponsors who guided and coached in the early career, and were advocates of the promising young future director.

- *Challenge*: Opportunities to prove oneself through challenging assignments.

- *Visibility*: Exposure to influential people.

Figure 2: The Career Success Cycle

As Figure 2 shows, this was a cyclical process continuing to have a positive effect on the directors' career development up through the organisation. The initial personal qualities led to visibility to sponsors. Then, having mentors and bosses who were prepared to support them as junior staff led to this group of future directors being identified as 'high-potential', and they were given a further chance to prove themselves. This in turn encouraged them to rise to the challenges they were given, which, when they succeeded, made them more visible within the organisation. This then led to them receiving yet higher level support, with even more senior managers willing to take a risk that they would deliver the goals.

These factors are consistent with previous literature on the career development of senior women managers, as was shown in Table 1, particularly with the models of Mainiero (1994b) and Ragins et al (1998). However, the British women did not talk particularly of developing a style with which the males would be comfortable. Indeed, some of the women seemed to want to keep the males guessing, so that they would not be stereotyped but instead be seen as extraordinarily competent and individual.

Significantly, the career development facilitators mentioned here appear to operate differently for men and women. Two linked features stand out. Firstly, the males said that they were the initiators of the mentoring relationships, and that they used those relationships for career advancement. In contrast, the females were more likely to say that mentors stepped in to help them develop as senior managers. But this could be simply a difference in the way men and women talk about their achievements (Tannen, 1994) rather than a real difference. Post-hoc rationalisation also has to be taken into account, as these directors may have recalled and reported the events differently from the actual event. Secondly, there was the male directors' stated willingness to seek out and accept challenges, fully confident that they would rise to overcome them, in contrast to most of the females, who said that they needed encouragement from their mentors before accepting these highly developmental challenges.

Undoubtedly, for both men and women in this talented group of directors, the initial visibility through support from their mentors led to further chances to prove themselves in more challenging roles, thereby making them visible to a higher tier of management. These results indicate that successful career development may depend on these processes happening early on in a manager's career, in this cyclical fashion. They do not operate in isolation, but each part of the process contributes to the next stage of career development. Women may enter through being noticed, whilst men say they engineer their own access to the arena. Nonetheless, once successfully integrated into this cycle, men and women alike set the foundations for later career achievements.

References

Astin, H.S. (1984) The meaning of work in women's lives: a socio-psychological model of career choice and work behaviour, *Counselling Psychologist* **12** (4), 117-126.

Davidson, M.J. and Cooper, C.L. (1992) *Shattering the Glass Ceiling: The Woman Manager,* Paul Chapman Publishing Ltd, London.

Dreher, G.F. and Cox, T.H. (1996) Race, gender and opportunity: A study of compensation attainment and the establishing of mentoring relationships, *Journal of Applied Psychology* **81** (3) 297-308.

Equal Opportunities Commission (1997) *Briefing on Men and Women in Britain: Management and the Professions*, EOC, Manchester.

Erikson, E. (1963) *Childhood and Society,* 2nd edition, Norton, New York.

Hall, D.T. (1976) *Careers in Organisations,* Goodyear, Santa Monica.

Hoschette, J.A. (1995) A mentor in hand, *IEEE Spectrum* **95**, Feb, 56-58.

Ibarra, H. (1992) Homophily and differential returns: Sex differences in network structure and access in an advertising firm, *Administrative Science Quarterly* **37**, 422-447.

Ibarra, H. (1995) The relationship paradox: Gender, homophily and the strength of network ties, *12th EGOS Colloquium*, Istanbul.

Kram, K.E. and Isabella, L.A. (1985) Mentoring alternatives: The role of peer relationships in career development, *Academy of Management Journal* **28** (1), 110-132.

Larwood, L. and Gutek, B.A. (1987) Working towards a theory of women's career development, in B.A. Gutek and L. Larwood (eds.), *Women's career development,* Sage, Newbury Park.

Levinson, D. (1978) *The Seasons of a Man's Life,* 2nd edition, Knopf, New York.

Lofland, J. and Lofland, L.H. (1995), *Analysing Social Settings*, Wadsworth, Belmont CA.

Mainiero, L.A. (1994a) On breaking the glass ceiling: the political seasoning of powerful women executives, *Organisational Dynamics* **22** (4), 5-20.

Mainiero, L.A. (1994b) Getting anointed for advancement: The case of executive women, *Academy of Management Executive* **8** (2), 53-67.

McRae, S. (1995) *Women at the top: Progress after five years*, Follow up Report to the Hansard Society Commission on Women at the Top, King-Hall Paper No 2, Hansard Society, UK.

Miles, M.B. and Huberman, A.M. (1994), *Qualitative Data Analysis: An Expanded Sourcebook*, Sage, London.

Morgan, S. Schor, S.M. and Martin, L.R. (1993) Gender differences in career paths in banking, *Career Development Quarterly* **41**, 375-382.

Morrison, A.M., White, R.P. and van Velsor, E. (1992) *Breaking the Glass Ceiling: Can Women reach the Top of America's Largest Corporations,* 2nd edition, Addison Wesley, Reading, MA.

Ohlott, P.J., Ruderman, M.N. and McCauley, C.D. (1994) Gender differences in managers' developmental job experiences, *Academy of Management Journal* **37** (1), 46-67.

Pazy, A. (1987) Sex differences in responsiveness to organisational career management, *Human Resource Management* **26** (2), 243-256.

Powell, G.N. and Mainiero, L.A. (1992) Cross-currents in the river of time: conceptualising the complexities of women's careers, *Journal of Management* **18** (2), 215-237.

Powell, G.N. (1990) One more time: do female and male managers differ? *Academy of Management Executive* **4** (3), 68-75.

QSR NUD.IST Qualitative Software, Version 4 (1996).

Ragins, B.R. and Sundstrom, E. (1989) Gender and power in organisations: a longitudinal perspective, *Psychological Bulletin* **105** (1), 51-88.

Ragins, B.R., Townsend, B. and Mattis, M. (1998) Gender gap in the executive suite: CEOs and female executives report on breaking the glass ceiling, *Academy of Management Executive* **12** (1), 28-42.

Schein, E.H. (1971) The individual, the organisation, and the career: a conceptual scheme, *Journal of Applied Behavioural Science* **7**, 401-426.

Schein, V.E., Mueller, R., Lituchy, T. and Liu, J. (1996), Think manager - think male. A global phenomenon, *Journal of Organizational Behavior,* **17** (1), 33-41.

Singh, V. and Vinnicombe, S. (1999) What does "Commitment" really mean? Views of British and Swedish engineering managers, *Personnel Review*, in press, Autumn 1999.

Stamp, G. (1986) Some observations on the career paths of women, *Journal of Applied Behavioural Science* **22** (4), 385-396.

Super, D.E. (1984) Career and life development, in D. Brown, L. Brooks et al. (eds.) *Career Choice and Development,* Jossey Bass, San Francisco, CA.

Super, D.I. (1957) *The Psychology of Careers,* Harper & Row, New York.

Tannen, D. (1994) *Talking from 9 to 5: Women at Work: Language, Sex and Power.* Virago: Reading.

Tepper, B.J. (1995) Upward maintenance tactics in supervisory mentoring and non-mentoring relationships, *Academy of Management Journal* **38** (4), 1191-1205.

Tharenou. P., Latimer, S. and Conroy, D. (1994) How do you make it to the top? An examination of influences on women's and men's managerial advancement, *Academy of Management Journal* **37** (4), 899-931.

Vinnicombe, S. and Colwill, N.C. (1995) *The Essence of Women in Management*, Prentice Hall, London.

Wahl, A. (1998) Deconstructing women and leadership, *International Review of Women and Leadership* **4** (2), 46-60.

White, B., Cox, C. and Cooper, C. (1992) *Women's Career Development: A Study of High Flyers,* Blackwell Business, Oxford.

THE PARADOX OF AFFIRMATIVE ACTION FOR
WOMEN DIRECTORS IN ISRAEL[1]

DAFNA IZRAELI
Bar-Ilan University
Ramat-Gan, Israel

1.   The Event

On March 16, 1993, the Israeli Knesset (Parliament) passed an amendment to the Government Companies' Act   (1975). The main purpose of the amendment was to depoliticize the appointment of directors. The amendment (Amendment 6) defined criteria and procedures for the appointment of directors to the boards of government companies.[2] Clause 18a of the amendment stated:

a)   In the makeup of the board of directors of a government company, appropriate[3] expression will be given to the representation of both sexes.
b)   Until that time as the said appropriate representation is achieved, government ministers will appoint, to the extent feasible under the relevant conditions, directors from the sex which is not appropriately represented at that time on the company board.

Clause 18a, is significant because it is the first piece of affirmative action legislation ever to be enacted in Israel.[4] In effect, the clause instructs ministers to give preference to

---

[1] I wish to thank Judith Lorber, Rachel Benziman and Neta Ziv for helpful comments on this paper. Material for this study was collected largely from personal participation in the various commissions and committees mentioned in this chapter and from interviews with numerous people associated with them.

[2] Government companies refer to government-controlled companies, that is, companies in which the government owns at least 51% of the voting shares. The government appoints directors proportionate to its shares of the respective companies.

[3] The Hebrew term <u>holem</u> could be alternatively translated as suitable, fitting, or adequate

[4] This situation is different from that in the United States, where women followed the movement for racial justice and the category women appears as an addendum, rather than a starting place, for the formulation of affirmative action (Bacchi, 1996).

R.J. Burke and M.C. Mattis (eds.), Women on Corporate Boards of Directors, 75-96.
© 2000 Kluwer Academic Publishers. Printed in the Netherlands.

women when making appointments to boards of directors[5]. Notwithstanding the gender-neutral wording of the clause, women, who are invariably underrepresented on these boards, have been the sole beneficiaries of the amendment. Before the amendment was passed, the concept of affirmative action as a basis for legal action was virtually nonexistent (Radai, 1995) and was largely rejected as a basis for social policy (Yishai 1997:147).

The increase in women's representation on boards of government companies that occurred between 1993 and 1998 is impressive. In 1993 there were approximately 170 government companies and some 900 state directors, 7% of whom were women.[6] This proportion rose to 29% by 1997 (Izraeli, 1998) and to 30% in 1998 (Comptroller General, 1998). In 1993 there were no women directors in 69% of the companies but by 1997 there were no women in only 21.5%. Of all the companies in which there had been at least one woman director in 1993, the number had increased in 64% of them by 1997; had remained the same in 28% and had decreased in 2.5%.

This short description of events leading to the appointment of women directors to government companies in Israel provides an unusual prism through which to explore women's struggle for access to positions that require knowledge and confer power. It begins by underlining the apparent contradiction inherent in the inclusion of an affirmative action clause in an amendment whose main purpose was to depoliticize the appointment of directors. Ministers frequently used such appointments as political patronage, which they distributed to party members. The 1989 annual report of the Comptroller General stated that 61% of the directors were members of the central committee of the political parties.[7] Those who were appointed frequently did not have the independence necessary to protect the interests of the general public against the narrow political considerations of the ministers. They also generally lacked sufficient competence to be effective directors, especially of large, complex economic concerns, such as the Israel Electric Corporation. The proposed amendment to the Government Companies Act, was intended, according to its sponsors,

> "To assure the existence of a proper (standardized) appointment procedure for directors that should be based on relevant considerations only and related to advancing the welfare of the company and the suitability of the candidate to serve in this role, to

---

[5] Section 60 of the amendment extended the application of the affirmative action clause to all corporations created by, law such as the Port Authority, Consumer Protection Authority, and the Authority for the War against Narcotics.

[6] In 1998 there were 689 state directors. (Comptroller General, 1998:17). The decline in total number of directors was largely the result of privatization.

[7] Ministers appointed directors of companies within their respective jurisdictions, in conjunction with the minister of the treasury. Each board is comprised of two kinds of directors: those representing the government and selected from among senior civil servants and those from the public at large.

secure adequate guarantees that the selection of candidates will be detached, as much as possible, from political tendencies or personal obligations." (Knesset Protocol, 1992).

The guidelines prescribed in Amendment 6 limited appointments to persons with relevant academic degrees and at least five years of managerial experience. Directors were also prohibited from having economic, personal or political interests in the companies or ties to the appointing ministers. Clause 18a of Amendment 6, known as the affirmative action clause, in contrast, introduced a consideration based on ascription into legislation aimed at institutionalizing a merit system. This chapter examines this apparent paradox -- that a law, ostensibly intended to establish a norm and practice of universalism and rationalism, should include an affirmative action clause that privileges gender.

Given only the information supplied in the opening paragraphs of this chapter, a person who is familiar with gender politics in Israel would find the impact of the legislation surprising. At the time of its passage there were many reasons to expect that Clause 18a would not be enforced. Israel has a history of well-intentioned equal-opportunity legislation, most of which remains more honored in the breach (Ben-Israel 1998). The phrase "to the extent feasible under the relevant conditions" provides an escape clause that ministers could have used to continue to appoint men in that they could have claimed conditions under which it was not feasible to appoint women. Furthermore, the law did not specify that giving preferential treatment to women when women were not appropriately represented on boards was a criterion for disqualifying men. This omission is in contrast to the educational requirement, political affiliation limitations, and other stipulations that the law delineated as criteria to be used by the supervisory committee responsible for authorizing that ministerial appointments are in keeping with the requirements of the law. Rather, it required the intervention of the Supreme Court to establish the new norm in practice.

2. The Theoretical Perspective

In the 20th century, states in most parts of the world have played an important role in changing women's status in society. Whereas social scientists may disagree about the nature of the impact that the state has had on women (see Connell, 1994), it is indisputable that the state is a major player in the power relations of gender. For example, the state limited the power of husbands in families, thus increasing women's autonomy, if not their power. Some have argued that this change is merely a shift from family patriarchy to state patriarchy. Others, such as Fox Piven (1984) have pointed to the positive contributions of the modern welfare state to the condition of women. The state has benefited women not only as a provider of welfare benefits and an employer, but as an object in relation to which to organize and use electoral power. It provides the arena in which gender relations in society are negotiated and is an important object for influence.

The structure and culture of the state shape the strategies that women's organizations adopt in their struggle for greater equality. Welfare states such as those in Europe and Israel, provide greater legitimacy for state intervention in the economy and therefore, greater cultural support for mobilization of groups around such demands than is the case for the United States. Furthermore, enterprises that are owned or controlled by the state are expected to be more responsive to the claims of citizens' groups than are privately owned enterprises. Consequently, they are more vulnerable to moral claims by contending groups.

A discussion of the role of the state needs to be premised on the understanding that the state is neither gender neutral nor monolithic. The state is gendered in at least two respects: First, the majority of the most powerful and prestigious positions are occupied by men and men like any powerful group, benefit from preserving their hegemonic position. Second, the fact that men have historically controlled the state, state institutions, and state laws reflect men's perspectives and interests (MacKinnon, 1987). As Connell observed, (1994) gender is both internal and external to the state. It is external in the sense that "the state as an institution is part of a wider social structure of gender relations" whose structure of gender relations, or "gender regime" provides the context within which state practices develop. Gender is internal to the state in that the state engages in a wide range of activities that impact on gender relations.

The state is not a monolithic or even a coherent structure but, rather, the site of competing discourses, practices and struggles. Competition is inherent in part, in the separation of functions that is characteristic of democratic states where, for example, the judiciary is a check on the legislature. Social policy, however, is determined not only by the state but by political parties and interest groups. Thus Scokpol (1992) emphasized the "polity", rather than the "state", and highlighted the importance of state, political party, and interest group organization, all of which serve to structure policy initiatives. According to Skocpol, (p. 58) there is a two-way relationship between politics and policies:

> "Politics creates policies and policies also remake politics......The overall structure of political institutions provides access and leverage to some groups and alliances, thus encouraging and rewarding their efforts to shape government policies, while simultaneously denying access and leverage to other groups and alliances operating in the same national polity. [T]his means that the degree of success any politically active group or movement achieves is influenced not just by the self consciousness and resource mobilization of that social force itself....[D]egrees of success in achieving political goals - including the enactment of social legislation - depend on the relative opportunities that existing political institutions offer to the group or movement in question [and simultaneously deny to other groups]."

Policies have feedback effects by transforming or expanding state capacities, shaping administrative possibilities as well as by affecting the identities, interests, and capacities of politically active groups. Therefore, according to Skocpol "any valid explanation of the development of a nation's social policies must be genuinely historical, sensitive to processes unfolding over time" (1992: 59).

This chapter analyzes the developments that led to the passage of Clause 18a – the affirmative action law requiring ministers to appoint women to the boards of government companies in order to achieve a gender balance, and to its ultimate enforcement. It traces the emergence and history of   women's demand for board representation as a social issue around which interested women's organizations mobilized. It argues that this demand emerged and was reinforced in the context of opportunities provided by state initiatives. The change in policies was not always related to gender and that it was legitimated somewhat differently at different points in time. Specifically, the shift from a "political loyalty" discourse to an "economic rationality" discourse created a window of opportunity for professional (Jewish) women. Women's choice of strategies was shaped by the changing legitimating ideologies of the state, the opportunities for access to information,   the development of organizational resources and the networking among women located at various strategic junctures within the state and   civil society.   The principle of women's representation on boards of directors was ultimately supported when the policy could be made to fit into a male-defined agenda and to resonate with men's interests. The practice of representation required the intervention of the Israeli Supreme Court.

3.   The Call to Depoliticize the Boards of Government Companies

Israel, established in 1948 as a socialist welfare state in the British tradition, developed a strong centralized and highly elaborate state-owned economy. In the early 1990s the government employed approximately one third of the labor force, and public sector spending represented 60% of the gross national product (Bank of Israel, 1998:274), among the highest in the world. From the pre-state period until 1977, Labor was the dominant political party. It established and sustained its power by politically driven appointments in all sectors of the polity.

Political considerations in appointments of personnel gained renewed importance following the election of the right-of-center Likud Party in 1977, and its return in 1981. The first time it was in power, the Likud used patronage to repay its supporters and strengthen its hold on the state apparatus (Izraeli, 1994). During the same period, there was mounting public criticism of the ineffectual operation of the governance function of companies belonging to the Histadrut -- the General Federation of Labor -- as well as of the banks. The growing deficit of the Histadrut-owned Koor Industries from the late 1970s, with the consequent loss of some 20,000 jobs, and the crash of the banks in 1982, highlighted the need for more effective and responsible governance. In 1983 the Knesset passed an amendment to the Companies Act (that governs companies publicly traded on the stock exchange) required the board of every publicly traded corporation to include two directors from among the public at large as representatives of the interests of stockholders. From the mid-1980s, numerous public reports emphasized the malpractice involved in the selection of directors to government companies and the need to depoliticize board membership (Comptroller General, 1989)

The proposed amendments to the Government Companies Act may also be understood in the context of the emergence of a new capitalist discourse that intensified during the 1980s. Social considerations associated with the goals of nation-building which had provided the guidelines for economic decisions in the past, gave way to a greater emphasis on profits and on achieving a competitive advantage in global markets. These developments took place within the context of a decline in collective values and the rise of greater individualism and materialism -- changes that affected women's priorities as well. The shift in national discourse from a focus on social/political goals to a focus on economic goals and from idealism to a greater emphasis on material success are reflected in the growing importance of paid work in the lives of women in general and of the achievement of careers for a growing sector of the female labor force (Izraeli, 1992).[8] The loosening hold of the collective created new social spaces, separating parts of the economy that operated in a more competitive market. Economic restructuring began in the late 1980s, and the number of companies that went public annually increased significantly each year (Izraeli and Talmud, 1997). In this context, the new importance attributed to the role of boards, in both the private and the governmental sectors of the economy, also widened the circle of those who became interested in serving on them, including women.

Throughout the 1980s, the government, especially the powerful minister of the treasury, resisted attempts to curtail the use of board appointments for patronage, as well as for ensuring control over company policies. Legislative initiatives aimed at depoliticizing and rationalizing appointments of directors that were brought to the 11th Knesset (1984-88) and again to the 12th Knesset (1988-92) died in committee. Shortly after the 1992 election, which returned a Labor coalition to power, the proposed amendment passed the first reading and was returned to the Constitution, Law and Justice Committee (hereafter called the Constitution Committee) for preparation for the second and third reading. What is important for this chapter is that none of the clauses of the various proposed amendments to the Government Companies Act that dealt with the appointment of directors, made reference to either gender or affirmative action. How then did gender get incorporated into the final version of the law, and how was it justified? A satisfactory answer requires taking a step back into history.

---

[8]The weakening grip of the collective and the new emphasis on individual rights and individualism is subversive of patriarchy. Women who had been incorporated into the Zionist collective primarily as "helpmates to men" began to demand more equal partnerships.

4. Women on Boards

Golda Meir not withstanding, women as a group have never had significant political clout in Israel, although traditionally, they had more influence in the parties of the Left than in others.[9] Although women were recognized as having special needs the expectation was that these would be dealt with by the women's auxiliary within the party. Their problems were not sufficiently important to be part of the national agenda (Herzog, 1996). The few women leaders in the ruling Labor Party were divided by their loyalties to the various competing factions within the party. The electoral system, at least until primaries were introduced, made women more dependent on powerful men in the Central Committee of the parties than on a female constituency. Nonetheless, the principle of women's right to representation on publicly constituted bodies, like the myth of their equality, was part of the ideological repertoire of Israeli politics. In the Labor Party, this right was translated into an informal policy of quotas for women. The quota system was formalized at the 1971 Labor Party convention, which, under pressure from the women's caucus and with the support of the then prime minister, Golda Meir, granted a 20% quota for women in all the institutions of the party, including the electoral list for the Knesset. The quotas, however, were never honored in practice, and women never achieved 20% representation in any of the party organs, including the party lists to the Knesset. The quota system not only put a ceiling on the number of women elected or appointed; it backfired. People often preferred not to "waste their vote on women" who would be appointed regardless of the number of votes they received, and thus ironically, the quota system resulted in women getting fewer votes than they might have otherwise received. The quota system primarily protected the positions of a handful of influential women, loyal members of the Labor Party coalition, who made it into the Knesset or were rewarded with other positions, including occasional appointments to the boards of government companies.

The issue of women's participation on boards was first aired publicly by the Report of the Prime Minister's Commission on the Status of Women (1978), known as the Namir Commission, in which the Subcommittee for Women's Representation and Involvement in Public and Political Life, recommended that "the government should initiate the appointment of women to such bodies as: boards of government companies, public councils and committees and investigative committees" (Namir commission, 1978:320). The subcommittee apparently did not attribute great importance to the issue of women's representation on boards. The one-sentence reference to it may be contrasted

---

[9] The official recognition of women as a special-interest group within the Labor Movement may be traced back to the founding convention of the Histadrut -- the General Federation of Labor (1920), when the leaders of the Women Workers' Movement protested their underrepresentation among the delegates and the failure of the convention to deal with the special problems that women pioneers faced in finding employment (Izraeli, 1981). The convention voted to reserve two places on the governing body of the Histadrut for representatives of the Women Workers' Movement.

to the detailed manner in which the subcommittee dealt with such issues as women's under-representation in the foreign service, in political parties, and at the higher echelons of the civil service. The term "appropriate representation" which later provided the rhetoric necessary for making the affirmative action clause palatable to different constituencies, was the contribution of the Subcommittee on Women in the Labor Force, which used the term in the following recommendation concerning women's representation in the elected bodies of the trade unions: "It should be aspired to [achieve] appropriate   representation of women on the elected bodies of trade unions and on workers' committees in places where women are employed" (Namir Commission, 1978:160). [10] The term "appropriate," like the term "equal,", has a positive emotive meaning, but is more ambiguous in its substantial meaning and allows for multiple definitions. It arouses less resistance than either "equality," which poses a threat to existing power arrangements, and "quota," which many considered to be undemocratic or reflecting badly on women.

5.   The Emergence of Affirmative Action as Rhetoric for Social Policy

The recommendation that the government should appoint women to boards disappeared from public view until April 1985, when it reemerged as a governmental decision. This government decision called for increasing the representation of women "in senior positions in the civil service, on government tender committees [which select candidates for senior positions in the civil service] as well as on boards of government companies." The decision was the achievement of the then advisor to the prime minister on the status of women, a position established in 1980, one of the few recommendations of the Namir Commission that was actually implemented. The position carried little authority and was endowed with minimal resources, but the person in the position, Dr. Nitza Shapira Libai; enjoyed close ties with influential politicians, especially in the Labor Party, including the then prime minister, Shimon Peres. After months of lobbying, and with "help from my friends" (as she put it), Shapira Libai succeeded in getting the issue of the status of women in governmental service onto the agenda of the weekly governmental meeting at which she presented her proposal for increasing women's representation.[11] The

---

[10] The former chairperson of the Subcommittee on Women in the Labor Force, Zohar Carthy, explained to me: "We ignored the subject of boards out of "naivete." We did not realize the economic power potential of boards; we were just not familiar with the whole issue."

[11] Nitza Shapira Libai explained to me: "I drafted the proposal; - Peres signed and brought it to Cabinet for approval. At the cabinet meeting, I lectured at length -- on international law, human rights, and discrimination. I think they did not really understand the implications of my proposal. The Liberal Party [part of the then coalition] argued -- What if there were no suitable women for senior positions? I brought names of women - the whole thing barely passed."

governmental decision is considered to be the first reference to affirmative action as social policy for women, although the term was not used at the time.

In the official statement to the media (prepared by the advisor on the status of women) the governmental decision was legitimated on three grounds. First, it was framed as the implementation of recommendations made by the Namir Commission. Presenting it as a proposal that had already been accepted in principle by the government increased its legitimacy Second, it was claimed to be based on the principle of social justice and equality of opportunity. The statement noted that women constituted 51% of those employed in government service but only approximately 15% of those in senior positions and only 2% of those on the boards of directors on government companies. Third, it stated that given their considerable human capital, women had an important potential contribution to make to service in the governmental sector that was not yet realized. This reference to women's human capital -- their educational and professional accomplishments--was a new theme in the rhetoric justifying the demand for women's increased representation. It resonated with the new capitalist discourse and the emerging emphasis on the need for greater rationality in public bureaucracies and a greater emphasis on merit and qualifications as bases for promotion and later provided the justification for including the affirmative action clause in the amendment.

6.   Women as Exclusive Beneficiaries of Affirmative Action

The 1985 government decision had no immediate practical effect on women's appointments to boards of government companies. It had, however, symbolic value, in that it put forth publicly the possibility of using affirmative action to redress past discrimination against women, but only women. It should be noted that Arabs in Israel constitute 20% of the population but only 5% of those employed in the civil service at any level. Other underrepresented groups include Jews who came or whose parents came from Moslem countries (known locally as Easterners), orthodox Jews, and new immigrants. The following case of the Koberski Commission reveals the dynamics by which Arabs were excluded and women, primarily women of Western origin, came to be exclusive beneficiaries of the 1993 affirmative action amendment, even though there were no Arab directors of government companies at that time.

In June 1986, Prime Minister Shimon Peres established the Koberski Commission "to examine government service and bodies supported by the government, with the purpose of improving the quality of the services provided by the state and promoting the aims of the state" (Koberski Commission, 1989). One of the commission's seven subcommittees was designated to deal with the status of two "special populations"--women and minorities--the latter being a euphemism for Israeli Arabs. The woman who was appointed chairperson of the subcommittee objected to linking women with Arabs and the two populations were subsequently dealt with by separate subcommittees. Each subcommittee approached the use of affirmative action policy differently. The report of the Subcommittee on the Status of Women in Government Service claimed that affirmative action was needed to compensate women for discrimination based on stereotypes and resulting in an unequal starting point in the competition for advantage. Furthermore, it recommended that affirmative action should be applied to occupational training. It called for the recognition of women as a population requiring special treatment with regard to training and promotion "comparable to [privileges given to] released soldiers, new immigrants and senior military officers" and reaffirmed the governmental decision of 1985 to include women on the boards of government companies (see Koberski Commission, 1989).

In contrast, the report of the sub-committee on the status of minorities explicitly objected to the use of affirmative action and devoted several pages to explaining its opposition. It listed the criticisms commonly leveled against affirmative action in other countries and reviewed "the failed attempts" by various government committees over the years to improve the situation of minorities in the public sector. The report then summarized the subcommittee's objection to affirmative action on two counts – legal and pragmatic (Koberski Commission, 1989:350): The legal objection was that "preference for the sake of equality" is not implementable because the appointment clause of the Civil Service Act (1959) made it illegal to reserve jobs for a specific ethnic group or nationality. The pragmatic objection was that affirmative action would not work because the governmental offices were unwilling to hire minorities. The report recommended instead undertaking an educational campaign to convince the government offices to adopt a more positive attitude to the subject. A minority opinion by an Arab male committee member (a judge) responded to the objections and made a case in favor of affirmative action.

The differences in the two subcommittees approaches to affirmative action cannot be attributed to legal constraints, since such constraints would be equally applicable to both Arabs and women. The reference to the resistance of the governmental offices to hiring minorities could equally well have led to the opposite conclusion, namely, that affirmative action would be a preferred and even necessary, strategy if the status of Arabs in the public sector was to be improved. It may be suggested that the difference relates to the perception of who was worthy of affirmative action or entitled to be a beneficiary of it - women yes, Arabs no. [12]

---

[12] The Subcommittee on Women was composed of 9 members: 7 women including the chair –one of them an Arab woman, and 2 men, both Jewish. The Subcommittee on Minorities was also composed of 9 members 4 Arabs, one of them a woman, and 5 Jews including the chair, none of them women. It is most probable that if the majority of the members of the minorities' subcommittee had been Arabs, the outcome would have been different. However, the fact that the Arabs were not the majority and did not fill the role of chairperson is indicative of the difference between Arabs and (Jewish) women in their status as citizens and in perceptions of their entitlements. In her study of the development of civil rights legislation in Israel, Ziv (in press) noted: "Israel was established as a Jewish nation state, and many of its policies and symbols manifest this ideological constitution through a clear preference of its Jewish citizenry. Associating its Arab citizens with the security

If affirmative action should be applied to women but not to Arabs, what is the fate of Arab women? One of the consequences of a conceptual scheme that defines people as either women or minorities is that it does not define a place for those who are both and hence who tend to get overlooked. As Spelman (1988:14) pointed out, "attempts to focus on gender in isolation from other aspects of identity such as race and class can work to obscure the effect race, class and gender have on each other. In particular...gender can be treated in a way that obscures the race and class of privileged women -- for example of contemporary white, middle-class women -- and simultaneously makes it hard to conceive of women who are not of that particular class and race as 'women'." The reports of both subcommittees made passing reference to Arab women's underrepresentation in governmental service. This was explained in terms of their underrepresentation in the civilian -labor force because of the constraints of traditional Arab culture. Moreover, neither report made any recommendation that would improve opportunities for Arab women. In both cases, Arab women (like Jewish woman of Middle Eastern and North African origin) became invisible. On matters related to the redistribution of power, what Molyneaux (1985) termed women's strategic needs, women spoke in a singular voice. The claim for more representation for women in general masked the fact that the beneficiaries would most likely be middle-class Jewish women of Western or European-American origin.

The Koberski Commission submitted its report in 1989. Its recommendations regarding women remained at the level of rhetoric, as an idea available in the public arena for possible future use by interested political contenders.

7. Affirmative Action Becomes Legislation

The 1988 elections had returned the right wing Likud Party to office. Now in the opposition, Mapam -- the Israeli socialist party headed by Yair Zaban, with three member of Knesset (MKs) and Ratz -- the civil rights party that was founded and headed by a woman, Shulamit Aloni, with four MKs left the Labor coalition and acted as autonomous parties. As the political adviser to Mapam, explained to me, "Yair [head of Mapam] had more freedom to act [to initiate legislation] when in the opposition than he had had as a minister in the Labor coalition." However, the support services allocated to small parties are inadequate for conducting intensive parliamentary work. These parties often rely on extraparliamentary organizations with which they engage in an exchange relationship for legal and other services. In the words of the same adviser to Mapam:

---

threats from neighboring Arab states, Israel had treated its Arab minority as a collective security threat for years. These two factors resulted in a mixture of discriminatory and restrictive policies towards the Palestinian Citizens of Israel."

"Mapam saw itself as a provider of parliamentary services to some 35 grass-roots organizations. We sent them material on what was going on in the parliamentary committees, and they supplied us with professional backup services. For example, we had an idea for a law and they drafted it, or we drafted and they polished, or they supplied the ideas and the draft, and we had the apparatus to push things through. At the time many of them had legal and other professional staff who could supply us with services we needed.... We had such a close working relationship with the Israel Women's Network. The Israel Women's Network (IWN), established in 1984, was as a multi-issue feminist lobby, particularly active in promoting feminist legislation. It was the only national multi-issue women's organization established since statehood (1948) and the only one that was not dependent on party or governmental funds.[13] Most of the leading members of IWN were high-profile feminist academics with links to the political establishment, predominantly of the Left. The IWN's   legal department formulated feminist legislation for which it then sought sponsors among Knesset members. The issue of board representation for women was consonant with its agenda, and promoting it provided IWN with an opportunity for visibility."

Both Mapam and Ratz received most of their electoral support from Jews of Western origin particularly women who sympathized with the goals of the feminist movement. Both parties presented themselves as champions of women's rights and gender equality. In 1989, Zaban, the head of Mapam, submitted a legislative proposal requiring that one of the two directors representing the public at large in publicly traded corporations should be a woman. In 1991 he submitted a second proposal regarding boards of government companies: "A director of one sex shall not be appointed to the board of a government company unless, at the time of appointment, there is at least one director of the other sex." The first proposal was endorsed by the four Mapam MKs, the second, by 20 MKs from a wide spectrum of political parties.. There was more support for legislating women's participation on boards of government companies than on companies in the private sector, where the general push was for reducing government intervention in the economy. Both proposals, however, passed only the preliminary hearing and were killed in the constitution committee.

The 1992 elections returned a Labor coalition. It was the first time that the newly formed left-of-center party Meretz, which incorporated both the Mapam and Ratz parties in 1992 formed part of the coalition. MK Dedi Zucker of Meretz was granted the chairmanship of the constitution committee. Zucker together with fellow party member MK Haim Oron, resubmitted Amendment 6 to the Government Companies Act, with no reference to gender. In July 1992 Labor Party MK Avrum Burg ,one of the original 20 co-signers of the proposed legislation that required the board of a government company to have at least one woman director resubmitted that bill. The latter proposal came before the Knesset for a preliminary hearing in December 1992. The Meretz MKs suggested that the proposed legislation should be incorporated into Amendment 6 that the constitution committee was then preparing for a second and third reading.

---

[13] IWN was initially totally funded by the U.S.-based New Israel Fund.

Policy innovations may come from career-minded state actors such as politicians who view certain policies as opportunities to promote their visibility or attractiveness to their constituency. In 1992, Meretz had the largest proportion of women MKs of any political party. For the two men MKs from Meretz, the feminist clause had symbolic value signaling their commitment to gender equality.[14] The mainly symbolic importance is suggested by the fact that no steps were taken to ensure implementation of the affirmative action clause. As was noted in the introduction to this chapter, the law did not specify affirmative action as one of the criteria to be used by the supervisory committee when approving the appointment of directors. This omission suggests that the MKs did not attach great importance to the enforcement of the clause.

The women lawyers who were working with the constitution committee and in the Ministry of Justice were uneasy about the idea of affirmative action for women, and in interview, some openly objected to it. They did not want to be identified on the basis of gender or to be stigmatized as "disadvantaged" (mekupachot). They also considered it an insult that they should be thought of as needing to be appointed by mandate of law. The success of their careers, they thought, was proof that capable women did not need to be given preference. Furthermore, such preference threatened to cast a shadow on their hard- earned and well-deserved achievements. However, not all the governmental lawyers were of like mind on this issue. For example, Carmel Shalev, the legal adviser in the ministry of health and a committed feminist, favored affirmative action and helped her colleagues find an acceptable formulation. The original formulation requiring "at least one woman" was not acceptable to those who wanted more than lip service to equality. This criticism was voiced by David Libai, then the minister of justice who explained to the Knesset at the preliminary hearing: "the Government had decided to reject the proposal because its demand for only one woman was too minimal. The purpose of such legislation is to increase the representation of women, not to set such a low ceiling on it."   The solution was a gender-neutral wording, and the phrase "appropriate representation"-- which was ambiguous enough -- if not to satisfy all groups, at least to quiet their fears or ignite their hopes -- was adopted.

The constitution committee was divided between those who wished to limit the proposal to the first half of clause 18a(a), expressing the principle of appropriate representation, and those who wished to include clause 18a(b), instructing ministers to prefer women. The committee chair brought the issue to the Knesset plenary, which voted in favor of including the affirmative action clause.

The affirmative action clause was among the least debated clauses of the amendment. Apart from a remark from the floor by an Arab male MK about the absence

---

[14] The populist appeal of the amendment is indicated in a handwritten note I found in the constitution committee's file in which the MK from the Labor Party who reintroduced the affirmative action legislation admonished the members of Meretz for failing to indicate that he proposed the clause and reminded them to acknowledge his contribution.

of Arab directors, the only objection came from Dan Meridor, the former minister of justice in the previous Likud government who contended: "Here we come to prevent the intrusion of foreign considerations, to correct the non-relevant considerations. The whole political appointment is an example of such a foreign consideration. What do we do? We force the appointment of a woman even in a case that the woman is not appropriate."(Knesset Protocol, 1993). His reservation that the woman appointed must be equally qualified as the man was not supported. The minister of the treasury did not oppose the clause because, first, there was no outlay of money involved and second, the phrase "to the extent feasible under the relevant conditions" provided an escape for ministers who could always claim that the choice of a woman was not feasible.

Affirmative action was legitimated on the grounds that women constituted over 50% of the public and only discrimination prevented their representation on public bodies. The women lawyers, economists, and other governmental professionals had proven their competence. In a personal interview, the governmental lawyer who had drafted the legislation later justified the clause in terms of the goals of the legislation. Rather than introduce an irrelevant consideration, the appointment of women as directors would be proof that patronage had been eliminated, that ministers were paying more attention to talent than to politics. "Women are not in any special way different from men except that they are discriminated against by the political protecstia (patronage) that men have and give each other. So, if politics are out, - women will be in. Assuring women's entry by affirmative action also ensures that politics are out because women are outside the political networks."

8. Women as Agents of Change

Once passed, the law was not applied in practice. Ministers continued to appoint men as before. The law, however provided women's organizations with that ammunition they could use to pressure ministers and to appeal ministerial evasions in court. This was an era of growing public-policy-interest advocacy in general, and in the legal arena , women were the first "minority group" to chart this course (Ziv, in press). In the late 1980s women had won two important Supreme Court decisions which established the right to equality as a basic fundamental right (Ziv, in press).

A number of women's organizations[15] whose members were potential candidates in the expanding market for directorships sponsored initiatives to enhance their chances for appointment. These initiatives included the establishment of a training

---

[15] Such organizations included Naamat, the largest and oldest women's organization in Israel; the Senior Women Managers' Forum within the Israel Management Center; the Women Managers' Forum within the Manufacturers' Association, and the Women's Forum within the National Association of Lawyers

course for women would-be directors (the first of its kind in Israel)[16] and the creation of computerized data banks containing   curriculum vitae submitted by hundreds of professional women including senior civil servants, .who wished to serve as directors. The strategic purpose of both activities was to counter the common argument that no women were available with the competence and willingness to fill the positions. The lists were forwarded to the adviser to the prime minister on the status of women, who supplied the names of suitable candidates to the various ministers. In addition, individual women, who were connected to one or more ministers or their advisers, served as power brokers for their friends.

A serendipitous development provided an opportunity and incentive for greater cooperation among women's organizations on the issue of their representation on the boards of government companies In May 1993, after the affirmative action law was passed the governmental ministerial committee for coordination and administration (chaired by Minister Shetreet) established a public commission to implement the Koberski Commission's   recommendations submitted   in 1989, regarding the advancement of women in the government sector . The mandate of the new commission, popularly referred to as the Ben-Israel Commission was embedded in its name: The Commission to Enhance the Advancement and Integration of Women in Government Service. The commission was given few resources with which to operate and was essentially window dressing for the chair of the ministerial committee who convened it. Headed by a prominent Law Professor Ruth Ben-Israel and comprised of about 40 people, most of them high-profile women who were representative of different sectors of society and noted for their involvement in women's issues, the commission provided a framework within which women could meet and discuss strategy. It also provided a public platform from which women could legitimately address their demands to ministers and get access to the information they needed to devise strategies. Information such as the gender makeup of company boards, the dates when current directors would complete their terms, and the openings available for new directors, was not available to the public.[17] The work of the commission created an informal information-and-support network that linked the women members of the commission with feminists working in the civil service, and various voluntary women's organizations. When despite repeated appeals to ministers to comply with the affirmative action clause, the ministers continued to appoint men, this network was instrumental in bringing the ministers' noncompliance to the attention of the Supreme Court.

---

[16] At the time there were no courses in Israel for training men to become directors.

[17] Information control is a well-established tactic that authorities use to ward off encroachment on their power. The then head of the Government Companies Authority had refused to grant such information about directors on grounds of confidentiality, until Professor Ben Israel threatened to appeal to the Supreme Court.

9. The Supreme Court Intervenes

In December 1993, a senior woman in the civil service informed a member of the Ben-Israel Commission that the cabinet was about to approve the appointment of a man to the Ports and Railways Authority board that had no women directors. The member passed the information on to Rachel Benziman, director of the legal center at the Israel Women's Network, with the recommendation that IWN take legal action. At the same time, Benziman noted an announcement in the newspaper that the government had approved the appointment of two men to the all-male board of the Oil Refineries Corporation. Within about two weeks, IWN filed two petitions in the Supreme Court demanding that the government and the relevant ministers explain why they did not appoint women as directors. On November 1, 1994, the Supreme Court presented its judgment. It instructed the relevant ministers to reopen the appointment procedure and follow the requirements of the law by making a more serious attempt to find suitable women candidates.

The judgment sent a clear message to all the ministers that they could no longer ignore the law as they had done previously. According to the Supreme Court, taking affirmative action to achieve equality in practice was the main principle. The qualifying clause --"to the extent feasible under the relevant conditions" -- was to be used sparingly. It did not free the ministers from the obligation to make a serious effort to make the conditions feasible. Whereas the ministers in question had failed to make appointments in accordance with the requirements of Clause 18a of the Government Companies Act, the Supreme Court annulled the appointments. The ministers pleaded in their defense that they had not been sufficiently aware of the weight they were required to give to the appointment of a woman. However, even given that they had not made a serious-enough effort to find suitable women candidates, they argued, voiding the appointments would cause damage to the men, whose qualifications no one questioned. The judges rejected the plea, emphasizing the importance of the goal that the law sought to achieve, namely, equality in practice for women in the economic sector, a sector fully under the government's control. "If additional evidence is needed that enforcing this law is essential, it is [precisely] the ministers' claimed lack of awareness of their obligations under the law." The claims made by the ministers in their own defense "only strengthen the assessment that the essence of the obligation that clause 18a(b) imposes on the ministers was not properly understood" (High Court, 1994, Clause 34).

The favorable judgment encouraged women's organizations to continue to pursue affirmative action as a strategy. It confirmed the legality of affirmative action and provided the moral justification for its use (Radai, 1995). "The goal of affirmative action legislation was to establish a new norm and enforce it through the positive action of implementing suitable representation for both sexes."(High Court 1994 [18]. The judgment viewed the paucity of women directors as merely a specific case of general inequality in the public arenas, that needed correction:

> "It is not unreasonable, therefore, that the innovation inherent in Clause 18a should be interpreted in the light of its relationship to a wider social need; namely the need to strengthen women's part in the employment system in general, and among the levels of management in particular, in all sectors and branches of the economy." (Clause, 24).

The judgment preempted tokenism. "Appropriate representation" did not mean simply any representation. What the Supreme Court would accept as "appropriate," were the case to arise, would depend on the requirements of the position and the availability of suitable women. The Court warned against using the qualifying clause "to the extent feasible under the circumstances" in bad faith by defining the requisites in a way that by definition excluded women.[19]

10. The Aftermath of the Court Decision

The strong position taken by the Supreme Court with regard to the importance of establishing new norms of behavior came as a surprise to most people I interviewed. For example, "They exaggerated" (Heegzeemu) was the response of the woman lawyer who was instrumental in drafting the clause. The phrase implies that in annulling the appointments, rather than merely warning the ministers to appoint women in the future, the Supreme Court acted more severely than, in her opinion, was deserved. The strong position had an almost immediate impact on appointments to the boards of government

---

[18] The judgment quoted extensively from leading feminist scholars and pro-feminist legal opinions from the United States and Canada.

[19] The following incident, referred to in the judgment,, reveals the way in which the judge "educated" the lawyers representing the Israel Women's Network to look after women's interests. The judge asked the lawyers whether they demanded that preference be given to women only in cases in which women had the same qualifications as the male candidates or whether it was sufficient that women have adequate qualifications. The lawyers, presumably concerned about not devaluing the achievements of women who would be appointed as a result of affirmative action, insisted that the women should be preferred only when they had identical qualifications to the male candidates. The judge retorted that he would adopt a more flexible test, one that scrutinized the relevance of the relative advantage of the male candidates, in light of the centrality of the principle of affirmative action. "For example, if the advantage of the male candidate over a competing female candidate stemmed from his having a wealth of experience, especially from having served on a number of boards, I would tend to view this advantage as a basis for preferring him only if it were proved that, under the circumstances, such experience was worthy of being granted special weight as for example, if there were few experienced directors on the board...." (High Court, 1994 Clause 28). In the future, in every case in which preference was not given to the woman candidate, the burden of proof that a suitable woman could not be found, given a reasonable effort, would rest with the appointing minister.

companies. Ministers became more receptive to the recommendations of the advisor on the status of women who fed them names of female candidates to fill vacating directorships.[20] Ministerial advisers approached female acquaintances whom they knew to be strategically located, to recommend other women as candidates for board appointments. The committee responsible for approving ministerial board appointments took a more vigilant stand about returning ministerial appointments made to boards that had no women members. More women than before initiated contact with ministers either directly or through "friends" and "friends of friends" to request appointments. A study (Markovich, 1998) of 20 women members of boards of directors of government companies found that those appointed after the law was passed were more likely than those appointed prior to its passage to say that they had initiated the contacts. The fact that ministers needed to appoint women empowered these women to take advantage of this window of opportunity

The final report of the Ben-Israel Commission recommended that affirmative action should be introduced into the civil service. In 1995 Article 15a (Appointments) of the Government Service Act (1959) was amended to include a declaratory affirmative action order in the government service. The order, however, left it to the discretion of the civil service commissioner to determine whether affirmative action was required and what measures should be taken.[21] On August 14, 1998, a government decision extended the application of Article 15a to all local councils. In 1998, an amendment to the Companies Act introduced a limited form of affirmative action regarding appointments of directors at large of publicly traded corporations. In other words, the introduction of affirmative action, which began within the government sector for boards of directors of government companies and was extended to managerial positions in the civil service was later extended beyond the government sector to board positions representing the public in the private sector. The wording of the affirmative action clauses regarding the civil service and boards of publicly traded corporations, however, was significantly less obligating and limited the ability of the court to order direct appointments of women when the spirit of the law was violated.[22]

Ministers continued to make political board appointments, behavior that was criticized by the comptroller general who wrote: "It was found that the ministers select many of the candidates for the position of director from among their acquaintances and those close to them" (Comptroller General, 1998:39). The comptroller general found that

---

[20] Names were supplied by a number of women's organizations whose members wished to become directors.

[21] The Ben-Israel Commission's recommendation required that the civil service commissioner appoint women to all positions in which they were under-represented. The original legislation proposed by Mapam in 1989 required that in every case, one of the two directors at large must be a woman. The 1998 law is a watered-down version that states that when there are no women directors on a board, one of the two directors representing the public at large should be a woman.

among directors representing the public at large, 37% of the men and 20% of the women were political appointees. She also noted the minute representation of women among board chairpersons and CEOs.

11. Women in Support of Women

Researchers have inquired into the extent to which women directors play an activist role and become champions of women's issues as part of their board responsibilities (Burke, 1994; Mattis, 1993). Affirmative action for women directors in Israel was legitimated primarily within the terms of the new rationality discourse. That is, women's human capital, their professional qualifications made them worthy of board membership. Women were not appointed to represent women's interests or because they (or women in general for that matter) were assumed to have a special women's perspective. Rather, it was their similarity to men that entitled them to be included in the boardroom.

Furthermore, women believed that emphasizing their gender would detract from their being perceived as professionals (Markovitch, 1998). They saw a conflict between competence and femininity.[23] The feeling that they needed to prove that they were competent professionals (Talmud and Izraeli, in press) put pressure on them not to bring attention to themselves as women With few exceptions, the women members of boards of directors who were interviewed by Markovitch (1998) insisted that their being women was not relevant in the boardroom or to the subjects on the boards' agendas. The only difference they perceived between themselves and their male colleagues was that they believed that they were better prepared for board meetings[24] and were less likely to speak up when they were not well-informed. The message was that they had less margin for error than men did. Almost all the women interviewed resisted the idea of raising the issue of gender differences, since they believed that this issue would detract from their being perceived as professionals, the equivalent of men. Several women reported "horror stories" following an attempt to promote a women's cause. For example, Rachel told me the following incident that occurred during the first months after she and Shira were appointed to the board of a bank. Someone had raised the issue of the need to recruit more qualified economists to the firm. Shira stated many competent women economists were available. "This was the first time she spoke up at a meeting and after that no one took anything she said seriously. She should have waited." There were indications, however, that this "status anxiety" decreased after women thought they had passed the "initiation rites." Women who felt more comfortable about the possibility of supporting

---

[23] This conflict is implicit in Mathis' (1997:18) finding for U.S. directors who wanted "to be recognized for their expertise rather than their gender."

[24] Huse's 1998 finding for Scandinavian directors was similar.

women's issues, if they were to arise, were those who believed they had proved themselves and that their professional competence was recognized by their fellow board members.

It would probably require some outside force to prod these women to action on behalf of the women in their respective companies. For example, an initiative from the adviser on the status of women to organize the women directors into a support group could encourage them to consider acting on behalf of women's interests.

12. Conclusion

Connell (1994, 150) suggested that the historic shift from economic systems dominated by political patronage to those that promote professional expertise represents a transition from one form of hegemonic masculinity to another. The form of masculinity that prized the ability to mobilize constituencies at polling places and that worked through patronage obligations and exclusionary social networks was displaced by a new form of hegemonic masculinity that is organized around the theme of rationality, calculation, and economic expertise.

The legislation to depoliticize and rationalize director appointments to the boards of directors that was discussed in this chapter may be seen as part of this broader transition. Whereas the rationality discourse still privileged men, who were perceived to be the embodiment of rationality, it, nonetheless, created more favorable conditions for women than did the old regime. Savage (1992), however, argued that whereas women have gained considerable professional expertise in recent decades, they have not attained organizational power or gained control of organizational hierarchies. Becoming a board member requires knowledge, it does not confer power, which may explain why the affirmative action clause was not actively opposed. Board membership is largely a prestigious position. Directors generally do not determine the career trajectories or opportunities of the company's employees. Furthermore, they are appointed for a limited term of office. Board power usually resides in the hands of the chair, the CEO, senior executives and board members whose power base is external to the board.

Board membership, in this case, provided a few hundred women with the opportunity to gain experience in this high-status position. It granted them access to strategic information, resource-rich social networks, and the possibility of being appointed to other boards.[25] Whether they will be able to transform these resources into

---

[25] McGregor (1997) in a study of women directors in New Zealand noted that once on a board of directors, a woman's acculturation increases the likelihood of her being invited to join additional boards. "In the acculturation process, the female director becomes socialized into boardroom culture, and gains acceptance through familiarity and through the female director's desire to accentuate her similarity rather than her difference to other board members. She is then more likely to be considered suitable on knowing and will be regarded as safer than an untested novice who could alter the dynamics of boardroom proceedings" (p. 6).

positional power remains to be seen. Equally, if not more important than the achievement of several hundred women is the fact that affirmative action legislation, legitimated and backed by the courts, created normative changes in attitudes toward women's participation in senior positions in the developing capitalist economy.

References

Bacchi, C.L. (1996) *The Politics Of Affirmative Action: Women Equality And Category Politics*, Sage, London.

Bank of Israel, (1998) *Annual Report*, Jerusalem. (Hebrew).

Ben-Israel, R. (1998) *Equal Opportunity And Anti-Discrimination At Work*, Open University, Tel-Aviv. (Hebrew)

Burke, R.J. (1994) Women on corporate board of directors: Forces for change?, *Women in Management Review* **9**, 27-31

Comptroller General (1989) *Annual Report*, no. 40, Jerusalem.(Hebrew).

Comptroller General (1998) *Report On The Appointment Of State Directors In Government Companies*, Jerusalem. (Hebrew).

Connell, R.W. (1994). The state, gender and sexual politics: Theory and appraisal. in H. L. Radtke and H.J. Stam (eds.), *Power/Gender: Social Relations In Theory And Practice, Sage*, London, pp. 136-173.

Fox Piven, (1984) Women and the state: Ideology, power and the welfare state, *Socialist Review* **14**, 11-19.

Herzog, H. (1996) Why so few? The political culture of gender in Israel. *International Review of Women and Leadership*, **2**, 1-18

High Court of Israel (1994) 453/94, 454/94 *Israel Women's Network v. Government of Israel et al.*, PD (5) 501.

Huse, M. (1998) How women directors challenge theories of boards of directors, Paper presented at the annual meeting of the Academy of Management, San Diego Aug. 7-12.

Izraeli, D.N. (1981) The Zionist women's movement in Palestine — 1911-1927: A sociological analysis, *Signs*, **7**, 187-114.

Izraeli, D.N. (1992) Women and work: From collective to career, in B. Swirski and M. Safir (eds.), *Calling the Equality Bluff*, Pergamon, N.Y., pp. 165-177.

Izraeli, D.N. (1994) Outsiders in the promised land: Women managers in Israel, in N.J. Adler and D.N. Izraeli (eds.), *Competitive Frontiers: Women Managing in a Global Economy* Blackwell, Cambridge, MA, pp. 301-324..

Izraeli, D.N. (1998) *Women's Representation In Boards Of Government Companies: 1993-97,* Unpublished report, Bar-Ilan University, Israel. (Hebrew)

Izraeli, D.N. and Talmud, I.(1997) Getting aboard: Mode of recruitment and gender composition: The case of women directors in Israel, *International Review of Women and Leadership* **3**, 26-45.

Koberski Commission (1989) *Report Of The Public-Professional Commission For The General Investigation Of Government Service And Bodies Supported By The State Budget.* Jerusalem. (Hebrew)

MacKinnon, C.A. (1987). Difference and dominance: On sex discrimination, in C.A. MacKinnon (ed.), *Feminism Unmodified: Discourses On Life And Law,* Harvard University Press, Cambridge, MA, pp. 32-45.

Markovitch A.D. (1998) The impact of affirmative action: A case study of directors in government companies in Israel, Unpublished master's degree thesis, Bar-Ilan University, Israel. (Hebrew).

Mattis, M.C. (1993) Women directors: Progress and opportunities for the future. *Business and the Contemporary World*, **5**, 140-156.

Mattis, M.C. (1997) Women on corporate boards: Two decades of research. *International Review of Women and Leadership* **3**, 11-25.

McGregor, J. (1997) Making the good woman visible: The issue of profile in New Zealand corporate directorship, *International Review of Women and Leadership* 3, 1-11.

Molyneux, M. (1985). Mobilization without emancipation? Women's interests, the state and revolution in Nicaragua, *Feminist Studies* **11**, 227-54.

Namir Commission (1978) *Prime Minister's Commission on the Status of Women,* Jerusalem.

Radai, F. (1995) On affirmative action, *Law and Government,* **3**, 145-172 (Hebrew)

Savage, Mike (1992). Women's expertise and men's authority: Gendered organization and the contemporary middle class, in M. Savage & A. Witz (eds.), *Gender and Bureaucracy.* Oxford: Blackwell.

Scokpol , T. (1992) *Protecting Mothers and Soldiers: The Political Origins of Social Policy in the United States,* Harvard University Press, Cambridge, MA:

Spelman, E.V. (1988) *Inessential Woman: Problems of Exclusion in Feminist Thought,* Beacon Press, Boston.

Talmud, I. and Izraeli, D.N. (in press) The relationship between gender and performance issues of concern to directors: Correlates or institution? *Journal of Organizational Behavior*

Yishai, Y. (1997) *Between The Flag And The Banner – Women In Israeli Politics,* State University of New York Press, N.Y.

Ziv, N. (in press) Civil rights and disability law in Israel and the United States: A comparative perspective. *Israel Yearbook of Human Rights,* Tel- Aviv University.

WOMEN ON CANADIAN CORPORATE BOARDS OF DIRECTORS: STILL A LONG WAY TO GO[1]

RONALD J. BURKE
York University
4700 Keele Street
North York, Ontario
CANADA M3J 1P3

Increasing research attention has been devoted to understanding the roles and responsibilities of boards of directors of North American corporations (Gillies, 1992; Lorsch & MacIver, 1989; Fleischer, Hazard & Klipper, 1988). Initially, boards had honorary or at best advisory roles to CEOs appearing as "ornaments on a corporate Christmas tree" (Mace, 1971). They also have functioned as "old boy's clubs" (Leighton & Thain, 1993). Board Members were appointed exclusively at the request of the CEO. But events of the 1970s and 1980s have brought about changes in both the composition and functioning of boards. A majority of board members now come from outside the corporation (outside directors), board membership has grown, corporate boards have created more committees, corporate directors take their jobs more seriously, and directors bring a greater variety of abilities and skills to the boards on which they serve. Despite these changes, corporate boards of directors continue to be criticized.

Patton and Baker (1987) suggest that board members do not live up to their responsibilities because of a "let's not rock the boat" mentality. They cite several reasons for this. These include: the dual authority often claimed by CEOs as chiefs of management and as Board Chairmen, the large size of corporate boards makes good discussion difficult, many board members are themselves CEOs who value each others friendship and want to keep their seats on the board, board members are too busy to

1 This research was supported in part by the School of Business, York University. I would like to thank Mary Mattis and Catalyst for permission to use their survey. Rachel Burke and Elizabeth Kurucz assisted with the collection of the data and Cobi Wolpin helped with data analysis. Parts of this chapter were published in French in Gestion (1998)

R.J. Burke and M.C. Mattis (eds.), Women on Corporate Boards of Directors, 97-109.
© *2000 Kluwer Academic Publishers. Printed in the Netherlands.*

devote enough time to their board responsibilities, and the fact that few directors have large amounts of stock in the companies on whose boards they sit.

One way to deal with some of the concerns raised about the effectiveness and relevance of corporate boards of directors is to appoint more qualified women to them. Why qualified women? First, there are not enough qualified male CEOs to go around. Second, male CEOs do not have enough time to serve on all the boards they are invited to join. Third, many male CEOs do not have enough time to do justice to the boards on which they currently serve.

Finally, women are developing the necessary experience, track records and abilities to qualify for board membership, though they are often "invisible" to male CEOs (Schwartz, 1980).

1. Characteristics of Women Directors

Directors were almost exclusively white males until the 1970s. A few token women were then appointed. Women have continued to be appointed to corporate boards, but given the short period of time that has elapsed, the absolute number of women directors is still very small.

It is not surprising that male CEOs dominate corporate board memberships, given that the recruitment and selection process has relied so heavily on CEOs' suggestions (Patton & Baker, 1987). Male CEOs get to know and feel comfortable with other male CEOs. Lorsch and MacIver (1989) indicate several pluses and minuses in having corporate boards dominated by CEOs. CEOs understand the difficulties of leading complex organizations. CEOs also provide excellent resources, knowledge and information. The negatives associated with CEO dominance of boards is that board members may be too supportive (i.e., not critical enough) of the CEO who appointed them (Patton & Baker, 1987). Most directors still feel they serve at the pleasure of the CEO (Lorsch & MacIver, 1989). CEOs are in limited supply; there are not enough CEOs to fill all board openings so many are overworked and unable to devote enough time to their responsibilities as board members (Patton & Baker, 1987).

A recently completed survey (Burke, 1997) using data available from 951 companies from the *Report on Business* Top 1000 Canadian companies for 1996 has found that, of 5252 external corporate directors, 310 (6%) were women and 4942 were men (94%). In addition, for those 480 corporate boards with complete information, 360 had no external women directors (75%), 86 had one external women director (18%), 30 had two external women directors (6%) and 4 had three external directors (1%). Two boards with incomplete information had four external women directors while one board had five external women directors. These figures indicate fewer external women directors serving on corporate boards of directors in Canada than found in similar studies conducted in the United States, where a recent finding indicated about 11%.

It appears women are increasingly being asked to serve on corporate boards. Their absolute numbers remain small resulting from their low initial base level, the small increase in their appointments, and the limited time that has elapsed. Women serving on corporate boards have more varied backgrounds and experiences than male counterparts, are younger and have shorter board tenure (Mattis, 1993).

2. Changes in Characteristics of Women Directors

The 1991 Catalyst study (Mattis, 1993) considered levels of education of women directors. It reported that all but 11% had at least one university degree; 25% had three or more university degrees. In a 1976 study, women directors had levels of education generally similar to that of men directors. Less than twenty percent did not have university degrees; thirty-nine percent had a Ph.D; and a further 16% had specialization in law. The Burson-Mosteller study indicated that few women directors had risen to the highest organizational levels. But many had been highly successful in education and law. In general, women's career fields were more diversified and less business oriented than men's. There seemed to be a different profile in the 1991 Catalyst study. The "new generation" of women directors were more likely to have a focussed business-oriented career (42% were corporate). There were fewer women directors having only not-for-profit experience and fewer women directors with a mixture of business and not-for-profit experience.

It appears that the "new generation" of women being appointed to corporate boards, in comparison with early women board pioneers, are younger, more likely to have business experience and corporate careers, and expected to bring expertise and skill to the board room. They are less likely to window-dressing.

3. Selecting and Electing Directors

The identification and nomination of women for corporate board appointments is very much dependent on personal contacts with a few key people. This process is undoubtedly similar in many respects to the identification and nomination of men to corporate boards. It probably makes it more difficult for women to be identified than men, however. The process seems to be becoming dependent on a wider variety of contacts which may increasingly operate to women's advantage. Although many women believed they were appointed because they were women, they did not see this as necessarily a liability.

4. Joining and Serving on Boards

There is very little information on the motivation of women, and men, in joining corporate boards. There appear to be some differences in sources of motivation but this conclusion must be treated with caution. Both women and men seem to be motivated by opportunities to learn and by challenge, and not motivated by compensation and perks (Mattis, 1993). Women may be more concerned about time demands and conflicts with home responsibilities.

5. Percentage of Board Seats Held by Women Directors

Data were obtained from the Report on Business Top 1000 Canadian companies for the 1996 calendar year. This list included 1049 companies. At least partial information was available for 946 companies. A total 8247 directors were listed by name for these Canadian companies. The gender of a particular director was not clear for 416 individuals (5%). Of the 7831 directors for whom identifying information was available, 450 were women (6%) and 7381 were men (94%).

Of the 450 women directors, 143 were internal directors (32%) and 308 were external directors (68%). Of the 7381 men directors, 2494 were internal directors (33%) and 4887 were external directors (67%). Thus women and men corporate directors were similarly represented as internal and external directors. Of the 7831 board members, 2637 (33%) were internal and 5194 (67%) were external.

A tally was made of the absolute number of women present on the 930 companies providing useable data on their corporate boards of directors. Six hundred and forty-two boards had no women (69%), 206 boards had 1 woman (22%), 64 boards had 2 women (7%), 10 boards had 3 women (1%), 4 boards had 4 women (.4%), 2 boards had 5 women (.2%), 1 board had 6 women (.1%) and 1 board had 8 women (.1%).

The number of internal board appointments for women on these boards ranged from 0 to 4; the number of external board appointments for women ranged from 0 to 6. The number of internal board appointments for men ranged from 1 to 14; the number of external board appointments for men ranged from 1 to 24.

6. Descriptive Statistics

The following comments are offered in summary. The organizations had an average size of 3245 employees. The average Board of Directors had 8.5 members (8.1 men, .4 women). There were about twice as many external than internal directors (5.7 vs 2.8). External directors typically consisted of 5.3 men and .4 women; internal directors consisted of 2.7 men and .1 women. Larger organizations, not surprisingly, had larger boards of directors ($r=.39$, $p<.001$); and both internal and external women and men ($r_s=.18$, $.43$, $.55$ and $.87$ respectively).

7. No Measures - No Movement

Catalyst is fond of saying that without a measure of the number of women serving on corporate boards of directors - there will be little (or no) movement in increasing their numbers. Towards that end, Catalyst has conducted an annual census of women serving on Fortune 500 organizations in the United States. It puts those organizations having twenty-five percent or more women, board members into a "blue ribbon" category and singles out, by name, those organizations achieving gender parity. Their census also identify organizations having nor women directors. This places subtle pressure on these latter organizations. It is increasingly
common for shareholders to ask why there are no women directors at annual meetings. In a few cases, when the Catalyst census has been made public members of the local media have called organizations in their area without women directors and asked why none were present.

8. Why Are There So Few Women on Corporate Boards?

Elgart (1983) conducted a survey of Fortune 500 firms inquiring specifically about reasons for not recruiting more female directors. She obtained responses from 143 companies. One hundred and twenty-six companies in her study indicated reasons for not having women directors. Seventy-six firms provided one reason; 36 firms, two reasons, and 17 firms, three or more reasons. The most common reasons were: already filled with qualified candidates, not enough qualified women, and companies were against constituency representation.

Mattis (1993) identified at least three barriers to the appointment of women as directors: the director selection process which relies to a great extent on the "old boy's network," risk aversion by corporate board leadership, and corporate boards not being aware of the roles that women members can play in promoting the advancement of women in their own companies.

Leighton and Thain (1993) argue that the director selection process is fundamentally flawed. Male CEOs and male board chairmen are more comfortable with others like them (other white male CEOs). They are more likely to have other men in their personal networks. Qualified women are less likely to be visible to these men. Organizations are unwilling to take risks by appointing women who are not already serving on corporate boards. Organizations claim they have no empty seats. Organizations state there are not enough qualified women and that they do not know where to look for qualified women. Some writers (e.g., Lorsch & MacIver, 1989; Fleischer, Hazard & Klipper, 1988) even suggest that a homogeneous group of directors can deliberate and arrive at decisions more efficiently than they might if the director group was more diverse. Finally, legal mandates prescribing the role and responsibilities of boards of directors works against the appointment of representatives of excluded or minority groups, though it is hard to argue that 52% of the population is a minority!

9. Reasons for Having More Women on Boards

There are several reasons why appointing more qualified women to corporate boards has a solid business rationale. First, there are not enough qualified male CEOs to go around. CEOs currently on boards decline three times as many board invitations as do directors from other professions. A Korn-Ferry survey (1982) reported that 62% of all CEOs had declined at least one invitation to join a corporate board compared to only 22% among all other outside directors. The continuing reliance on male CEOs results in lower quality men being appointed. Given this situation, it is necessary that the selection of board members go beyond the traditional search for male CEOs as candidates.

In addition, male CEOs serving on boards indicated a variety of constraints on their contributions (Lorsch & MacIver, 1989). About one-fifth mentioned each of lack of expertise, little time for preparation and lack of information as constraints on their ability to contribute.

Nation's Business (1990) indicated that women serving on corporate boards can serve as role models for company recruits and indicate to potential female recruits that women can be upwardly mobile. That is, the appointment of women can have important symbolic value, both within and outside the organization. In a similar vein, both Mattis (1993) and Schwartz (1980) argue for lots of interaction between women on corporate boards and the managerial women in these organizations. In fact, Mattis argues that the two are interdependent. That is, appointing more women to boards will be associated with having more women in management, and vice-versa.

A survey by Heidrick Partners observed that more women <u>without</u> corporate board experience were now being named as corporate directors. These women were selected because of their enhanced business experience and management knowledge, instead of specific board experience. Interestingly these women board members had higher educational qualifications than their male counterparts. This suggests the increasing appointment of women to corporate boards is likely to continue.

10. Do Women on the Board Make a Difference?

Women serving on corporate boards want to be seen as directors first, women second. They want to be known for their competence on board issues rather than as feminists. It also seems that women may bring particular sensitivities with them on issues important to women. In addition having women on corporate boards may also influence the tone of board discussions making them less sexist. We do not have an answer to the question of whether women serving on corporate boards have, as part of their implicit mandate, responsibilities for supporting the career aspirations of the managerial and professional women in these organizations. This is not normally specified in the job description of women directors. Some organizations would look on these initiatives favorably, others would not. Some women directors would feel comfortable with these activities, others would not.

11. Canadian Women Directors

There has been relatively little research conducted on Canadian boards of directors in general and on women directors in particular. We undertook a study of the characteristics and experiences of Canadian women serving on corporate boards of directors (Burke, 1994) to address this situation. Names and addresses of Canadian women directors were obtained from the 1992 Financial Post *Directory of Directors* (Graham, 1991). Each was sent a questionnaire. The final response (N=278) represented about a fifty percent response rate.

12. Background Areas and Expertise

The personal and career demographic information indicates that Canadian women directors are an impressive and talented group. Almost ninety percent are university graduates and over forty percent have competed one or more graduate degrees. In addition over one-fifth of them possess one or more professional designations. In addition to these impressive formal credentials, women directors brought a variety of backgrounds and expertise to their director responsibilities. About forty percent had professional backgrounds (law, accounting, medicine or health care). Over half had not-for-profit or public sector experiences. Finally, many areas of business functional expertise were also represented (48%, general management; 36%, finance; 26%, PR or advertising; 24%, marketing or sales; 22%, human resources).

These women were also active on a variety of private, public and voluntary sector boards. One women served on 13 boards; 60 women served on only one board. The typical woman director served on three boards. Most women served on boards in different sectors (private, public, not-for-profit). Besides serving on boards, the women in the sample also had other employment. Most worked full-time for organizations (57%), were owners of business (13%), or were consultants or independent contractors (7%).

As a consequence of both their skills, education, type of employment and board service, these women received sizeable incomes. Almost half earned between $100,000 and $200,000, and fifteen percent earned over $200,000.

We (Burke & Kurucz, (1998)) developed a more recent profile of demographic characteristics of Canadian women corporate directors. Data were obtained from the Report on Business Top 1000 Canadian companies for 1996. A total of 254 women directors were identified by name in the listings; 220 of these women were listed in the 1998 Financial Post Directory of Directors (87%). Considerable data were missing on demographic characteristics since the data in the Directory of Directors were based on information provided by those listed and several directors chose not to provide particular information, e.g., age, marital status, and education.   Thus the description of these women that follows should be considered tentative.

Of the 176 women indicating a current job title, 71 (40%) were presidents/CEOs and 46 (24%) were Executive VPs, Associative VPs, Assistant VPs or VPs. Of the 98 women indicating age, the range was from 30 years to 77, with a median age of 50 years. University education was indicated by 114 women. These women had obtained a total of 222 degrees, an average of almost two per woman. Most common were BAs, BSCs, BBAs, LLBs, MBAs, and MAs. Marital Status was indicated by 78 women directors. Of these, 37 (47%) wee married; 41 (53%) were single, divorced, or widowed.

Eighteen of the 220 listings were new to the Directory of Directors likely representing first-time board appointments. Almost all of the women directors served on private sector boards (*n=216, 98%*), considerably fewer also serving on voluntary or not-for-profit boards *(n=37, 17%)* and public or government sector boards *(n=9, 4%)*. Women directors served on an average of 1.9 private sector boards, .4 voluntary or not-for-profit boards, and .1 public or government sector boards.

The women described in this study, not surprisingly, are a talented, educated, successful group. The explanation for the low representation of women on corporate boards that qualified women are few does not appear valid. The vast majority had pursued successful careers in the private sector, consistent with recent American findings (Catalyst, 1997) which indicate an increasing number of women having mainstream business experience are now serving as corporate directors. The group was also diverse in terms of educational background and business experience. A surprisingly small number of these women served as directors of voluntary and public sector organizations. It may be that other talented nonbusiness oriented women fulfill the latter directorships.

13. Characteristics for Attaining Directorships

There was considerable agreement on the most and least important characteristics for attaining directorships. The former included a strong track record, business contacts, an understanding of business and advanced education. These indicate a successful career in traditional business organizations. Somewhat surprisingly, several skills and abilities (leadership qualities, objectivity, diplomacy and tact, communication ability) and character traits (integrity, intelligence) were not seen as very important. It may be that many women at this level have these so the former become the "extras" one needs to attain directorships. Interestingly, not-for-profit experience was seen as unimportant.

The data indicated, as have others (Lorsch & MacIver, 1989; Leighton & Thain, 1993), that being visible to male CEOs, male board chairmen and male board members was the most common route to board nomination. The "old boy's network" is still alive and well. Personal contacts and visibility to these gatekeepers was critical. Somewhat surprisingly, professional search firms seemed to have little impact here.

The reasons given for their selection as directors were somewhat consistent with the critical criteria for attaining directorships already reported. Thus, having the right expertise, holding the appropriate job (business) title, being a woman, having high visibility, and fitting a desired regional profile were important reasons. These women directors, as has already been reported (Mattis, 1993; Sethi, Swanson & Harrigan, 1981) realized they were selected because they were women. They did not see this as a negative. Somewhat surprisingly, having previous board experience was not seen as an important reason for selection. It may be that these women were often the first women to serve on corporate boards, and they had to start somewhere. Once again, not-for-profit experience, having a knowledge of women's issues, or being a minority were seen as unimportant reasons for their selection to corporate boards. The last finding is not surprising since a very few of the women in the sample were members of minority groups.

Women directors generally reported considerable benefits from their board experiences. Most of the areas of potential benefit were rated at least somewhat important. The most important benefits emphasized the acquisition and sharpening of skills, applying these skills through participating in strategy development, and learning more about corporate governance. Similarly, less important benefits included income, raising women's issues, helping their own careers, personal prestige and additional business contacts. Many of these women were either beyond those concerns or were aware of the "dangers" of carrying the women's banner.

The pattern of findings contained elements of both optimism and pessimism regarding increasing the numbers of women serving on corporate boards. The optimistic conclusions are based on the importance of a strong track record, business expertise and appropriate business job titles in attaining directorships. More and more women are acquiring these credentials. In addition, being a women was also seen as influencing their appointments to corporate boards. The reasons women joined boards would also appeal to male board members because they were board and business related. Finally, the many benefits these women reported from their experiences on boards would pass on positive signals to other women interested in board service.

The pessimistic slant on these findings stems from the fact that the nomination process is still pretty much the result of the "old boy's network". Many qualified women would not be visible to this small, important but insulated group of men. Thus it is unlikely that the small percentage of current board members that are women will change appreciably in the short run. But Leighton and Thain (1993) offer useful suggestions for organizations interested in changing the composition of their boards; and Barrett (1993) suggests several motivations for doing so, as does Schwartz (1980).

14. Types of interaction with Senior-Level Company Women

The women directors in this study seemed to be active in raising and/or discussing policy issues of relevance to women. The vast majority believed each of the seven policy issues was appropriate for board discussion (over 80%) almost fifty-eight percent of respondents felt it was their responsibility to address these issues and about forty-three percent felt it was expected of them. Equal opportunities for women and work and family policies were typically ranked among the top three policy issues.

Almost two-thirds of the women had raised one or more of these policy issues for discussion. But the two most widely initiated policy issues (equal opportunity for women, work and family policies) were raised by less than one-third of the respondents. These data indicate that women directors on private sector corporate boards are indeed serving as potential forces for change on issues relevant to women in the broader society.

About two-thirds of the women directors had interactions with senior-level women in the companies on whose boards they served. But these interactions seemed narrowly focussed on board-related matters and meetings. These data suggest that women directors are having little direct impact on the managerial and professional women in the companies on whose boards they sit. It is possible that they might serve as role models for such women and benefit them indirectly through the advancement of more "women friendly" policies.

Women serving on corporate boards seemed to be playing an active role in raising and discussing issues of concern to women, both inside and outside of their organizations. This was consistent with observations of others (Mattis, 1993: Schwartz, 1980), and supports the conclusion that women directors are functioning as champions for change on women's issues. This picture is increasingly likely to be the case as more women get appointed to corporate boards, though such progress is likely to be slow.

It may also be possible for organizations to reap additional benefits from women directors once they realize the potential advantage of fostering interaction between women directors and senior-level women (Mattis, 1993; Schwartz, 1980).   Such interaction, beyond routing board-management contacts might impact on career development of senor-level women, reducing their attrition, increasing retention, and influencing the attractiveness of the organization in the recruitment of women.   This requires some significant change in the expectations and roles of women directors, and perhaps directors in general.

15. Why Aren't More Women Directors?

Women directors believed that the current mix of board members was inadequate. They wanted more women, board members with more varied experience and background (small business, different racial and ethnic backgrounds) and fewer CEOs.

Women directors attributed the absence of women on corporate boards primarily to attitudes of male CEOs and Board Chairmen.   Male CEOs were seen as thinking that women were not qualified, were afraid to take on new and untried women, or were fearful that women might have a women's agenda.   In addition, women directors believed that organizations were not looking to put women on their boards or did not know when to look for women.   Women themselves were seen as shouldering some of the responsibility for their absence by not making their interests known.   The women directors in the study seemed to have identified, quite realistically, the reasons why so few women serve on corporate boards.

These findings suggest that women will continue to be absent from the boards of Canadian private sector organizations.   There is no obvious punishment from failing to do so.   The perceived attitudes of male CEOs and Board Chairmen remain an obstacle to such appointments.   For this picture to change, male CEOs and Board Chairmen will have to approach the director selection process differently (Leighton & Thain, 1993; Barrett, 1993).   This will obviously involve a more extensive search process.   Related to this would be looking at levels below the CEO to find qualified but still invisible women. An important question that remains is what role women currently on corporate boards will or should play in this process.

In order to find more qualified corporate women, CEOs will have to look lower than the CEO level to get talented - but invisible - women. Motivation for this will come, in part, from the difficulty companies say they are having in recruiting nominees for board positions (e.g., conflict of interest, exposure to liability, amount of time involved). Schwartz (1980) identifies two challenges for organizations in this regard: identifying and selecting the best of this "unknown" pool of candidates, and defining and communicating their expectations for women directors.   Board chairmen need to articulate a "contract" with women directors.   What are their (the board's) expectations on expertise and perspective and her ability to perform?   This would include women directors contributions via expertise and perspective, as well as enhancing morale and productivity of women inside the organization. This results from their presence as role models, as well as their active communication with internal women so that their specific needs and problems are addressed. This, of course, needs the consent and encouragement of top management. Women directors may be able to more freely ask questions than male directors, and serve as modest forces for change. Recruiting women to corporate boards then becomes a source of competitive advantage and a bottom-line business issue.

16. Prospects for the Future

What are the prospects that the numbers of women board directors will increase over the next few years? The best bet is that these numbers may gradually improve. The most recent American Censuses conducted by Catalyst have shown continued but slower increases in the numbers of women directors.

Increases in the number of women directors can be achieved by adding new directorships held by women or replacing men directors by women directors. There is no evidence that board size is increasing; in fact there is some evidence that corporate boards are becoming smaller.

A considerable number of Canadian corporate boards (almost seventy percent) were found to have no women directors. Adding a woman director to these boards, seems reasonable, but these boards were typically smaller and more likely to be in less women-friendly sectors (e.g., mining). It is also important to the difficulties such pioneering women may face as tokens (Kanter, 1977).

References

Barrett, M. W. (1993). Restructuring the board. *Business Quarterly*, 57, 34-40.
Burke, R.J. (1994) Women on corporate boards of directors. In J. de Bruijn & E. Cyba (eds) *Gender and organizations - Changing perspectives*. Amsterdam, NL: VU University Press, pp. 191-222.
Burke, R.J. (1997) Women Directors on *The Report on Business Top 1000 Canadian firms*, Toronto: School of Business, York University, unpublished manuscript.
Burke, R.J., (1998) Les femmes au conseil d'administration des societies Canadiennes: il ya loin de la coupe aux leures. *Gestion*, 23, 121-126.
Burke, R.J. & Kurucz, E. (1998) Demographic characteristics of Canadian women corporate directors. *Psychological Reports*, 83, 461-462.
Catalyst, (1997) *Women board directors of the Fortune 500*. New York: Catalyst
Elgart, L. D. (1983). Women on Fortune 500 boards. *California Management Review*, 25, 121-127.
Financial Post (1997) *Directory of Directors*. Toronto: The Financial Post Company.
Fleischer, A., Hazard, G. C., and Klipper, M. Z. (1988). *Board Games: The Changing Shape of Corporate Power*. Boston, MA: Little Brown and Company.
Gillies, J. M. (1992). *Boardroom Renaissance*. McGraw-Hill: Toronto.

Graham, J. (1991). *Directory of Directors*. Toronto: The Financial Post.

Kanter, R.M. (1977) *Men and women of the corporation*. New York: Basic Books.

Leighton, D. and Thain, D. (1993). Selecting new directors. *Business Quarterly*, 57, 16-25.

Lorsch, J. W. and MacIver, E. (1989). *Pawns or potentates: The reality of America's corporate boards*. Boston, MA: Harvard Business School Press.

Mace, M. (1971). *Directors: Myth and reality*. Boston, MA: Division of Research, Harvard Business School.

Mattis, M. C. (1993), Women Directors: Progress and Opportunities for the Future. *Business and the Contemporary World*, 5, 140-156.

Nations Business (1990). Companies court women for boards, January, 78, 52.

Patton, A. and Baker, J. C. (1987). Why directors won't rock the boat. *Harvard Business Review*, 65, 10-12, 16, 18.

Schwartz, I. N. (1980). Invisible resource: Women for boards. *Harvard Business Review*, 16-18.

Sethi, S. P., Swanson, C. L. and Harrigan, K. R. (1981). *Women Directors on Corporate Boards*. Richardson, TX: Center for Research in Business and Social Policy, University of Texas at Dallas.

WHAT DISTINGUISHES WOMEN NONEXECUTIVE DIRECTORS FROM EXECUTIVE DIRECTORS?

Individual, Interpersonal, and Organizational Factors Related to Women's Appointment to Boards

ZENA M. BURGESS
Student Services
Swinburne University of Technology

PHYLLIS THARENOU
Department of Management
Monash University

1. Background

Little is known about the factors that help women become company directors, with few research studies done. Studies from the United States (Catalyst, 1995a, 1995b), Britain (Holton, 1995a, 1995b, 1995c), Canada (Burke, 1995; Burke & Kurucz, 1998; Mitchell, 1984), and Australia (Korn/Ferry International, 1997) offer extensive and useful descriptions of women directors from frequencies of demographic, experiential, and organizational characteristics. However, the relative importance of factors is not assessed for appointment to boards, nor the importance of other factors, such as social processes. The aim of this study is to add to our understanding of women's appointments to boards by assessing the relative importance of a broader range of factors than previously examined, using an Australian sample.

Women company directors in Australia hold only 4% of board positions (Korn/Ferry International, 1996, 1997). Boards of governance of Australian companies usually consist of a mixture of outsider directors, called nonexecutive directors, and a small number of senior executive staff from within the company itself, called executive directors (Korn/Ferry International, 1995). This study assesses the factors linked to women attaining nonexecutive as opposed to executive board status. Women nonexecutive directors are more freely selected (invited, elected) than women executive directors who are on the board often because they work for the company or are owners. Because there are so few top executive women, the choice of women executive directors in an individual company is limited to very few women, perhaps one or two. This comparison therefore provides an avenue for assessing the factors that help women to be freely chosen for boards (i.e., nonexecutive directors) rather than being on boards because they work for, or own, the company (i.e., executive directors).

R.J. Burke and M.C. Mattis (eds.), Women on Corporate Boards of Directors, 111-127.
© 2000 *Kluwer Academic Publishers. Printed in the Netherlands.*

Hence, the aim of this study is to extend understanding of how women are appointed to boards in Australia by identifying distinguishing individual characteristics and situational factors with regard to nonexecutive compared to executive status. Studies of the correlates of women directors' board representation (Burke, 1995; Mattis, 1997; McGregor, 1997) have rarely examined situational factors or evaluated the relative importance of individual and situational factors (there are exceptions, Bilimoria & Piderit, 1994). The situational factors examined comprise both interpersonal and organizational factors.

1.1   INDIVIDUAL FACTORS

Individuals' skills and knowledge are important influences on their being appointed to boards. Human capital theory proposes that investments in human capital, such as education and company tenure, result in economic advantages of advancement and higher salaries (Becker, 1993). Investments in human capital increase women's skills and knowledge for senior positions, as for men, but also bring them to the attention of decision-makers. Women may need to invest substantially in human capital, perhaps even more than their male counterparts, in order to come to the attention of decision-makers for board positions and to overcome being women, who are not usually on boards. Based on this argument, although women executive directors are likely to have substantial human capital to reach high management levels, women nonexecutive directors may have more still, helping them have the skill, knowledge and visibility to be freely chosen for boards. Women nonexecutive directors may therefore have greater investments in human capital than executive directors.

The links of human capital investments to women's gaining board status have not been assessed. The demographic characteristics, work experience, skills, and background of women directors found in U.S., Canadian, and British studies (Burke, 1994, 1995; Catalyst, 1995a, 1995b; Holton, 1995a, 1995b, 1995c; Korn/Ferry International, 1995, 1996; Mitchell, 1984) are descriptive and based on simple statistical analyses of individual items. They show that women company directors have substantial education and tenure in their occupations. Howe and McRae (1991) found that human capital investments that increased visibility, networks, and public profile were seen as important for director selection.

The human capital variables selected for this study comprise those reflecting skill development through developmental activities (e.g., education) and length of experience (age, company tenure, work continuity). Two other developmental variables, those of training and development and challenging work assignments, are considered in this study as part of the organizational factors, because they are less under women's control and more likely to be awarded by the organization. However, they are also investments in human capital.

In addition, managerial advancement is examined as a form of human capital. Board members are usually chosen from chief executive officer (CEO) or top executive ranks, including women board members (Mattis, 1997). Hence, women selected for boards are likely to have advanced considerably in management. Managerial advancement reflects both the skill and knowledge for board work, and also the senior levels needed for consideration for appointment to boards. It is argued that women freely chosen for boards are likely to have had higher managerial levels throughout their careers than the women on boards because they work for, or own, the company.

The other personal variables considered in this study are exploratory in nature. Individuals high in masculine gender roles are perceived as leaders (Lord, De Vader, & Alliger, 1986), and may fit with male board members, whereas those high in feminine gender roles are not. Women high in masculinity may be more likely to be appointed to boards than other women. However, traits in general, including gender roles, have weak links to advancement to top positions (Tharenou, 1997a), thus they are unlikely to differentiate women nonexecutive board members from those in senior roles in their organizations. Marriage and children are also taken into account. Specific predictions are not made between executive and nonexecutive directors. Because the hours involved in board work per week are low, and attendance at stipulated times, it is not thought that family duties will restrict board representation, including differently for executive versus nonexecutive status.

Hence, Hypothesis 1 proposes that women nonexecutive directors will have greater human capital investments (education, age, company tenure, work continuity, managerial advancement) than executive directors, but that gender roles and home factors are less likely to differentiate the groups.

Despite the importance of personal factors of human capital, a combination of individual qualities and situational factors is most likely to predict women being appointed to boards. Those considered are interpersonal and organizational factors.

1.2   INTERPERSONAL FACTORS

Lack of interpersonal support and gender dissimilarity are likely to create direct barriers for women to be appointed to boards, and also indirectly through limiting their advancement to top management positions. Although social factors, such as networks, are likely to be important, interpersonal factors are rarely directly measured in studies of women's board appointments. The "social" factors considered in prior studies can be considered in terms of support (Catalyst, 1995a) and women's similarity to other members of the board (Smith, 1994).

Social similarity (e.g., from education, demography) may be especially important for appointment to boards. Social similarity means that individuals will often have shared values and attitudes and derive self esteem from group membership (Jackson, Stone & Alvarez, 1992). Individuals are attracted to, and prefer those similar to themselves (Byrne, 1969). Similarity leads to self-validation, ease of communication, and trusting relationships (Kanter, 1977). The preference for those that are perceived as similar is particularly prevalent in situations of uncertainty and lack of familiarity (Baron & Pfeffer, 1994). Choosing who to appoint to boards is an uncertain situation as there are likely to be a range of factors that may make

individuals effective board members. Similarity reduces uncertainty, thus likely helping men's appointment to boards.

Appointment as company directors was found to be influenced by similarity to the existing members of the board and to the CEO (Westphal & Zajac, 1995), supporting similarity-attraction principles. Similarity was in terms of leadership and communication styles, age, functional background, similarity, and educational level.

Lorsch and MacIver (1989) examined new director selection and change over three years in large U.S. industrial and service firms. The results suggested that relatively powerful boards facilitate the appointment of demographically similar new directors, but also frustrate the attempts of the CEO to do likewise. CEOs used their influence over the nominating process to appoint demographically similar and sympathetic individuals to the board. The pattern was consistent for both nonexecutive and executive appointments. Overall, similarity to existing members of the board appears to help gain men appointment to boards.

By contrast, women are automatically dissimilar to boards because of their gender. The fact that they are women, and thus dissimilar, may of course gain them appointment to boards. However, usually only one woman is appointed to a board, including in Australia (Korn/Ferry International, 1997). A survey of Canadian women directors found that they thought their appointment was because of gender and due to their public visibility (Mitchell, 1984). Women recognised their "token" status. The three most common reasons women thought for their appointments were their community profile (23%), the increasing representation of women (21%), and their business expertise (14%). Overall, it may be that gender dissimilarity to the board will result in women being selected for the board.

However, gender similarity usually helps women rise in rank in management. The women freely chosen for boards are likely to come from organizations where women could rise in rank. Women rise to upper manager, executive and CEO ranks when in less than more "male" managerial hierarchies (Konrad & Pfeffer, 1991; Pfeffer, Davis-Blake, & Julius, 1995; Tharenou, 1995). Hence, it is likely that women will be appointed to boards when women work in organizations with less male managerial hierarchies. As well and by contrast, nonexecutive women who are suitable for appointment to boards are likely to work in the core business of their organizations (general management, line positions); that is, "male" positions. Hence, working in a more "male" than "female" position may lead to women being selected for boards, unlike women executive directors who are on the board because they work in, or own, the company. Overall, women nonexecutive directors may have more of the circumstances for board appointment than executive directors in terms of gender similarity to their own organizations (in less male managerial hierarchies) and gender dissimilarity (working in more male positions, on more male boards). However, these proposals are speculative.

The other category of interpersonal variables considered in this study is career support. Women who gain more support from a mentor and more encouragement for their careers from others (colleagues, superiors) may persist in their attempts to rise to top management ranks and to gain board membership than others. However, gender similarity/dissimilarity is likely to be a more potent influence on women's board appointments than career support is. Moreover, women who reach senior positions in their organisations (the executive directors) may have gained just as much career support as those appointed to boards. Overall, career support is thought to be a less potent influence for women's appointment to boards than is their gender similarity/dissimilarity. Hence, Hypothesis 2 proposes that women's gender similarity (to their own managerial hierarchies) and dissimilarity (to the board, their positions) will be higher for nonexecutive directors than executive directors, but career support is likely to be similar.

1.3   ORGANIZATIONAL FACTORS

The nature of the organization in which a woman is employed is likely to be related to her selection for board positions. This study considers both structural and developmental organizational factors. Executive women who work in larger rather than smaller organizations may be more likely to be chosen for appointment to boards. Large organizations offer women visibility, credibility through their having executive roles in large enterprises, and more chance to gain the kind of experience board chairs and company CEOs think board members should have. As well, the public sector (government, community services) has a higher proportion of women top executives than does the private, profit-making sector (International Labour Organization, 1997). Hence, women who are appointed to boards may be more likely to be executives in the public sector than in the private sector; that is, the profit-making sector. In addition, women should also be more likely to be chosen as board members when in the highest level occupational categories, that of managers and administrators, rather than in lower occupational types. Those working for the company or owners of it may be in lower occupational types (e.g., sales and service).

The other major category of organizational variables examined is developmental. Women who experience more training and development and challenging work assignments throughout their careers may develop more of the knowledge and skill for selection for board positions, and also establish more credibility to overcome their being women. They may become more visible to decision-makers who appoint women to boards. However, developmental factors may be similar for women nonexecutive directors as executive directors. The latter are likely to have had substantial development to get to the top (e.g., executive levels) in their own organizations. Hence, Hypothesis 3 proposes that women nonexecutive directors will work more in the public than private sector, in larger than smaller organizations, and in higher than lower occupation types than executive directors, but may have had similar developmental opportunities.

Overall, this study is an exploratory investigation of the factors that help women gain appointment to boards. It employs a broader range of factors than previously assessed, takes a multivariate approach taking into account interrelationships between factors, and compares the factors distinguishing women who are more freely chosen as board members from those less freely chosen.

2. Method

1.4   RESPONDENTS AND DATA COLLECTION

As there is no directory of women company directors, names were obtained from a number of sources, including the Australian Business Who's Who 1995 and the Jobsons Yearbook 1995, professional associations (e.g., Australian Institute of Credit Unit Directors), executive search companies (ProNed, Waite), and personal contacts. Questionnaires were mailed to 1859 women company directors. The overall response rate was 31% (572 women). An analysis of the representation of the respondents from the population sampled showed that they were generally representative, apart from their representation from some industries (construction, manufacturing, wholesale trade, service). Respondents were asked on the survey for their board position in terms of nonexecutive or executive director status. It was possible to be both. Of the sample, 224 (39%) held only executive director positions; 348 (61%) were nonexecutive directors (167 of them were also executive directors).

As shown in Table 1, the women nonexecutive directors worked in more "female" industries (i.e., those with more female employees and senior women managers and executives, Affirmative Action Agency, 1996; International Labour Organization, 1997), those of finance, property and business services; community services; recreation, personal, and other services: and public administration and defence, than the executive directors. The executive directors worked more in "male" industries (more male employees and executives) of wholesale and retail, manufacturing, and construction than the nonexecutive directors.

Table 2 presents a description of the boards of the companies by the women's executive versus nonexecutive status. As shown, more of the nonexecutive than executive directors were on the boards of statutory authorities and not-for-profit organizations, but fewer on boards of private companies, in which more executive directors held positions. The latter were most likely family businesses. More nonexecutive than executive directors were on the boards of larger than smaller companies. More nonexecutive than executive directors were recruited by invitation to the board by the chair or by election or by informal networking, and less likely recruited from ownership of the company or family affiliation. The recruitment of the nonexecutive directors is thus consistent with their being more freely chosen than the executive directors who were more likely to be on the board because they owned the business.

TABLE 1. Description of the Industries in Which the Women Directors Work

Item	Executive Director:		Nonexecutive Director:	
	Number	%	Number	%
Industry				
Mining	3	1.4	8	2.3
Manufacturing	56	25.2	24	7.0
Electricity, gas and water	0	0.0	6	1.8
Construction	14	6.3	11	3.2
Wholesale and retail trade	53	23.9	33	9.6
Transport and storage	10	4.5	9	2.6
Communication	24	10.8	38	11.1
Finance, property and business services	37	16.7	98	28.7
Public administration and defence	5	2.3	21	6.1
Community services	7	3.2	54	15.8
Recreation, personal and other services	13	5.9 (222)	40	11.7 (342)

Note. There were some respondents who did not complete all demographic items.

1.5   MEASURES

1.5.1   Individual variables

Human capital was measured by education level, age, years organization tenure (all single items, Tharenou, 1998), work continuity (multi-item scale, Tharenou, 1995; α = . 79), and managerial advancement. Managerial advancement usually combines managerial level, pay, and promotions (Tharenou, 1997a). Because the nonexecutive board appointees may be retired, the managerial level items asked also about earlier levels reached. Managerial advancement averaged six items: the managerial level of one's current, last, and second last positions, number of supervisory or overall promotions over one's career, and current salary (α = . 82). The factor emerged as a distinct factor from factor analysis, supporting construct validity.

Marital status was 1, spouse (married, living together) or 2, no spouse (single, divorced, separated, widowed). Number of dependent children was a 6-point item from 0, no children, to 6, six or more children. Gender role traits were measured by the Bem Sex Role Inventory (Bem, 1981), which consisted of 30 adjectives: 10 masculine items, 10 feminine items, and 10 filler items. The items were averaged for masculinity (α= .87) and femininity (α = .89).

TABLE 2. Description of the Boards of Which Women are Directors

Item	Executive Director			Nonexecutive Director		
	Number	%		Number	%	
Type of Board [a]						
Publicly listed company	21	8.2		59	10.2	
Publicly unlisted company	20	7.8		67	11.6	
Private company	165	64.7		162	28.0	
Trust	24	9.4		42	7.3	
Partnership	6	2.4		7	1.2	
Statutory authority	5	2.0		105	18.2	
Not for profit	14	5.5	(255)	136	23.5	(578)
Source of Recruitment [a]						
Invitation by chair	41	15.9		132	27.3	
Invitation by executive	45	17.5		89	18.4	
Election	21	8.2		97	20.1	
Ownership of company	112	43.6		88	18.2	
Family affiliation	33	12.8		37	7.7	
Being a consultant	3	1.2		10	2.1	
Informal networking	2	0.8	(257)	30	6.2	(483)
Number of Boards						
None	0	0.0		0	0.0	
1-2 boards	166	74.1		190	54.8	
3-4 boards	38	17.0		104	29.9	
5-6 boards	9	4.0		30	8.6	
More than 6 boards	11	4.9	(224)	24	6.9	(347)
Board Company Size						
Fewer than 25 employees	84	37.5		102	29.7	
25 to 50 employees	54	24.1		51	14.7	
51 to 100 employees	38	17.0		54	15.6	
100 to 200 employees	17	7.6		38	11.0	
201 to 500 employees	16	7.1		34	9.8	
501 to 1000 employees	8	3.6		18	5.2	
1001 to 2000 employees	3	1.3		10	2.9	
2001 to 4000 employees	3	1.3		12	3.5	
4001 to 8000 employees	0	0.0		12	3.5	
More than 8000 employees	1	0.4	(224)	15	4.3	(346)

[a] Respondents could give more than one response to some items. Some respondents did not complete all items.

1.5.2   *Interpersonal variables*

Gender similarity was measured by four variables, two concerned with gender similarity to the women's own employing organizations (male managerial hierarchy, male position) and two with gender similarity to the board (male board, years working with women directors). Male managerial hierarchy ($\alpha = .70$) measured the extent to which senior positions in the woman's own organization's managerial hierarchy comprised men (Tharenou, 1998). Male position measured the extent to which participants' current positions were occupied by men ($\alpha = .71$). The scale was developed for the study from items derived from the results of earlier research (Konrad & Pfeffer, 1991; Pfeffer et al., 1995; Tharenou & Conroy, 1994). The construct validity of the male managerial hierarchy and male position constructs was supported by factor analysis in which the scales emerged as distinct factors. Male board was a single 5-point item that assessed the gender composition of the board from 1, all women, to 5, all men. Gender similarity was also measured by asking the women for the number of years they had worked closely with women board members using a 5-point item from 1, none to 5, 5 or more years.

Two variables measured career support: career encouragement and career mentoring. Career encouragement (Tharenou & Conroy, 1994) measured the extent of encouragement for one's career development and advancement over one's career from peers and superiors ($\alpha = .83$). Mentor support (Dreher & Ash, 1990) measured the amount of career support given by a higher ranking individual who had played the most significant role in the respondent's career ($\alpha = .92$).

1.5.3   Organizational variables

Of the organizational variables, three measured structural variables and three measured developmental factors. The structural variables were from the women's employment: the size of their employing organizations (Tharenou, 1998), their employment sector, and the occupational categories in which the women worked. Occupational category was measured by asking respondents to place themselves on the Australian Standard Classification of Occupation Code categories: 1, manager and administrator; 2, professional; 3, paraprofessional; 4, tradesperson; 5, clerk; 6, sales and personal service; 7, plant and machine operator; and 8, laborer and related worker. Employment sector was coded as private sector (1) and public sector (2) by collapsing 11 industry categories from the Australian Standard Classification of Industries into two. The industries are given in Table 1. Public administration and defence and community services were coded 2, and the remaining industries were coded 1.

The development variables were training and development and challenging work. Training and development (Tharenou, 1997b) measured participation in courses and on-the-job activities ($\alpha = .76$). Challenging work measured the extent of challenging work in the first three months of the present position and subsequently (Tharenou, 1998; $\alpha = .72$).

3. Results

Logistic regression is used to predict group membership from a set of variables when the dependent variable is dichotomous. It does not include assumptions about the distribution of the predictors (i.e., that they are normally distributed, linearly related, or of equal variance within each group; Tabachnick & Fidell, 1996). Logistic regression also calculates if blocks of variables add to the prediction of the dependent variable, using chi-square tests to do so.

TABLE 3. Results of the Logistic Regression Analysis for Women Executive Directors
Versus Nonexecutive Directors

Variable	B	SE	Step	df	Chi-square Improvement
Individual Variables					
Marital status	-.30	.25			
Dependent children	-.07	.10			
Masculinity	.05	.14			
Femininity	-.19	.14			
Age	.17*	.08			
Education	.12**	.05			
Managerial advancement	.46*	.21			
Work continuity	.13	.16			
Organization tenure	-.11	.07			
			1	9	62.65***
Interpersonal Variables					
Career encouragement	-.06	.07			
Mentor support	-.24*	.10			
Male managerial hierarchy	-.48**	.16			
Male position	-.02	.16			
Male board	.37**	.14			
Years working with other women directors	.17*	.08			
			2	6	35.94***
Organizational Variables					
Occupational category	.29*	.12			
Employment sector	.92**	.30			
Organization size	.15**	.05			
Training and development	.13	.10			
Challenging work	-.23**	.08			
			3	5	43.44***
Constant	-1.94	1.41			

Note. At the first step, 65.04% of the respondents were correctly classified; at the
second step, 70.00% were correctly classified; and at the third step, 72.20%. At the
third step, 59.80% of the executive directors were correctly classified, and 80.74% of
the nonexecutive directors.
$p < .05$, ** $p < .01$, *** $p < .001$.

The results of the logistic regression are presented in Table 3. With respect to
the hypotheses, supporting Hypothesis 1, nonexecutive directors overall had more
human capital than executive directors. As shown by the significant coefficients,
women nonexecutive directors had higher education levels, were older, and had more
managerial advancement than executive directors. Nonexecutive and executive
directors were not different on other human capital variables, or family variables, or
gender role traits, consistent with Hypothesis 1. Overall, supporting Hypothesis 1,
human capital rather than gender roles and family distinguished nonexecutive
directors from executive directors.

Hypothesis 2 received partial support. Overall, gender similarity/dissimilarity
distinguished nonexecutive directors from executive directors more than career
support did. Supporting Hypothesis 2, women nonexecutive directors worked in
organizations with less male managerial hierarchies and were dissimilar in gender to
the board, being on boards with more male directors than were executive directors.
Not supporting Hypothesis 2, women nonexecutive directors did not work in more

male positions than executive directors, and had worked longer with other women board members than had executive directors. Not supporting Hypothesis 2, where a measure of career support was significant, women nonexecutive directors had less mentor support than women executive directors.

Overall, there was partial support for Hypothesis 3. The organizational structural variables differentiated the nonexecutive from executive directors more than did the developmental variables. Women nonexecutive directors worked in larger than smaller organizations and in the public rather than private sector. Not supporting Hypothesis 3, the executive directors were more likely to be managers and administrators than the nonexecutive directors (the low score is the highest category). Contrary to Hypothesis 3, women nonexecutive directors reported less challenging work than the executive directors.

Discriminant analysis (DA) was also conducted to distinguish the two groups. The canonical correlation squared revealed that 25 percent of the variance was explained. Moreover, all the variables that were significant in the logistic regression were also significant in the DA, except challenging work. Only those variables significant in both analyses were interpreted, resulting in the omission of challenging work.

4. Discussion

The aim of this study was to add to our understanding of how women gain appointment to boards of directors. This was done by examining those factors characterizing nonexecutive directors, who are chosen by companies, compared to those characterizing executive directors, who are on boards because they work for, or own, the company. The results reveal that becoming a nonexecutive director (versus an executive director) is related to individuals' skill, knowledge and expertise from education, advancement in management, and age. This is consistent with women being appointed to boards based on their professional background and business acumen (Korn/Ferry International, 1996; Mattis, 1997). Becoming a nonexecutive director is also related to being employed in organizations with opportunity -- large organizations and in the public sector. Nonexecutive board status as opposed to executive board status is also related to gender similarity through the women working in less male managerial hierarchies and having lengthy close relationships with other women board members, but also with dissimilarity through being appointed to male boards, suggesting women's token status. By contrast, gender role traits, family variables, and career support, apart from lack of mentor support, are not relevant for distinguishing the nonexecutive from executive directors of this sample.

1.6   THE IMPORTANCE OF EXPERTISE AND SIGNALING

Women are thought to gain nonexecutive director status by traditional pathways such as education and top executive jobs (Daum, 1994; Mattis, 1997). The results of this study support this view. The human capital variables consistently related to nonexecutive director status – education, managerial advancement, and age - not only reflect knowledge and skill, but also signal to decision-makers that women are suitable, make the women visible, and reduce the perceived risks from selecting them. The overall pattern suggests that women freely chosen for boards have the kind of organizational experience needed in terms of experience as executives.

The nonexecutive directors of this sample are more likely to hold postgraduate degrees (PhDs, MBAs, honours) than the executive directors, and less likely to hold undergraduate degrees or less. The education levels of nonexecutive directors are consistent with other studies (Mattis, 1997). The results suggest that women who are chosen for boards are so partly through the knowledge and problem-solving ability they gain from high education and by the signals sent by education to decision-makers. Because women are rarely on boards, high education levels may help decision-makers overcome their uncertainty about individual women's capabilities and appoint women based on their qualifications and credibility.

Another traditional way of getting onto boards is by being, or having been, a CEO or top executive (Lorsch & MacIver, 1989; Mattis, 1997). It is thus logical that women who gain advancement to senior executive ranks will be those offered board appointments, as shown by the result for managerial advancement. Taking this into account, women nonexecutive directors were also older than executive directors. This is consistent with other studies that find nonexecutive directors are in their mid to late 40s and 50s (Catalyst, 1995a; Izraeli & Talmud, 1997; Mattis, 1997). Because the preferred director is a retired executive, it is likely they are older. Moreover, the women nonexecutive directors' older age is consistent with women with a high and positive industry profile being chosen for appointment to boards (Kesner, 1988).

1.7   GENDER SIMILARITY

The women of this sample seem to gain board positions both from their similarity and dissimilarity by gender. Women nonexecutive directors work in organizations with less rather than more male managerial hierarchies. Perhaps when women gain executive jobs from working in less male hierarchies, they learn how to advance to the top and are confident that they can do so, including gaining board jobs as well. Less male managerial hierarchies provide women with top executive women in their own organizations as role models who can provide advice and encouragement. The nonexecutive women directors also have the experience of working closely with other women directors for a number of years, unlike the executive directors. Hence, nonexecutive women directors may get the support of other women facing the same difficulties as they do, be able to gain advice on how to handle barriers, and have role models on whom to model behaviors. Women directors may also recommend other women directors for appointment. Overall, similarity-attraction effects are supported, as well as other women acting as role models and advisers. By contrast, it is not career encouragement over one's career that is related to women being appointed to boards, but lengthy ties with other women going through the same circumstances.

This link of women's nonexecutive board status with years of working with other women directors is consistent with explanations of how close ties help women advance. When women have strong interpersonal ties, they have sponsors for their mobility (Izraeli & Talmud, 1997). Working closely for substantial time periods with other women board members likely provides the nonexecutive director with strong ties to other women directors, but also encourages greater trust by other board members. Working with other women board members, as well as having experience on male boards, may also provide opportunities for learning norms, rules, and values of the boardroom. It may provide insider information assisting the women to identify company boards with a forthcoming vacancy, and identify boards that would be prepared to appoint a female director.

By contrast, the finding that women nonexecutive directors are appointed to "male" boards suggests that women may be appointed as tokens. Consistent with similarity-attraction theories (Baron & Pfeffer, 1994) and homosocial reproduction approaches (Kanter, 1977), directors are appointed from a small group of white, educated men (Leighton & Thain, 1993; Westphal & Zajac, 1995). Through a process of appointing those who are similar to the board, company boards remain closed gendered circles (Izraeli & Talmud, 1997). However, there are now governmental, stakeholder, and shareholder pressures to appoint women directors (McGregor, 1997). So, women are more likely to be chosen to be directors when the board is all male. Thus, the women nonexecutive directors appear to be "tokens", unlike the women executive directors.

A surprising finding of this study was that women appointed more freely to boards than others report less mentor support. Women nonexecutive directors may have needed less mentor support and sought less assistance from mentors, like men who reach top levels (Burt, 1998; Schor, 1997). They may be exceptionally robust and hardy women. Overall, the women nonexecutive directors may need less mentor support and rely more on their expertise, credibility, and visibility from their age, education and managerial advancement than the executive directors, to advance onto company boards.

1.8   OPPORTUNITY

The results for the organizational variables suggest that opportunity is important for women to be appointed to boards. For example, the nonexecutive directors work in the public sector (community services, government) more than the executive directors do. The public sector has a greater proportion of women top executives than the private, profit-making sector, so it is logical that this should be the sector that provides the pool of potential women. Although some public sector organizations have boards (e.g., statutory bodies, community service organizations), they have them less than private, profit-making companies do. So, when companies appoint internal women directors, they must work more in the private than the public sector.

Women freely appointed to boards work more in larger than smaller organizations. Women who are top executives and upper managers in larger companies are likely more visible and have a higher profile than those in smaller companies. The operations of smaller companies may not provide the relevant experience or level of difficulty for women (e.g., financial responsibility) to handle the decisions needed on boards. Moreover, the advancement opportunities in larger companies may assist executives to gain sufficient seniority to be considered for nonexecutive director appointments in other companies.

An unexpected finding in this study was that the executive women were more likely to be in higher occupational categories (i.e, managers and administrators) than the nonexecutive women. The means for occupational categories indicate that the women overall are either managers and administrators or professionals; i.e., the nonexecutive directors are more likely to be professionals. A survey of Australian company directors found that women were most likely to be accountants or lawyers or academics (Korn/Ferry International, 1996). It may be that the executive women, who were more likely to be on the board because they owned the company, class themselves as managers and administrators. The nonexecutive directors have more professional qualifications because they are more educated than the executive directors, and likely thus class themselves more as professionals. Hence, the nonexecutive directors are more likely professionals based on their educational background and the executive directors more likely managers based on theirs.

1.9   LIMITATIONS OF THIS STUDY AND FUTURE RESEARCH

This study has several limitations. The study was a cross-sectional study, and thus does not predict the factors that allow women to gain board appointments. Future research requires prospective studies in which women who are not board members but upper managers, executives, and CEOs are tracked longitudinally to assess the factors that predict whether they become board members or not. Some variables that were not important in this study could become important in longitudinal analyses (e.g., mentors).

The measures used in this study were self-report. Self-report measures can be inaccurate, such as when asking women to estimate the extent to which their managerial hierarchy or position is male. Hence, future research needs to employ objective measures to increase validity of measurement, especially of the situational variables.

The study explained one quarter of board status. Hence, other variables need to be measured. These include the types of organizations of which women are board members. For example, are women more likely to be appointed to boards in companies in more "female" industries (Kesner, 1988; Korn Ferry International, 1995; Mattis, 1997; McGregor, 1997) and in the public than private sector?. Moreover, are women more likely to be appointed to boards of larger rather than smaller companies, as found (Fryxell & Lerner, 1989; Harrigan, 1989; this study Table 2), with the attendant institutional pressures to conform and of visibility?. Are women more likely to be appointed nonexecutive directors when the CEO of the company has positive views towards women being on boards or in positions of power? Are women more likely to be appointed to boards when the business strategy of the company suggests they would fulfil these organizational needs (Harrigan, 1981; Holton & Rabbetts, 1989; Mitchell, 1984)?. The present study has not explored the characteristics of the companies to which women were appointed as board members.

This study suggests that women's social capital is important to their selection to boards, through their gender similarity to their own managerial hierarchies and their having long-term links with other women directors. However, the study did not examine the influence of social capital (e.g., networks). Women need close networks, especially of other women, and strong sponsors to advance to top positions (Burt, 1998). Because women are outsiders and lack legitimacy, they need to borrow the social capital of their sponsors, and gain their large disconnected networks (Burt, 1998). Future research needs to examine the links of women's networks and of the nature of sponsors to their selection to boards. This study examined mentor support for career advancement, rather than sponsorship for board appointment.

In this study, women themselves were not asked what were the barriers or facilitators to their board appointment. This may result in additional factors being found than those here, such as barriers of men's stereotypes about women (Bilimoria & Piderit, 1994), and facilitators such as women developing specialist expertise. Future research needs to ask women about the barriers and facilitators to their appointments and contrast those to the barriers and facilitators that male chairs of boards and CEOs of companies report. It may be that women board members and decision-makers give different reasons for why women are not on boards.

This study examined what helps women reach nonexecutive as opposed to executive board status. Women board members are atypical of women in general and of male counterparts, because they are so rare. Future research needs to compare men and women nonexecutive and executive directors to assess the differences between the factors linked to men and women reaching nonexecutive director status. The factors that cause women and men to be appointed freely to boards as nonexecutive directors are likely to be different (e.g., long-standing network links, social similarity).

1.10   PRACTICAL IMPLICATIONS AND CONCLUSIONS

Practical implications for women's advancement to company boards emerge from the results. At the individual level, women should be encouraged to enhance their human capital, especially education and managerial advancement. Especially relevant to more women gaining appointments is the number of women in executive positions in companies, because of the relationship found here between women in senior roles and women being nonexecutive directors. Thus, if the proportion of women executives increases, the likelihood of a woman being appointed to a board as a nonexecutive director should also increase. Because women now form a low 5% of top executives, and have increased by only 1% or 2% in the last 20 years (Korn/Ferry International, 1993), their appointment based on managerial advancement may indeed be difficult.

Women also need to increase their social capital and similarity by working in organizations where they are similar in gender to the managerial hierarchy, and by developing networks of other women directors. The important implication is that organizations need to reduce their homosocial reproduction in favor of men, both in their managerial hierarchies and on their boards, perhaps by adopting affirmative action policies. CEOs and company chairs need to take active steps to prevent these similarity-attraction effects. Women also need to work in organizations that give them a greater opportunity to learn executive skills, such as the public sector and large organizations.

In conclusion, the results of this study suggest that women are appointed to boards based on their human capital, their social capital, and opportunity. Women who have more skill, knowledge and expertise for executive work from age, education and managerial advancement are more likely to be nonexecutive directors than executive directors. Women who have more social capital, through similarity to the gender of the managerial hierarchies of their organizations and through having long-term contacts with women directors, are more likely to be nonexecutive directors than executive directors. However, women may be chosen to become nonexecutive directors to fulfil a token status as indicated by their being on male boards. There are also opportunities for women to be appointed nonexecutive board members if they are in the public sector and large organizations, which may have pressures on them to conform to external pressures. Women executives seeking to extend their board experience to nonexecutive director appointments should attempt to maximize their opportunities to gain advantage based on increasing their skills, knowledge, and expertise, increasing their social capital in terms of their similarity and networks, and enhancing opportunities through the types of organizations for which they work and the occupations in which they work. However, the onus should not be on women. CEOs and the chairs of boards need to reduce homosocial reproduction with respect to the membership of boards and the advancement of women to top positions in organizations.

References

Affirmative Action Agency. (1996) *Affirmative Action Agency: Annual Report 1995-1996,* Australian Government Publishing Service, Canberra.

Baron, J.N., & Pfeffer, J. (1994) The social psychology of organizations and inequality, *Social Psychology Quarterly, 57,* 190-209.

Becker, G.S. (1993) *Human capital*, University of Chicago Press, Chicago.

Bem, S.L. (1981) *Bem Sex-Role inventory: Professional manual*, Consulting Psychologists Press Inc, California.

Bilimoria, D., & Piderit, S. K. (1994) Board committee membership: Effects of sex-based bias, *Academy of Management Journal 37*, 1453-1477.

Burke, R.J. (1994) Women on corporate boards of directors: Views of Canadian chief executive officers, *Women in Management Review 9*, 3-10.

Burke, R.J. (1995) Why are there so few women corporate directors? Women and men see it differently, *International Review of Women and Leadership 1*, 55-60.

Burke, R.J., & Kurucz, E. (1998) Demographic characteristics of Canadian women corporate directors, *Psychological Reports 83,* 461-462.

Burt, RS. (1998) The gender of social capital, *Rationality and Society, 10 (1),* 5-46.

Byrne, D. (1969) Attitudes and attraction, in L. Berkowitz (ed.), *Advances in experimental social psychology 4*, Academic Press, New York, pp. 35-89.

Catalyst. (1995a) *The CEO view*, New York, Catalyst, NY.

Catalyst. (1995b) *Catalyst census - Female board directors of the Fortune 500*, New York, Catalyst, NY.

Daum, J.H. (1994) Women directors at work, *Directors and Boards 19*, 50-54.

Dreher, G.F., & Ash, R.A. (1990) A comparative study of mentoring among men and women in managerial, professional, and technical positions, *Journal of Applied Psychology 75*, 539-546.

Fryxell, G.E., & Lerner, L.D. (1989) Contrasting corporate profiles: Women and minority representation in top management positions, *Journal of Business Ethics 8*, 341-352.

Harrigan, K.R. (1981) Numbers and positions of women elected to corporate boards, *Academy of Management Journal 24*, 619-625.

Holton, V.D. (1995a) Women on the boards of Britain's top 200 companies, *Women in Management Review 10*, 16-20.

Holton, V.D. (1995b) Corporate governance report surveying the situation for women directors in the UK, *Corporate Governance 3*, 102-107.

Holton, V.D. (1995c) Women and equal opportunities: Creating a level playing field, *Equal Opportunities 31*, 904-907.

Holton, V.D., & Rabbetts, J. (1989) *Pow(d)er in the board room: Report of a suvey of women on boards on top UK industrial companies*, Ashridge Management Research Group, England.

Howe, E., & McRae, S. (1991) *Women on the board*, Policy Studies Institute, London.

International Labour Organization. (1997) *Breaking through the glass ceiling: Women in management*, International Labour Office, Geneva.

Izraeli, D.N., & Talmud, I. (1997) Getting aboard: Mode of recruitment and gender composition, *International Review of Women and Leadership 3*, 26-45.

Jackson, S., Stone, V., & Alvarez, E. (1992) Socialization amidst diversity, in B.M. Staw, & L.L. Cummings (eds.), *Research in Organizational Behavior*, JAI Press, Greenwich, CT, pp. 45-109.

Kanter, R.M. (1977) *Men and women of the corporation*, Basic Books, New York.

Kesner, I.F. (1988) Directors' characteristics and committee membership, *Academy of Management Journal, 31*, 66-84.

Konrad, A.M., & Pfeffer, J. (1991) Understanding the hiring of women and minorities in educational institutions, *Sociology of Education 64*, 141-157.

Korn/Ferry International (1993) *Decade of the executive woman*, Korn-Ferry International, Los Angeles.

Korn/Ferry International. (1995) *Boards of directors in Australia* (Fourteenth Study edition), Korn/Ferry International, New York.

Korn/Ferry International. (1996) *Boards of directors in Australia* (Fifteenth Study edition), Korn/Ferry International, Sydney, Australia.

Korn/Ferry International. (1997) *Boards of directors in Australasia* (1st edition), Korn/Ferry International, Sydney.

Leighton D., & Thain, D. (1993) Selecting new directors, *Business Quarterly 57*, 16-25.

Lord, R.G., De Vader, C.L., & Alliger, G.M. (1986) A meta-analysis of the relationship between personality traits and leadership perceptions, *Journal of Applied Psychology 71*, 402-410.

Lorsch, J.W., & MacIver, E. (1989) *Pawns or potentates: The reality of America's corporate boards*, Harvard Business School, Boston, MA.

Mattis, M.C. (1997) Women on corporate boards: Two decades of research, *International Review of Women and Leadership 3*, 11-25.

McGregor, J. (1997) Making the good woman visible: The issue of profile in New Zealand corporate directorship, *International Review of Women and Leadership 3*, 1-10.

Mitchell, M. (1984) A profile of the Canadian woman director, *Business Quarterly (Spring)*, 121-127.

Pfeffer, J., Davis-Blake, A., & Julius, D.J. (1995) AA officer salaries and managerial diversity: Efficiency wages or status? *Industrial Relations 34*, 73-94.

Schor, S.M. (1997) Separate and unequal, *Business Horizons 40 (5)*, 51-58.

Smith, A. (1994) Storming the board, *Management 41*, 42-47.

Tabachnick, B.G., & Fidell, L.S. (1996) *Using multivariate statistics* (3rd edition), Harper Collins, New York.

Tharenou, P. (1995) Correlates of women's chief executive status: Comparisons with men chief executives and women top managers, *Journal of Career Development 21*, 201-212.

Tharenou, P. (1997a) Managerial career advancement, in C.L. Cooper, & I.T. Robertson (eds.), *International Review of Industrial and Organisational Psychology*, Wiley, New York, pp. 39-93.

Tharenou, P. (1997b) Organisational, job and personal predictors of employee participation in training and development, *Applied Psychology: An International Review 46*, 111-134.

Tharenou, P. (1998) Predictors of advancing in management, in G. Griffin (ed.), *Management theory and practice*, MacMillan, Melbourne, pp. 358-378.

Tharenou, P., & Conroy, D.K. (1994) Men and women managers' advancement, *Applied Psychology: An International Review 43*, 5-31.

Tharenou, P., Latimer, S., & Conroy, D. (1994) How do you make it to the top? *Academy of Management Journal 37*, 899-931.

Westphal, J.D., & Zajac, E.J. (1995) Who shall govern? *Administrative Science Quarterly 40*, 60-83.

THE NEW ZEALAND EXPERIMENT-TRAINING TO BE ON BOARD AS A DIRECTOR

JUDY MCGREGOR
Professor, Human Resource Management Department
Massey University, New Zealand

1. Introduction

The first female head of state in New Zealand, Prime Minister Jenny Shipley, is conducting a radical experiment on the nation's boardrooms. She is personally committed to improving the status of women on boards of directors and regards boardroom representation as a symbolic 'marker' of women's progress. The New Zealand Prime Minister has pledged through the Ministry of Women's Affairs to improve the proportion of females on statutory boards to 50% by the year 2000. She retained the women's portfolio for a period after becoming Prime Minister to give strength to female policy issues around the cabinet table and within the coalition government's caucus. This gives her commitment political significance.

The Government's promise of gender balance on government boards and committees was made as part of its follow-up to the Beijing Women's Conference in 1995. It will become a highly visible symbol of women's progress because New Zealand is required to report on developments towards giving women full equality with men, as a signatory to the United Nations Convention on the Elimination of All Forms of Discrimination Against Women (CEDAW). The reports, compiled every four years, comprise a type of score-card on the status of women for women's groups and policy makers.

On the face of it, board representation is a promising and progressive Government initiative and in keeping with New Zealand's status as the first nation state to grant women the vote. The problem for the Prime Minister, though, when it comes to changing the male domination of boardrooms, is that as a head of the government Mrs Shipley can directly influence the state sector only. The corporate world has to date remained largely impervious to Mrs Shipley's radical experiment. It is in the private sector, with its enormous financial power and socio-economic significance, where male cultural norms are so pervasive. The boardrooms of corporate companies in the private sector remain citadels of patriarchal values.

This chapter firstly explores the issue of equal opportunities behind the boardroom in New Zealand, both in the state and private sectors. This material has

R.J. Burke and M.C. Mattis (eds.), Women on Corporate Boards of Directors, 129-144.

been gathered in the past five years by researchers interested in gender equity in the boardroom who have used interviews, surveys and analysis of the annual reports of top corporate companies to collect data.

The comparison between the two sectors is important, too, because the pace of market liberalism and de-regulation in New Zealand has been swifter and more dramatic than the laissez faire economic direction of many other Western developed states. A consequence of this process of "the bureaucratic revolution" (Boston et al, 1991) means that the private sector is assuming greater responsibility for political and economic development as the state sheds power and loses its legitimacy for some functions (McGregor et al, 1997). This has seen a widened ambit for the corporate model which is now increasingly applying to the public sector. For example, in New Zealand about 60 crown companies have converted to the corporate model with compelling legislation that prioritises profitability over social responsibility (Taggart,1993).Other countries are expected to follow New Zealand's lead in corporatising the public sector. The trend has profound implications for the role of governance and the question of women's participation in the process as directors of boards. It can be predicted that corporate governance in these new hybrid companies will inevitably become a focus of assertiveness in the equal opportunities debate (McGregor et al 1997), a movement perhaps anticipated by Jenny Shipley.

Secondly, the chapter provides a first-hand perspective of the training initiatives undertaken by the Ministry of Women's Affairs, as part of the Government's radical experiment to improve gender representation on boards. Women's membership of boards of directors is often debated in the context of the need to prepare women for the boardroom with potential and with the appropriate skills through training. For example, the Ministry of Women's Affairs publication, *Panui,* in an article on decision-making states," Equal opportunities and elimination of discrimination in the appointment process will help women participate more fully in public decision-making, but there is also a clear need for training" (p.4).

While the popular business press often carries "lists" of the skills and competencies needed for board membership which aspiring female directors should develop, there are few written accounts by female researchers of the scope and effectiveness of the available training options. Partly with the aim of collecting research data and partly because I have ambitions some day to be a director myself, I attended a Government-sponsored training course for potential directors on corporate governance and accountability and report in this chapter on my observations of the process and the outcomes. The observations of others who attended were subsequently solicited by email and are reported here in such a way as to preserve their anonymity. Clearly my participant status means that instead of writing *about* the process objectively I am writing *from* a personal perspective (Marshall, 1997). I would hope that in acknowledging my participant status and commitment to the reform of board composition I am practising the "critical subjectivity" that Reason and Rowan (1981) urge on researchers.

2. So where are the female directors?

2.1. CORPORATES

New Zealand is not alone in its poor female representation in the boardrooms of top companies. The figures confirm overseas trends (Johnston, 1997; Holton, 1995; Burke, 1994) and show that the resilience of boardroom culture should not be underestimated, even though it flies in the face of the changing demographic influence of women and business imperatives such as female consumerism. While a seat on the board is highly symbolic of power, status and leadership in business, the number of female corporate directors in New Zealand is depressingly low, according to the available, empirical data (Pajo, et al 1997) The annual reports of the top 200 companies were utilised to compile a list of female directors, in the absence of any reliable data base or public register of board membership by gender. In cases where the annual report failed to identify the gender of board members, a letter was sent to the company requesting the names and addresses of any female directors. The top 200 were identified on the basis of a range of financial indicators such as turnover and profit. Table 1 gives the number and percentage of companies with female representation at board level.

TABLE 1: Representation of women on corporate boards in New Zealand's top 200 companies

Total number of companies	Companies with female representation on the board	Total number of directors	Number of women directors
166	47(28.3%)	1,282	56(4.4%)

Note: Final sample was reduced from 200 as a result of company restructuring, mergers and in a few instances failure to respond to our inquiries.

It is evident that women are poorly represented. Only a little more than 28 per cent of the companies, for which information was available, had women directors on their boards. Companies with more than one woman (average number of directors per company was 7.7) are exceedingly rare. Only 5.4 per cent of the companies surveyed had more than one woman on the board. Female representation as a percentage of the total number of directorships was 4.4 per cent only.

The demographic characteristics of the women who did make it behind the boardroom doors suggest a profile of a middle-aged group of highly educated women. The majority of the female directors were aged 50 and under (80.6 per cent) and were clustered in the 41-50 age group. This differs from the Canadian experience

(Bradshaw 1990) where an older group of women was represented, but corroborates the British evidence (Holton, 1995) which suggests the female directors in the 1990s are likely to be younger than those in the 1980s. High educational status was a feature, as elsewhere, (Bradshaw, 1990; Burke, 1994) with over 80 per cent of the New Zealand sample completing post graduate study and over 90 per cent undertaking tertiary education.

Slightly more than half had professional backgrounds (54.8%) with law the most common (25.8) and the majority were Pakeha (European) New Zealanders (83.9 per cent) and less than 10 per cent Maori (New Zealand's indigenous people). These demographic features undermine the somewhat evanescent notion of "experience" so often used as the excuse to deny gender representation in the boardroom, and the corollary notion that the "school of hard knocks" is adequate education for corporate directorship (Pajo et al, 1997).

Following Canadian research (Burke, 1994) questionnaires were sent to the pioneer female directors of the top 200 companies in New Zealand (Pajo *et al*, 1997). Respondents were asked why they thought there were so few female directors and they rated how strongly they agreed or disagreed with a range of statements about gender equity in the boardroom. The reason most commonly attributed for the poor representation was that companies did not think that women were qualified for board service (68.9 per cent). There was also substantial agreement that companies did not know where to look for qualified women (62 per cent) and, of more concern, that companies were not looking to put more women on boards (58.6 per cent). More than half the respondents (55.1 per cent) thought that the companies were not appointing women directors out of concern that they would bring "women's issues" to the boardroom agenda.

Just under half of the women directors surveyed (46.7 per cent) believed that there were not enough qualified women available for board service and 40 per cent believed that qualified women were not making it known that they were interested in board service. There was very little agreement, 10.3 per cent, with the proposition that qualified women were not interested in board service. The female directors unequivocally (85 per cent) believed there should be more women in boardrooms to improve the mix. The findings suggest that women perceive top companies in New Zealand as culturally conservative about women in boardrooms despite their perceived need for greater boardroom diversity.

Interestingly public controversy in New Zealand about the absence of women from boards of directors of top corporates is occasionally fanned by angry shareholders (Corbett, 1997). The responses of the companies under attack suggest active male cronyism. One chairman indicated that "good women were hard to find" and the chief executive told that annual general meeting that the boardroom of a publicly listed company was an appropriate place for men, but not for women. There were different "general, social expectations" of women, he said (Corbett, 1997). However, the notion of good women being hard to find is now under siege in the New Zealand.

The active recruitment and selection of a cadre of good women for the boardrooms of the new, hybrid state companies is altering the gender dynamic of governance. No longer can corporate companies claim ignorance of suitable women for boardroom jobs or that female inexperience remains a barrier to their inclusion at the top. There is now clear evidence in New Zealand that crown companies have discovered a pool of potential talent overlooked by the corporate sector.

2.2. CROWN COMPANIES

Let's just look at the figures. There has been considerable progress in getting more women onto public boards and committees. The proportion of women appointed to the boards of statutory bodies increased from 25% in 1993 to 31% in 1996 and while these figures include lower-level boards as well as the newer, more important crown companies, the trend is to be welcomed. And when only the Crown companies in areas as diverse as health, forestry, electricity, gas, water, transport and broadcasting are examined, the figures at 19.7 per cent of female to 80.3 per cent male directors (Shilton et al, 1996) show a distinct improvement over the public sector figures. These Crown companies have an estimated net worth of more than NZ$8.5 billion and total assets of $14.5 billion, so their financial impact, as well as their socio-political influence, is considerable. In part the improvement is a reflection of the ambiguous equal opportunities environment in New Zealand. While the public sector has compelling statutory requirements relating to equal opportunities (State Sector Act, 1988), these do not apply to the private sector where equal opportunities are voluntary, although anti-discrimination legislation (Human Rights Act, 1993) is universal.

In part, too, the improvement in gender equity is a result of pro-active Government policy in the training, recruitment and selection areas underpinned by statute. The conversion of public sector structures in New Zealand and the new hybrid organisations means that Crown companies now emphasise corporate principles as opposed to the traditional rationale of public good. But as McGregor (1997) notes they are not totally de-regulated in terms of the recruitment and appointment process.

The higher number of female directors in Crown companies relates to the establishment of a recruitment mechanism in the Crown Company Monitoring Advisory Unit (CCMAU), which has a legal obligation to search for competent women. This breaks with the pattern of homosocial reproduction, the selection of new directors on the basis of social similarity (Kanter, 1977),which has traditionally characterised corporate board recruitment. And it means that in future women may be less reliant on their own personal initiatives to boost their profile in order to attract attention of Crown companies (McGregor, 1997).

The unit, which advises on board appointments to Crown-owned companies, was established in 1993 and is responsible for monitoring nearly 60 companies. The Crown company model follows normal business structures and crown companies are limited liability companies established under the Companies Act. This means that directors of these companies have the same responsibilities and liabilities as other directors of boards. The Crown Company Monitoring Advisory Unit advises shareholding government ministers on the appointment of directors to the boards of these companies. The Prime Minister Jenny Shipley, who retained the women's affairs portfolio until August 1998, is also a former Minister of State-Owned Enterprises. Her power means she is uniquely influential in achieving the aim of gender equity on crown boards by the new millenium. The political promise of gender equity is being keenly observed by female groups and women in public life in New Zealand.

Searching for potential female candidates for boards of directors is part of the monitoring unit's role in striving for a balance of representation and skills. It publicly advertises the existence of its database of potential directors, solicits curricula vitae from women interested in entering the boardroom and interviews potential candidates to assess their suitability. In this interview process, which is conducted with unit personnel and existing company directors out in the community, the potential candidate is encouraged to talk about her experience, skills, strengths and aspirations. After the interview process names of suitable candidates are forwarded to shareholding ministers for consideration when vacancies on the boards of crown companies occur.

As noted elsewhere, (McGregor, 1997), it is at this stage of the crown company appointment process, that political appointments and blockages can interfere. This phenomenon is not gender specific. As this chapter was being written NewstalkZB reported that a misdirected facsimile from the office of a prominent Labour Member of Parliament which had been sent to the radio station anonymously, listed the names of several people, including women, whom the politician suggested should not be appointed to public bodies in the event of a Labour victory at the next elections.

The extent of political bias in crown company appointments warrants further analysis. Its operation is notoriously opaque and covert. The Ministry of Women's Affairs suggested to me informally in research for this chapter that the outmoded exercise of undue influence by politicians may be over stated as a barrier to board appointments. Political bias needs to be put to the sword of empirical research which analyses statutory board recruitments against political affiliation to determine whether it is a real or imagined impediment to women's progress. But political interference and influence aside, overall women have fared better in the radical experiment with crown companies than in the private sector.

The bid to reach 50% female directorships of crown company boards by 2000 has seen a number of interesting recruitment and training initiatives. First, consciousness-raising amongst women has taken place through four regional seminars organised as partnerships between regional work trusts, enterprise agencies and chambers of commerce and the Ministry of Women's Affairs. The Ministry of Women's Affairs and the Crown Company Monitoring Advisory Unit (CCMAU) have linked with the Institute of Directors to develop governance seminars. These are aimed in particular at women with board potential. If the project works it should lead to greater diversity on Crown company boards through more women and more Maori directors. In 1998 three training seminars were held, involving 49 women and 19 men, all of whom had some governance or senior management experience. I was one of the participants in the second training seminar and I report on the experience below.

3. Getting On Board

Twenty four of us, 21 women and 3 men, assembled for two intensive days at a Wellington hotel for sessions about boardroom practice and relationships, strategic planning, evaluating performance, financial reporting, legal duties and working on a Crown company board. Case studies of actual board situations were simulated during the seminar. The teaching styles, course organisation and workshopping were not unlike an executive MBA teaching experience. The other female participants included a business school dean, a Queen's Counsel, several barristers, the director of a computer training company, a leading museum chief executive officer, a health insurance executive and several women who worked either as accountants or in financial services. Two of the female participants were Maori and one male was a Pacific Islander.

Many of us already knew each other, or of each other. For example, at least three of the women were at Auckland University Law School when I studied law as a mature student. With such a small population base, 3.6 million overall, New Zealand's professional and social circles often overlap. This prior knowledge helped the process of socialisation and informal linkage during the seminars. It also usefully serves as a reminder of how many women there are who have potential for boardroom positions and who are interested in governance. A participant in the first training seminar, Jan Beange, a lawyer and chairperson of the Tauranga Energy Consumer Trust, stated that the most useful thing about the seminar she attended was being exposed to women in similar positions and to women already in senior directorships. She said "the people I workshopped with all had sound governance and strategic skills, though none had been on a government board. It was exciting to see how transferable our skills were." (Panui, p.5).

The training sessions could usefully be described as a mixture of 'hard' and 'soft' skills development. In the technical area the participants were exposed to issues such as joint venture development, financial reporting to and by the board and the legal liabilities and duties of directors . More significantly, perhaps, were the 'soft' elements of the seminar which featured the experiences of New Zealand's

longest serving female 'pioneer' director, Alison Paterson, and of a session
examining the dynamics of the boardroom, again run by a female director, Juliet
McKee, of Wellington. The topical issues of boards evaluating their own
performance, the relationship between the board of directors and the chief executive
officer, and the question of coping with directors of difficult temperaments, featured
in this session.

Significantly, both formal and informal evaluation of those who presented at
the seminar favoured these two sessions from the dozen or so offerings. In part, it
was the candour of the two women director-presenters who exposed both the
negatives and the positives of board directorships to us. Alison Paterson, an
Auckland accountant, who chairs a major and difficult crown health enterprise as
well as holding other directorships, spoke of the gender dynamic in the boardroom.
"Gender can discriminate for as well as against. Where it is for, I accept it gratefully
but I hope I will never lie to myself. If I felt I was not performing, or was unable to
perform on the board, then I hope I would follow my own advice and get out" She
exhorted us to " all the time remember you are as good as anyone else," a reference
to the need for self- confidence by potential, first-time female directors.

The boardroom ethos, or the 'conspiracy of discretion' as it has been
described (McGregor et al, 1997), is not well understood by women who aspire to
directorships. The boardroom mystique expressed by a closed, clubby and elitist
culture transcends the sound commercial reasons for boardroom confidentiality. The
notion of the boardroom as the apex of business power has promoted the fallacy that
super-human qualities are needed to gain admission. What is seldom talked of,
though, is the need for complementarity of attributes. The value of another female
director's training session was the acknowledgement of the benefits of a necessary
skills mix on effective corporate boards. The director, Juliet McKee, irreverently
divided the competencies required in boardroom composition: there needed to be a
"strategist, a tactician, a conformist and a argumentative b....." on each board.
Seldom did one individual possess all these attributes, she said.

Both of the female directors emphasised possible negatives associated with
directorship, such as the legal liability and need for insurance and the loss of income
from highly paid professional practices which had greater earning potential than
directorship fees. The legal and financial implications of being a director was
sobering for some attendees, not all of whom will necessarily want to enter the
boardroom after the training session. Vickie Paterson, a practice manager for a
Dunedin-based health, economics and consulting company, who attended the first
training session, said afterwards, "I'd now go in (to the boardroom) with my eyes
open. As a director, you have to be individually responsible for all decisions. You
can't just hide behind the collective" (Panui, p.5).

In New Zealand the liabilities of directors have been hardened up by
changes to the Companies Act, following public and parliamentary concern about the
role and performance of directors in company collapses through the 1980s. One of
the women who attended my training session said in an email response to me:
"my most immediate reflection came during training and that was that I had been
provided with enough information to create considerable doubt in my mind as to the

personal value versus input and risk in regard to directorships in New Zealand. I have in the past considered it a natural professional progression, but am now somewhat sceptical about the role". Another said…"if anything I think training put me off the idea."

4. Clash of cultures

A clash of cultures underpinned the training seminar. The tension was induced in part by the mix of sponsoring bodies, the women's ministry and the crown's monitoring unit, both compelled by statute and moral imperatives to pursue principles of equality and diversity, and the Institute of Directors (IOD), a defender of the faith. While the IOD is a powerful lobby group on governance issues and operates a register for companies wishing to recruit directors, it has traditionally held conservative views about the issue of gender equity on boards. Corbett (1997), in a business press article on the issue of women on boards, noted that the inability of groups such as the Institute of Directors to provide information about suitable applicants, on the grounds of privacy, and the absence of a public register of names of potential women, as barriers to building up a reliable picture of gender representation in this important area.

The clash of cultures we experienced in the classroom as trainee directors is best expressed as a contrast between new and old values. The new values were reflected in the opening address by New Zealand's youngest ever minister, Deborah Morris, who, in her capacity as the then Associate Minister of Women's Affairs, talked wryly about the merit principle and how she hoped it would soon apply to directorships. The old values were reflected in the written materials provided by the Institute of Directors, which consistently used the male pronoun to describe both chief executive officers and directors. While there is debate about the influence of sexist language in a socio-political climate obsessed with political correctness, the male pronoun was consistently used also by institute personnel in oral presentation. Sexist language addressed to professional women in training for top jobs sponsored by a ministry committed to women's equality is an unfortunate expression of out-moded practice and attitude.

Not surprisingly, the women on my course were loud in their condemnation of such written advice as "The director with integrity knows a conflict when *he* sees one and will not profit from dealing in *his* shares through inside information", and "If there are going to be executive directors on the board then it follows that the chief executive must be one of them. *His* position in the company would be untenable if this was not the case". One of the participants dismissed one of the presenters on the basis that he was "nauseatingly pompous and chauvinistic". The significance of the sexist language used in the training for women, beyond its symbolic power, lies in how far it reflects the thinking of the Institute of Directors. The Institute is in a powerful position to influence corporate appointments through recommendations to companies seeking advice on new directors.

5. Judging the experiment

It is premature to judge the effectiveness of the training courses for potential female directors in providing momentum for them to take a seat on the board. As the Ministry of Women's Affairs points out, the pool of potential female directors who have undergone training has now quite dramatically increased while the available directorships remain static. There is likely to be a lag, perhaps of two to three years, before vacancies and turnovers occur on crown company boards. At the time of writing several women only who attended the first two training sessions have been appointed to a crown company. At one level the government- sponsored training courses have increased the expectation of women of the likelihood of quicker progress than current boardroom routines, processes and cultures can deliver. One of the participants on my training course emailed me to ask, what next? She said, "what strategies should we use to get positions-it wasn't good enough to tell us 'it's all about knowing the right people'. If you are going to have affirmative action in the form of free training you need to take the initiative further".

The New Zealand experience in boosting the number of women in crown company boardrooms can be seen below figuratively as a series of steps or a process. The current process does not contain follow-up, incubator initiatives at this stage. The process ends for some women only with appointment to a board.

**FIGURE 1: Pathway to Improving Female Representation on Boards The NZ
Crown Company Experience
The NZ Crown Company Experience**

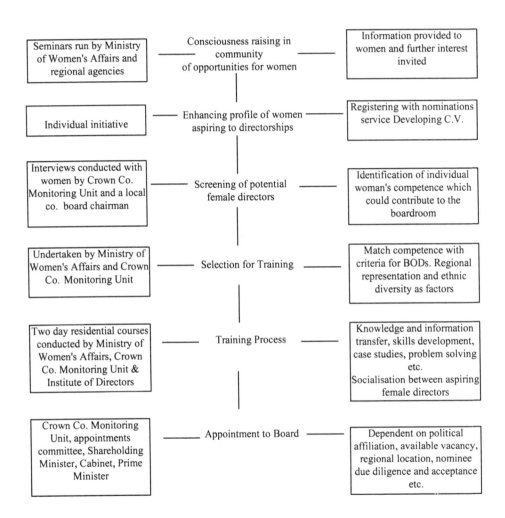

It is too soon also to say whether the first wave of women on crown company boards represents a new order or is an expression of tokenism to meet a political agenda. The issue of recruitment, appointments, vacancies and retention by gender needs longitudinal study. Will, for example, New Zealand follow the disappointing example of Australia? Still (1993) urges caution about the gains women appeared to have made in Australia.. In 1986 the Australian Federal Government, as part of its policy to improve gender representation on important boards, appointed a number of women as directors of government business enterprises. Still states that the women served their terms and were then mostly replaced by men. Affirmative action on boards is as vulnerable as any other women's issue which is subject to political whim.

At another level, there have been some interesting side benefits for some of the New Zealand training participants who may not yet have been appointed to a board but are using the skills developed during the governance training experience. For example, one female CEO on my course stated that "interestingly the most help it has given me is helping me realise what I should as a CEO be able to expect from my board. They certainly carry out half the functions they should be fulfilling". Another participant said, "as the recently elected Chair of a voluntary organisation with a turnover of NZ$15 million I felt more confident to introduce systems and practices of a board." And in my capacity as an academic staff member on my own university's governing body I adapted the template of board annual self evaluation referred to during training for use by a university council, a first for university governance in New Zealand.

There is evidence, too, of a ripple effect from the quest for greater diversity of board representation on crown companies. In Massey University research profiling the pioneers, 31 women directors on corporate boards, responded to a questionnaire on female representation (Pajo et al, 1997). The survey asked the female respondents how they came to the attention of corporate boards and what factors were important in their selection. Here it appears that being recommended by the Ministry of Women's Affairs or by the Crown Company Monitoring Advisory Unit was very important in terms of a second, or subsequent, board appointment, although less important in getting into the boardroom for the first time.

TABLE 2: Percentage of respondents indicating how their name was brought to the attention of corporate boards.

Method by which their name was brought to the attention of the board	First board appointment (n=30)	Most recent board appointment (n=24)
	0	8.3
Recruited by a search firm	6.7	25.0
Recommended by CEO of the company	23.3	8.3
Recommended by someone who knew CEO or board member	26.7	16.7
Recommended by a board member of their own organization	9.7	29.2
Was a shareholder in the company	23.3	8.3
Had a family affiliation with the company	10.0	4.2

The findings may suggest the two agencies, the women's ministry and the crown monitoring unit, are cautious in their approach, conscious of the need for track record and may want women to "prove themselves" before recommending them. The findings suggest the two agencies may be more effective in increasing the directorships of women who are already in the boardroom than in targeting new entrant female directors (Pajo et al, 1997). This is because the risk-averse nature of board appointments means that high profile women are more likely to be successful, at least partly as a consequence of their visibility.

While high profile and visibility are important factors in board recruitment, self-promotion collides head-on with women's social conditioning and value systems (McGregor, 1997). Women need to accept that self-promotion is legitimate on a personal and professional level even if they decide against mimicking male self promotional patterns. Monitoring whether a new girls network, the same group of professional, highly visible women, ends up paralleling the old boys network, the 30-odd, powerful men with multiple directorships, in New Zealand boardrooms is a future research direction. Leighton and Thain (1993) refer to corporate boards as "old boy's networks" and suggest that "many corporate directors are members of an 'old boys' network and appear to have been cut out with a cookie cutter". Is a smaller but nonetheless influential new girls network emerging, a network of a different age and gender, but of a cookie cutter similarity?

6. Sustaining the momentum

Despite her political clout and the radical nature of her experiment, New Zealand's Prime Minister Jenny Shipley is unlikely to be able to deliver on her political promise of gender balance on boards by the year 2000. Given the current rate of progress it is more likely to be between 35-40% in that time on all statutory boards and perhaps more likely to be 25% of the important crown companies. But when that figure is placed alongside the comparatively static progress of women in the top 200 companies the initiative is likely to be seen as a partial success story for New Zealand women aspiring to governance positions. So how can this momentum be sustained? Several factors will influence increased representation on boards of directors. These include:

6.1. MAINTAINING BOARD REPRESENTATION AS A POLITICAL ISSUE

The current momentum in the crown company arena represents increased political clout by female politicians, legislative imperatives and the policy push of the Ministry of Women's Affairs. Women must insist the political commitment is kept up through lobby initiatives on political parties and within electorates. It is helpful in this regard that a parliamentary election is due in 1999.

6.2. CONTINUING WITH DIRECTORSHIP TRAINING

The crown company process described in this chapter has broadened the scope of recruitment and selection beyond antiquated and self-perpetuating notions of homosocial reproduction. Women are asked to submit curricula vitae, are then interviewed and selected for training. The training seminars address the question of skills which has been one of the excuses traditionally used to lock women out of boardrooms. They also increase women's understanding of the technical requirements of directorships, and provide a pool of female candidates waiting 'in reserve'.

6.3. LINKING CROWN AND CORPORATE SECTORS

While it is clear that some women who are appointed to a crown company then come to notice for a second directorship in the corporate sector, there needs to be a much greater recognition by the top 200 companies of the pool of female talent which the crown company process has uncovered. Female board directors need to be profiled and their achievements publicised as a consequence of the crown company process.

Mattis (1997) provides another compelling reason for highlighting visible success stories. She states that "corporate leaders are motivated by the success of industry peers and other highly regarded companies" (p.23). She suggests more work needs to be done to document the positive relationship between diversity results and business results in companies who pioneered recruitment of women to boards and who have more than one female director i.e. the linkage between diversity in corporate governance and revenue/profitability.

6.4. MONITORING THE MONITORS

While the Ministry of Women's Affairs and the Crown Company Monitoring Advisory Unit are clearly committed to the pipeline growth of women on boards, there is a need for reliable monitoring of data, of community initiatives, of the training processes and of follow-up as well as the issue of reappointment of women on boards once they have penetrated the boardroom. Currently this data, which allows an independent eye on the performance of the agencies as monitors, is scattered through official government reports and comments or lies with individual researchers. What is needed is a monitor of the monitors.

Activism at a number of levels, by politicians, policy agencies, women's groups and individual women, is necessary to ensure there is a new age of female representation in corporate governance. Researchers have an important role, too, in scrutinising the role of women on boards and in ensuring that their findings receive the oxygen of publicity.

References

Boston, J., Martin, J., Pallot, J. and Walsh, P   (Eds.) (1991)*Reshaping the State: New Zealand's Bureaucratic Revolution*. Oxford University Press
Bradshaw, P.(1990) Women in the boardroom: two interpretations. Unpublished manuscript, Faculty of Administrative Studies, York University, York.
Burke, R.(1994) Women on corporate boards of directors: Forces for change?, *Women in Management Review*, 9,1,27-31.
Corbett, J.(1997) A good woman is hard to find. *The Independent*, 7 February, 16-17.
"Getting on Board: Women in Decision-making"(1998), *Panui*, An occasional publication of the Ministry of Women's Affairs, February, 4-5.
Holton, V.(1995) Women on the boards of Britain's top 200 companies, *Women in Management Review*, 10,3,16-20.
Johnston, P. (1997) Women still locked out of the boardroom. *The Weekly Telegraph*, 285, 42.
Kanter, R.M. *Men and women of the corporation*. New York: Basic Books.
Leighton, D and Thain, D. (1993) Selecting new directors. *Business Quarterly*, 57, 16-25.
Marshall, J. (1995) Researching women and leadership: Some comments on challenges and opportunities, *International Review of Women and Leadership*.1.1.1-10.

Mattis, M.C. (1997) Women on corporate boards: Two decades of research, *International Review of Women and Leadership*. 13.2. 11-26.

McGregor, J. (1997) Making the good woman visible: The issue of profile in New Zealand corporate directorship, *International Review of Women and Leadership*. 3.2. 1-10.

McGregor, J., Pajo, K., Cleland, J., Burke, R. (1997) Equal opportunities and the boardroom: The challenge of corporatisation, *Equal Opportunities International*. 16,8 1-8.

Pajo, K,. McGregor, J. Cleland, J (1997) Profiling the pioneers: Women directors on New Zealand's corporate boards, *Women in Management Review* 12, 5, 174-181.

Reason, R. and Rowan, J.(Eds.) (1981) *Human inquiry*. Chichester: Wiley.

Taggart, M (1993) State-owned enterprises and social responsibility: A contradiction in terms, *New Zealand Recent Law Review III* 343-364.

TAKING A SEAT ON THE BOARD: WOMEN DIRECTORS IN BRITAIN

V.M. HOLTON
Ashridge, Berkhamsted,
Herts, U.K.
HP4 1NS

Abstract

During the eight year period between 1989 to 1997 Ashridge surveyed the situation for women directors among the UK Times Top 200 companies. The 1997 data indicates that whilst more women than ever before are taking a seat on the board, they remain a distinct minority. Trends show a growth in the number of women appointed, the number of companies with a woman director and in the small group of companies with more than one woman director. However, women's overall share of director appointments is tiny, at less than 5 per cent. Similarly, women are more likely to gain the less important, non-executive, rather than executive directors' role. The pace of change has been very slow and it cannot be said that women directors in the UK are on a par with their male colleagues.

The article discusses the survey data, together with the barriers that block women directors, and changes that might affect a faster rate of change.

1. Hitting the Headlines

Women directors in Britain are rare, so much so that a major appointment of a woman is likely to make headlines in the national business press. The announcement of Marjorie Scardino as chief executive at Pearson Group, a blue-chip FTSE 100[1] company in 1997, is one example. Being the first woman to run a FTSE company was one element of the press coverage, and in addition to her business qualities she became newsworthy for breaking new ground for women. Ashridge surveys of the UK situation indicate that whilst more women than ever before are taking a seat on the board, they remain a distinct minority. The situation has improved in recent years. Before looking at the detail of the survey findings, it may be helpful to outline the general situation for women, together with some of the major changes that have occurred in recent years.

---

[1] FTSE 100 is an index of the largest 100 companies listed on the London Stock Exchange, often called the 'Footsie'. It was introduced in January 1984 and provides a minute by minute indication of how the market is moving.

R.J. Burke and M.C. Mattis (eds.), Women on Corporate Boards of Directors, 145-155.

The most significant change is the sheer number of women who now go on to further education, and in fact take it for granted that this will happen. At Hull University for example, a university with over 8,000 students, women are 52 per cent of the population.[2] A similar proportion of women in 1998 applied for higher education places in the UK[3]. In common with the international situation, few of their mothers and even fewer of their grandmothers were likely to have had such opportunities. A ceremony earlier in 1998 celebrated the achievements of some of the first British women admitted to one of the most prestigious universities, Cambridge. Many of the group, now in their 70s and 80s, did not formally receive a degree award at the time. It was considered too avant garde by the authorities for the social conventions of the time and only now, 50 years later, have formal degrees been awarded.[4] Over the past twenty years or so, there has been a three-fold increase in the number of women graduates, illustrated in Table 1.

Amongst this present generation of students, an increasing number of women are studying business related topics. Table 2 shows the number of women students in four key areas - computer science; engineering and technology; law; and business and administrative studies. However, the number of women studying engineering and technology remains low, only some 15 per cent of full-time undergraduates are women. In contrast, the number of women studying law and accountancy has increased two and three-fold compared to the situation during the 1960s and early 1970s. The impact on the business world of these changes is striking. In one major accountancy firm in 1997 two thirds of the student intake was female.

The overall number of women managers also continues to increase, albeit from a very low base. Data in Table 3 shows that women hold just over 15 per cent of management jobs. In just over two decades the number of women managers has catapulted, moving from 1.8 per cent in 1974 up to 15.2 per cent. However, the general situation is a mirror image of most other countries and continents. Women are far more likely to be at the bottom rungs of the management ladder. Fewer operate at middle and senior management levels, and only a handful of women hold the most senior, board level, appointments.

---

[2] Statistics provided by Hull University, 26 August 1998

[3] UCAS (Universities and Colleges Admissions Service) 1998 data shows that of 332,455 applications, 178,711 (54 per cent) are from women.

[4] Cambridge's Studied Act of Contrition' reported in The Times, 4.7.98, page 19 by Valerie Grove

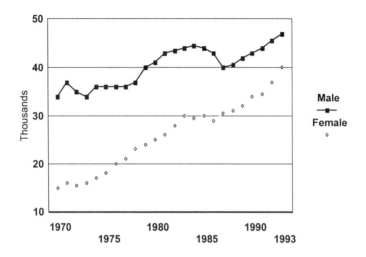

Table 1 : UK New Graduates by Gender

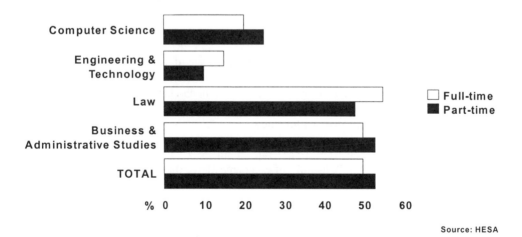

Source: HESA

Table 2: Percentage of Female Undergraduates by Subject

	1974 %	1983 %	1994 %	1995 %	1996 %	1997 %
DIRECTOR	0.6	0.3	2.8	3.0	3.3	4.5
FUNCTION	0.4	1.5	6.1	5.8	6.5	8.3
DEPARTMENT HEAD	2.1	1.9	8.7	9.7	12.2	14.0
SECTION LEADER	2.4	5.3	12.0	14.2	14.4	18.2
ALL MANAGERS	1.8	3.3	9.5	10.7	12.3	15.2

Source: National Management Salary Survey;
Institute of Management

Table 3 : Percentage of UK Managers who are Women, 1974 - 1997

2. Ashridge Survey Findings : A Slow Pace of Change

The Ashridge research[5], in 1997, is the third survey to look at the situation for women directors. The key findings reveal extremely good news in some respects. As noted earlier, the cadre of women directors, and the number of companies likely to appoint women at board level have increased during the timespan of the three surveys, from 1989 through to 1997.

There is a significant increase in the number of women directors among major UK companies. The number of appointments has, for the first time, moved into three figures; there are 97 women holding 109 board appointments. Eighty four, nearly half, of the Times Top 200 companies now have a woman director on the board. To illustrate how big this increase is, it is useful to benchmark against the 1989 data. At that time only 21 companies had a woman at board level.

However, alongside such good news, women still remain at the margins and the pace of change has been disappointingly slow. Women hold less than five per cent of the 2,000 or more director appointments in the 200 companies surveyed and are also more likely to hold the less important non-executive appointments. Most UK boards comprise a mix of executive and non-executive appointments. The former are usually the majority group, full-time staff within the company who have been appointed at director level. By contrast, the non-executive role is usually for a short period of time and held by someone outside the company.

The key question is of course just how much change has occurred over the years? Whilst the actual number of women directors is increasing, most remain the sole woman at board level within their companies. A more positive trend is the growing number of companies with more than one woman director. As noted in Table 5, this has risen from a base rate of nil, to 14 per cent in 1989, and most recently to 24 per cent. A handful of companies have more than two women. These include retailers such as the Co-operative Wholesale Society with five women

---

[5] The research was sponsored by Opportunity 2000 and member companies Unilever, BUPA Wellcome and Glaxo Wellcome. Holton, V and Rabbetts, J. 1997. Women on the Boards of Britain's Top 200 Companies, 1997. Published by Ashridge. ISBN 0903542 29 7. Whilst the authors took every possible effort to ensure survey data was accurate, they take responsibility for any omissions or inaccuracies.

directors, and Marks & Spencer with three women directors. It is an important trend as it is easier for critics to level the claim of "tokenism" at companies with a single woman director.

At the time of the first survey a quarter of appointments held by women directors were executive. The gap between executive and non-executive appointments has widened slightly and by 1997 only 17 per cent of women directors are appointed as executive directors; a much higher proportion (83 per cent) are non-executive directors. As illustrated in Table 4 the current ratio is 83 : 17, between non-executive and executive appointments.

	Non-executive Appointments n=	Executive appointments n=	Ratio of non-Executive to Executive %
1989	18	6	75 : 25
1993	46	11	81 : 19
1997	91	18	83 : 17

Table 4. Ratio of non-executive compared to executive appointments of women directors, 1989-1997

	Number of Companies	%
1989	-	0
1993	7	14
1997	20	24

Table 5 : Times Top 200 companies with more than one woman at board level, 1989 - 1997

It is possible to regard these trends as an indication that all is well for women and that soon they will be as likely as men to take any senior appointment in the business arena. This interpretation would however be incorrect. The Ashridge survey shows that beyond the Times Top 200 companies, the number of women directors drops significantly. As shown in Table 6, women's share of appointments plummets from 42 per cent (among the Top 200 companies) to only 11 per cent, amongst the Top 300-500 companies.

	Executive appointments n=	Non-executive appointments n=	Number of Companies	%
Times Top 200	18	91	84	42
Times Top 300-500	15	25	32	11

Table 6: Number of women directors - the Times Top 200 and Top 200 Companies Compared

Sector variables can also be observed. Women directors (in the Times Top 200) are more likely to be found among banks, building societies and retailing. The reverse can be observed among engineering and investment trust companies. Companies with women directors are likely to be members of the Opportunity 2000 Campaign, the national initiative in the UK to improve the situation for women. Examples include Littlewoods, Marks & Spencer and J Sainsbury.

2.1 BARRIERS THAT BLOCK WOMEN DIRECTORS

The barriers that hold women back can be divided into four key themes, as noted below in figure 1:

---

1. Unclear or closed recruitment process at board level
2. Conservative and old-fashioned attitudes about the role of women
3. Stringent criteria requiring major plc experience for candidates
4. Difficulties for companies in identifying suitable candidates

---

Figure 1. Barriers that block women directors

The first barrier concerns board level recruitment processes. Appointments, whether executive or non-executive, are rarely advertised and this means it is difficult for women to know what opportunities are available. The selection process often is made via personal contacts of the chief executive (CEO), chairman or senior managers; this generally excludes, rather than includes, women candidates. Likewise it is hard for individuals to know what qualities and experience are required whilst recruitment remains a closed process.

Old fashioned attitudes can create another barrier. Individuals may say for example that "it's OK to have women at senior level but I don't want a woman on my board"; others who have worked with women secretaries but have little or no experience of working with women as equals, sometimes have old-fashioned and conservative attitudes towards the role of women managers. In practice, this often means that they find it hard to accept women at senior or board level.

Another issue, particularly relevant to major UK companies, is the requirement for board level candidates to have experience of working at board level for a major plc (public limited company), preferably a leading blue-chip company. This creates a near impossible situation for women. Women remain far less likely to have such experience than men and this effectively blocks those with experience gained in other spheres. There are of course examples of companies successfully recruiting directors outside of this small clique of senior managers but until general opinion changes this will continue to block a significant number of women.

The fourth barrier is that companies often say it is difficult to find suitable women candidates, although a cadre of capable and able women exists in the UK. A few small scale initiatives have helped in the past, such as a database for non-executive appointments. Some exist elsewhere and more could, and should, be done to create a central/national or preferably an international database of such experience and expertise. Efforts by the Opportunity 2000 Campaign such as the 1997 conference for HR (human resource) practitioners focused on women at senior levels have undoubtedly been helpful. A future event aimed at a target audience of CEOs, chairmen and board directors would be likely to create more energy around this topic. Many of the barriers in Figure 1 are not UK specific, they are apparent in other countries.

3. International Comparisons

The situation for women directors in the UK is more positive than in many other countries with the exception of USA. In Switzerland, Spain and Italy, Israel, New Zealand and Australia, South Africa, the Netherlands, and Greece, the situation is similar to the UK with few women at director level. In Belgium women hold hardly any board level appointments. In France and Sweden there have been greater advances in public sector than in the private sector, whilst in Norway women hold less than 10 per cent of appointments.[6]

International and national data is hard to find. The Ashridge survey in 1989 for example was one of the first to review the UK situation. In other countries there exist few formal sources of information. The press and public in Germany talk about the "mythical twelve" women who supposedly are directors, but no one knows for sure who they are or how many.

4. Creating a Faster Pace of Change for Women Directors

There is a danger in making the statement that 'the number of women directors could and should be increased', as it could be assumed that this implies appointments are made in order to fulfil a gender quota. This is not what is advocated, and would in any case be illegal under UK law. Rather, there is now a significant pool of talented women with many of the necessary qualities that would enable them to contribute at board level. If more companies made more effort to seek out women candidates, or to help their own women employees, this would help increase the pace of change. This would require searching beyond the first point of call for information. For example, Gro-NED, an organisation acting as a broker service between prospective non-executive directors and companies, has only 4 per cent women candidates on its lists.

Some companies say they wish to remain "gender blind", rather than actively seek out women candidates. However, if the short-list and first or second interview process does not include any women an alternative interpretation is that it is an approach that is gender biased in excluding women.

Most commentators agree that the situation is unlikely to change substantially without effort and energy to bring about change. A survey of EWMD members during 1998 sought to understand more about what might help. Whilst one respondent noted, "I expect the level of change to be slow", a number of approaches

---

[6] Other sources include Bay, N. and Petit, C. (1988) Company Boards: Looking for Balance, *Australian CPA*, Vol 68, Issue 3, 29-32, and Bilimoria, D. and Huse, M. (1997) A Qualitative Comparison of the Boardroom Experiences of U.S. and Norwegian Women Corporate Directors, *International Review of Women and Leadership*, 3 (2), 63-76. Adler, N and Izraeli, D. 1993. Competitive Frontiers: Women Managers in a Global Economy. Blackwells.

were identified that could help improve the pace of change. Survey respondents were asked to rate a number of options. The result, in rank order, is noted below and emphasises the importance of the company role. At the top of the list is a database of candidates but the role of the company, as outlined in the previous paragraph, is seen as critical. The interest of companies to short-list women and having an interest in the topic are both key factors for change.

1st A national (or international) database of high-quality women candidates
2nd An interest by companies/senior managers to see more women appointed
3rd A campaign to identify suitable women candidates
4th A commitment by companies to short-list women
4th Support and funding for national initiatives that would
help women   - by national governments
                  - by the European Union
6th Job advertisements for all board level appointments
7th Ways to publicise the achievements of women directors already appointed (acting as role models for other younger women)

Additional suggestions highlight the need to promote women's involvement and review the work environment. Comments made include the need to "create thinking groups in companies on the advantages of diversity and ways to implement it"; "projects to show the economic benefits of increasing the number of women directors and (thus) women managers". Another topic mentioned is the need to create "a change in working conditions", such as creating a more family-friendly environment. In the UK for example few senior roles are available on a part-time or job share basis.

Creating more interest among UK companies would undoubtedly help women. A recent survey found that the current level of company interest is low. Fewer than a fifth of just over 300 companies had actively recruited women for board appointments. Companies that have taken an active interest include Unilever, BUPA and Glaxo Wellcome. In addition to sponsoring the Ashridge survey of directors, they took part in research to look at the situation for women at senior levels in each company. Looking in detail at the career experiences of a matched group of men and women revealed a number of key areas where companies can help women more. For instance whilst the majority of managers said that promotions are handled fairly, only half the group are clear about the process. Nearly two thirds of managers do not find it easy to combine work and home responsibilities, a finding that applied equally to men and women.

4.1 CHANGE AGENTS : ACTION PLANS FOR WOMEN AND FOR COMPANIES

The two main stakeholders that can help the process of change are companies (along with their respective managing directors and CEOs) and individual women. Advice to each group, drawn from the EWMD survey, is noted below in figures 3 and 4. The lists are not intended to be comprehensive and many other approaches could also help.

Figure 1. Action Plan for Women

1. Be visible, both within the company and via external initiatives such as the Veuve Clicquot Annual Award to successful businesswomen in different countries. One respondent advised "seizing the opportunity to be involved in project groups and initiatives outside the company creates a knock on effect later down the line. People remember that you were involved in various events and as a result other invitations happen".
2. Recognise and help other women as you become more successful yourself.
3. Join a women's network and don't forget the value of networking within your company.
4. Create a working group or women's network within the company.
5. Be yourself, rather than a copy of other "male-like" managers

Figure 2. Action Plan for Companies

1. More effort to find women e.g. require headhunters and HR to identify women candidates on any short-list, advertise appointments
2. The recruitment process is often referred to as something that happens "behind closed doors". More effort to create an open recruitment process would encourage more women to apply. As one respondent said "make more effort to find women, they are out there somewhere".
3. Support women's networks within the company.
4. Use a variety of processes within the company to help nurture talent and to provide the necessary exposure to board level discussions. e.g. project groups within the company to help provide the opportunity for the younger generation to contribute; one-year 'learning' appointments at subsidiary board levels; formal job shadowing and identifying women mentors to help younger women.

Other influential groups are business commentators such as the journals and press. An international web-based 'Harvard Business Review Database' of women candidates would be a useful intervention with a prestigious brand image. Alternatively, in the UK the database might be a Financial Times Register or across every continent sponsored by major newspapers such as Der Speigel, the Australian Observer, Le Figaro, the Times of India, the Malaysia Daily News, etc.

Training providers such as the major business schools, and professional institutes could also collectively or nationally consider ways to take a more pro-active role. Individual intervention will also undoubtedly continue to help change and a number of companies (and CEOs) will privately admit that action was instigated as a result of persistent questions about the issue raised at Annual General Meetings or in the press.

4.2 ADMIRED COMPANIES

It is no surprise to find from the EWMD survey that only a few companies in each country were named as companies actively trying to improve the situation for women directors. Asked to identify 'good practice' examples, the following list emerges :

ABN AMRO and ING Group Banks in the Netherlands
Douwe Egberts
Sara Lee
Avon Cosmetics
NHO (the Norwegian Employer's Confederation)
StatOil

In Norway, state owned companies are described as being the most positive, followed by banks. USA companies everywhere are seen to be more positive about the issue, in part respondents believe this is because of "pressure from home".

Multinationals may, over the next few years, set a positive example in the change process. This is already evident in such issues as the recruitment of women in traditional labour markets such as Greece, Italy and Japan[7]. It is early days yet, but if multinationals are less conservative than local companies they may be more likely to appoint women managers, and therefore more senior and board level women. As noted earlier, North American companies may be particularly aware of what is now termed 'political correctness', and that pressure from home about the topic may influence international recruitment policies and practices.

5. Does it matter?

The final question of this article is possibly the most important. Does it matter whether the number of women directors increases? Opinion in general is divided into two groups of people. Those who already see that the issue is important and that action should be taken to improve the number of women directors. These often tend to be the same group who see a rationale for equal opportunities and diversity and can appreciate the business case of recruiting women and providing them with the same equal opportunities as their male colleagues. The second group are those who are uninterested or unclear about the need for change.

It is this latter group that need to appreciate that it does matter whether more women become directors, for two important reasons.

1) Until women are equally likely as men to take any business appointment

---

[7] Reported in private company discussions.

it can not be said they have achieved parity.

2) If women remain in the management arena but operate mostly as marketing managers, company secretaries, HR professionals or in any other capacity rather than taking an equal share of key decision making roles, they have not reach the top level of business.

6. Looking forward to the Year 2010

Though women directors remain a rare group in the UK, the Ashridge survey reveals that the current situation is better than ever before. However, this should not create a sense of complacency, as the data reveals that women remain a minority and women have not made significant advances at the executive, appointment level. If companies, business observers and other interested parties considered ways each might help, this would create a faster pace of change.

Across the public and private sector in the UK exists a group of organisations with an interest in improving the situation for women. Government departments have recently announced plans to improve the number of women (and ethnic minorities) to public bodies. However, unless a wider group appreciate, and promote, the need for change, we are likely to see the same overall trends in the future. Looking forward to the Year 2010, just over a decade away, if women make significant advances in the UK and elsewhere, this will create a better work environment. This would mean that many more organisations will have created a career environment that offers advancement and rewards on pure merit alone. It is the kind of environment that the younger generation of managers, both men and women, want and expect to see from their employers.

References

Holton, V., Rabbetts, J and Stone, R. 1998 Women Managers – Reflecting on the Glass Ceiling
Radford, J and Holdstock, L. 1995. Does Psychology Need More Boy Appeal, the Psychologist, Volume 8, No. 1, January
See references and comments in Ashridge report, 'Women on the Boards of Britain's Top 200 Companies, 1997.' By Viki Holton and Jan Rabbetts. ISBN 0903542 29 7
Data gathered in part from the EWMD survey noted in footnote 6
The survey about women directors was undertaken with members of EWMD (European Women's Management Development) during Summer, 1998. Survey findings can be obtained from the author. EWMD is an international network that aims to advance women's management development. For more information contact: Angelika Poth-Mogele.
A survey undertaken by executive coaching organisation, GHN
See www.open.gov.uk/m-of-g/doors98/opa-dept.htm

COMPANY SIZE, BOARD SIZE AND NUMBERS OF WOMEN CORPORATE DIRECTORS[1]

RONALD J. BURKE
York University
Schulich School of Business
4700 Keele Street
North York, Ontario
M3J 1P3

Increasing research attention has been paid to corporate boards of directors (Demb & Neubauer, 1992). Recent writing has focussed on evaluating corporate director performance (Conger, Finegold & Lawler, 1998), corporate director influences on CEO pay (Cochran, Wood & Jones, 1985) and relationships between director characteristics and company performance (Daily, 1995, Zahra & Pearce, 1989). Relatively little consideration has been given to the makeup of coprorate boards of directors particularly the low participation of qualified women serving on them (Gillies, 1992; Lorsch & MacIver, 1989).

Increasing the number of qualified women serving on corporate boards makes sense for a number of reasons (Burke, 1994). First, there are a number of qualified women available. Second, there are not enough qualified men to fill available board seats. Third, men currently serving on boards do not have enough time to serve on all the boards they are invited to join. Finally, some men on boards do not have enough time to do justice to the boards on which they currently serve. Thus increasing the available talent pool to go beyond what some have termed the "old boy's network" seems desirable (Leighton & Thain, 1993).

The available literature which examines women corporate directors is small, scattered and piece-meal (Burke, 1994). This is typical in new areas of research. Two types of research seem to be required in this area. One type accurately documents the

---

[1]This research was supported in part by the School of Business, York University and Catalyst. Elizabeth Kurucz, Celia Moore and Rob Carson assisted with data collection and analysis.

R.J. Burke and M.C. Mattis (eds.), Women on Corporate Boards of Directors, 157-167.

numbers and location of women currently serving on corporate boards of directors (Catalyst, 1997). The second type goes beyond the numbers in comparing characteristics and experiences of women and men directors, board processes and dynamics as a function of numbers of women board members, and efforts by companies to move to a more balanced board composition.

Several researchers have come up with estimates of the percentage of board directorships held by women, but these have typically been based on incomplete information. With the exception of the work of Catalyst, a US based research and advisory group on women's career advancement issues, few researchers have invested the effort and resources to get the numbers of women directors accurate and verified. In addition researchers in the same country have often used different data bases in their analysis. It is not clear what difference this makes on their figures. Finally, more macro-level measures such as industry sector and company size are usually ignored.

This chapter reports the empirical findings from two studies which examine the links between company size, industry sector and numbers of women and men directors serving on corporate boards of directors. A consideration of these structural factors, some of which cannot be changed (e.g., industry sector) and some of which can be changed (e.g., board size), as predictors of the number of women serving on corporate boards may reveal opportunities and constraints to increasing women's board representation. These factors have been given little consideration to date in the published literature.

Two studies were undertaken using Canadian data which address the following questions.
1.   What percentage of Canadian corporate board directorships are held by women?
2.   How many company boards of directors include women?
3.   What influence does industry sector, company size and board size have on the number of women board members?
4.   What implications do these data have for the presence of women corporate directors in the future?

1. Women on Canadian Corporate Boards of Directors – Study One

Data were obtained in late 1997from the Report on Business Top 1000 Canadian companies for the 1996 calendar year. This list included 1049 companies. At least partial information was available for 946 companies. A total 8247 directors were listed by name for these Canadian companies. The gender of a particular director was not clear for 416 individuals (5%). Of the 7831 directors for whom identifying information was available, 450 were women (6%) and 7381 were men (94%).

Of the 450 women directors, 143 were internal directors (32%) and 308 were external directors (68%). Of the 7381 men directors, 2494 were internal directors (33%)

and 4887 were external directors (67%). Thus women and men corporate directors were similarly represented as internal and external directors. Of the 7831 board members, 2637 (33%) were internal and 5194 (67%) were external.

A tally was made of the absolute number of women present on the 930 companies providing useable data on their corporate boards of directors. Six hundred and forty-two boards had no women (69%), 206 boards had 1 woman (22%), 64 boards had 2 women (7%), 10 boards had 3 women (1%), 4 boards had 4 women (.4%), 2 boards had 5 women (.2%), 1 board had 6 women (.1%) and 1 board had 8 women (.1%).

The number of internal board appointments for women on these boards ranged from 0 to 4; the number of external board appointments for women ranged from 0 to 6. The number of internal board appointments for men ranged from 1 to 14; the number of external board appointments for men ranged from 1 to 24.

1.1 DESCRIPTIVE STATISTICS

Table 1 presents descriptive statistics on a number of measures developed in this study. The following comments are offered in summary. The organizations had an average size of 3245 employees. The average Board of Directors had 8.5 members (8.1 men, .4 women). There were about twice as many external than internal directors (5.7 vs 2.8). External directors typically consisted of 5.3 men and .4 women; internal directors consisted of 2.7 men and .1 women.

Table 2 presents the intercorrelations among the study measures. The majority (39 of 45, 87%) were significantly different from zero (p=.05), reflecting both the large sample sizes and the fact that some measures were combined with others to form composites. The following comments are offered in summary. Larger organizations, not surprisingly, had larger boards of directors (r=.39, p< .001). Larger boards of directors likewise had more internal and external directors, (r_s = .40 and .45, p < .001); and more internal and external women and men directors (r_s =.18, .43, .55 and .87 respectively).

2. Industry Sector Comparisons

Organizations in the study represented a variety of industries; dozens of SIC codes were present. Three SIC codes included fifty or more organizations (see Table 3). These three industries (mining/minerals, oil and gas, conglomerates) were compared on the ten measures in the study using a one-way ANOVA. Significant industry effects were

present even of the ten measures. There were no differences across the three industries on higher than the other two industry sectors on all measures. It should be noted that many of these measures were significantly intercorrelated, reflecting to a great extent the larger organizational and board sizes of the conglomerates.

There were significant relationships between industry sector and both company and board size and between company size and board size; not surprisingly larger boards contained more women directors. These larger organizations were typically found in financial services and conglomerates, sectors having significant number of women employees and clients as well.

TABLE 1. Descriptive Statistics – Study One

Measures	X	SD	N
Total directors	8.5	4.09	871
Total men	8.1	3.72	871
directors	.4	.80	871
Total women	2.8	1.57	871
Total internal	2.7	1.47	871
Internal men	.1	.38	871
Internal women	5.7	3.26	871
Total external	5.4	2.92	871
External men	.3	.70	871
External women	3245	9520.70	727
Organizational			
Size			

TABLE 2. Intercorrelations Among Measures – Study One[a]

	2	3	4	5	6
1. Total directors					
2. Total men directors	.98***	.55***	.45***	.43***	.18***
3.Total women directors	--	.39***	.43***	.44***	.07***
4. Total internal		--	.27***	.16***	.52***
5. Internal men			--	.97***	.36***
6. Internal women				--	.13
7. Total external					--
8. External men					
9. External women					
10. Organizational size					

TABLE 2 – continued

	7	8	9	10
1. Total directors				
2. Total men directors	.90***	.87***	.55***	.39***
3.Total women directors	.88***	.89***	.40***	.36***
4. Total internal	.49***	.34***	.89***	.33***
5. Internal men	.02	-.00	.12***	.08*
6. Internal women	.02	-.01	.11***	.08*
7. Total external	.02	.01	.07*	.04
8. External men	--	.98***	.56***	.40***
9. External women		--	.39***	.36***
10. Organizational size			--	.36***
				--

TABLE 3. Industry Sector Comparisons – Study One

Measures	Mining Minerals (N=90)	Oil/ Gas (N=102)	Conglo merates (N=142)	P
Total directors	7.1[a]	7.4[a]	8.6[ab]	.01
Total men directors	7.0[a]	7.2[b]	8.1[ab]	.05
Total women	.2[a]	.2[b]	.5[ab]	.001
Total internal	2.6	2.6	2.7	NS
Internal men	2.5	2.5	2.5	NS
Internal women	.1	.1	.1	NS
Total external	4.5[a]	4.8[b]	6.0[ab]	.001
External men	4.5[a]	4.6[b]	5.5[ab]	.01
External women	.1[a]	.2[b]	.4[ab]	.001
Organization size	687[a]	712[b]	5895[ab]	.0

3. Women on Canadian Corporate Boards of Directors – Study Two

The study, conducted in mid-1998 used companies included in the Canadian Financial Post 500. Each company was contacted and asked to verify the membership of their corporate board of directors and the gender of each individual member.

3.1 DESCRIPTIVE STATISTICS

Table 4 shows the descriptive statistics for all measures used in this study for the full sample of 500 companies and a sub-sample of 290 companies that were publicly held. The public companies were larger, had more directors, more men directors, more women directors, fewer internal directors, fewer internal men directors, about the same percentage of internal women directors. more external men directors, more external women directors, had greater revenues and assets and a larger profit margin.

TABLE 4. Descriptive Statistics – Study Two

Measures	All Companies (N=500)	Public Companies (N=290)
Total directors		
Total men directors		
Total women directors	8.3	10.0
Total internal	7.8	9.4
Total internal men	.5	.6
Total internal women	3.4	2.4
Total external directors	3.2	2.3
Total external men	.2	.1
Total external women	5.0	7.5
Company size	4.6	7.0
Revenue	.3	.5
Assets	4914	6506
Profit margin	146753.12	1624552.36
	1826426.26	2478344.00
	.06	.07

Table 5 shows the intercorrelations among all measures in the study for all 500 companies, the pattern of correlations in the 290 publicly held companies was generally very similar. The following general comments are offered in summary. First, the general pattern of correlations was similar to those obtained using the Report on Business Top 1000 Companies (Table 2). Second, larger companies had larger boards of directors. Third, larger companies and larger boards, had more external women and men directors, more internal men directors, but not necessarily more internal women directors.

The empirical results reported here have implications for increasing women's representation on corporate boards of director's. Specifically, larger boards had more women directors. An obvious recommendation would be to increase board size. If every corporate board added a woman director their numbers would change dramatically. Figure 1 presents a model indicating the hypothesized relationships between particular structural variables and the number of women board directors. Only one of the three antecedents is changeable – board size. One way to increase the number of women directors is to increase board size. It is unlikely for this to happen. In fact there is a belief that board sizes may in fact be decreasing and with the increase in company mergers and acquisitions, fewer boards will exist, reducing the numbers of both women and men directors. As a consequence, women will continue to face the likelihood of very limited gains in board memberships.

On the positive side, more companies are increasing their numbers of external directors while often reducing the numbers of internal directors. This may work to women's advantage since women currently represent a greater percentage of external than internal directors.

Given these observations, what might the future hold regarding the number of women directors? It appears that the best one might anticipate would be very small gains over time. There is some evidence (Catalyst, 1997) that women's board memberships, while increasing, are increasing at a slower rate. In addition, some recent Canadian data shows a decrease in women's board participation (O'Callaghan, 1998).

TABLE 5. Correlations Among Measures – Study Two[a]

Measures	Men	Women	Inside	Outside	In Men	Out Men	In Women
Directors	.98***	.41***	.18***	.79***	.19***	.76***	.63***
Men	--	.19***	.16***	.78***	.22***	.78***	-.12**
Women		--	.13**	.28***	-.00	.18***	.62***
Inside			--	-.46***	.98***	-.48***	.34***
Outside				--	-.46***	.99***	-.19***
In Men					--	-.46***	.14***
Out Men						--	-.20***
In Women							--
Out Women							
Revenue							
Assets							
Employees							
Profit							
Margin							

[a]Ns range from 319 to 500

*** p=.001
** p=.01
* p=.05

TABLE 5.-Continued

Measures	Out Women	Revenue	Assets	Employees	Profit Margin
Directors	.49***	.28***	.38***	.32***	.06
Men	.35***	.23***	.35***	.28***	.06
Women	.75***	.30***	.25***	.24***	.03
Inside	-.12**	.09*	.08	.04	-.15**
Outside	.52***	.19***	.29***	.26***	.15**
In Men	-.12**	.08	09	.04	-.14**
Out Men	.39***	.16***	.26***	.23***	.16**
In Women	-.05	.09*	-.05	-.00	-.04
Out Women	--	.30***	.32***	.30***	.05
Revenue		--	.69***	.65***	-.08
Assets			--	.52***	.03
Employees				--	-.01
Profit Margin					--

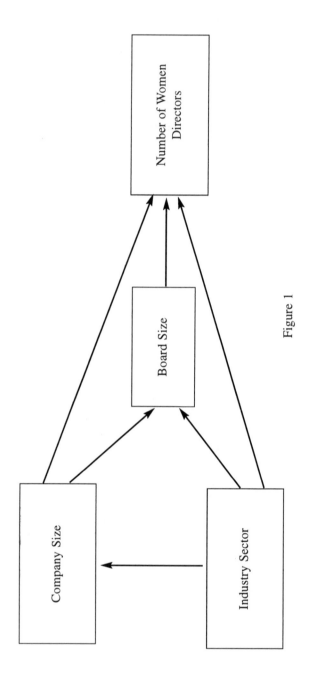

Figure 1

References

Burke, R.J. (1994) Women on corporate boards of directors. In J. deBruijn & E. Cyba (eds.) *Gender and organizations - Changing perspectives*. Amsterdam: VU University Press, pp. 191-222.

Catalyst (1997) *Women board directors of the Fortune 500* New York: Catalyst.

Cochran, P.L., Wood, R.A., & Jones, T.B., (1985) The compensation of Boards of directors and incidence of Golden Parachutes. *Academy of Management Journal*, 28, 664-671.

Conger, J.A., Finegold, D. & Lawler, E.E. (1998) Appraising boardroom performance. *Harvard Business Review*, 1998, Jan.-Feb., 136-148.

Daily, C.M. (1995) The relationship between board composition and leadership structure and bankruptcy reorganization outcomes. *Journal of Management*, 21, 1041-1656.

Demb, A. & Neubauer, F.F. (1992) *The corporate board: Confronting the paradoxes*. Oxford: Oxford University Press.

Gillies, J.M. (1992) *Boardroom renaissance*. Toronto: McGraw-Hill Ryerson.

Leighton, D. & Thain, D. (1993), Selecting new directors. *Business Quarterly*, 57, 16-25.

Lorsch, J.W. & MacIver, E. (1989) Pawns or potentates: The reality of America's corporate boards. Boston: Harvard Business School Press.

O'Callaghan, P. & Associates (1998) *Corporate board governance and director compensation in Canada*. Vancouver, B.C.: Patrick O'Callaghan & Associates.

Zahra, S.A. & Pearce, J.A., (1989) Boards of directors and corporate financial performance: A review and integrative model. *Journal of Management*, 15, 291-334.

PART THREE

Women Directors and Board Dynamics

WOMEN ON BOARDS OF DIRECTORS: GENDER BIAS OR POWER THREAT?

NANETTE FONDAS
Independent Scholar

"Choosing a Board of Directors based on race and gender is a lousy way to run a company."

- Cypress Semiconductor Corporation chief executive officer T.J. Rodgers, reacting to a letter he received from a Catholic nun, suggesting he put qualified women and minorities on the company's board of directors (Pollock, 1996: A1).

"No study has proved that diversity makes a better board."

- Nucor chief executive, Ken Iverson, reacting to TIAA-CREF's proposal that Nucor add women and minorities to its board of directors (McMenamin, 1995: 174).

1. Introduction

Companies have come under pressure within the last decade to appoint more women and minorities to their boards of directors. This pressure has come from institutional investors such as state retirement associations, individuals such as a Catholic nun, women's rights activist organizations such as Catalyst, and scholars who work in the area of women on corporate boards.

This pressure, however, has not produced the kind of change for which most advocates have lobbied: an increase in the number of women on boards so that their representation more closely resembles their proportion in the population, labor force, and management. According to Bilimoria and Wheeler (1995), women's representation on boards has remained largely unchanged over time. There has been some improvement in the last decade, but women's boardroom participation rate hovers around six percent in the large industrial and service companies in the United States.

Why has progress stalled? This chapter provides an answer to that question. At first glance, it appears that a backlash is occurring in the attitudes of chief executives, such as those quoted at the start of this chapter, who are so instrumental in facilitating the

171

R.J. Burke and M.C. Mattis (eds.), Women on Corporate Boards of Directors, 171-177.

nomination of women to boards. A closer look, however, reveals that CEO power and organizational legitimacy are not served by further increasing the number of women on corporate boards. This chapter will explore that thesis by examining women's role in the board's governance, institutional, and strategic functions. In doing so, it will also suggest a framework--or way of thinking about--the contribution of women directors to board functioning.

2. Governance Function

The first function of the board--governance--is to represent and safeguard the interests of stakeholders and to ensure that organizational actions align with their interests. In this capacity, boards must check managerial opportunism by exerting control over important decisions, some of which may be at odds with management's self-interest (Goodstein and Boeker, 1991). For example, boards are expected to curb managerial opportunism when management increases the company's size beyond that which maximizes profit in order to increase managers' compensation (e.g., undertaking unrelated diversification); when management makes compensation less contingent upon performance or sets up shark repellents, golden parachutes, or other anti-takeover devices; or when management fails to divest an unprofitable business.

Much of the literature on the board's governance function contains the strong theme that boards do not work. As Burke (1994:3) noted: "Historically, many board appointments, as well as boards themselves, seemed to have only symbolic value. Individuals were appointed to boards, but the CEO managed the organization in whatever fashion he/she chose.... Boards were often irrelevant because board members refused 'to rock the boat'." Board members frequently seem uncomfortable with their role as monitors of managerial decisions, preferring to exercise more of an advisory role. There are many examples of boards giving the CEO *carte blanche*, few of boards holding the CEO accountable for missteps. One reason is that directors may feel obligated to the chief executive for their positions on the board, since the CEO and/or management often nominates candidates for open director seats. Directors do not feel free in their evaluations of the people who appointed them, particularly when management performance is substandard (Johnson, Daily, Ellstrand, 1996).

So within this historical context of boards performing their governance function less than ideally comes the infiltration of women into board seats. A question then is whether women will succumb to the same temptation as some of their male counterparts to compromise the interests of shareholders and employees, or whether they will have a beneficial effect on the board's mandate to monitor and control management.

The research evidence suggests that women may enhance the board's performance of its governance role. Burke (1993) reports that a study by Bradshaw, Murray and Wolpin (1992) found that boards with larger proportions of women on them were less inclined to let CEOs dominate proceedings and more likely engage in "power sharing." Fondas and Sassalos (1999) found that boards with one or more female directors had significantly more influence over management decisions than boards without female directors. They suggested that the increased influence was due to a number of factors. First, the women selected had crossed such a high hurdle to appointment (in terms of their accomplishments and career history), and they were so highly motivated and prepared, that they brought a higher expectation of a board member's responsibility. This, combined with their more varied personal and professional backgrounds, gave them a different "voice" or perspective from the typical male board member. But in order for this perspective to have impact on the board's decisions, it had to be voiced in a setting where norms of collegiality, equality, consensus, and private decision-making prevailed. These norms characterized boards' proceedings; thus, even small numbers of women directors could affect a board's influence over management, that is, its execution of the governance function.

In addition to the explanations proposed by Fondas and Sassalos, women directors are usually outsiders and, therefore, more likely to be objective and independent. Outside board members are more capable of resisting self-interested efforts by inside managers to influence board decisions (Kosnik, 1987; Singh and Harianto, 1989). For example, Kosnik (1987) found that boards with more outsiders resisted greenmail payments more often. Agency theorists argue that the board can only act as an effective governing and monitoring mechanism if it is independent (Fama, 1980).

This independence may explain partially why the presence of women enhances board influence over management. It also suggests one reason women still hold so few director seats. Since top managers, particularly the chief executive, usually nominate candidates for open director seats, women can be at a disadvantage if they are not known by the nominators, in terms if being in the same social circle, executive circle, and/or members of other corporate boards. In addition, if a woman's politics are unknown, in terms of whether she carries a feminist agenda (Catalyst, 1995), she is at a further disadvantage. All of these unknowns may make her too independent in the eyes of the chief executive. He may not have a gut feel that she will rubber-stamp his decisions. Therefore, it is not her femaleness *per se* that places her at a disadvantage but the fact that she is an outsider, unknown, and potentially highly independent.

3. Institutional function

The second board function is an institutional function. It refers to board activities that link the organization to its environment, reduce uncertainty, and secure from external constituencies resources critical to the organization's success. These resources include access to capital but also prestige and legitimacy. Directors who are representatives of specific institutions (banks, for example) are often fulfilling this function (Pfeffer, 1972, 1973; Pfeffer & Salancik, 1978), as are directors from other companies, community groups, or particular constituencies. Indeed, firms will create larger, more diverse boards in order to establish and maintain linkages to other business, government, and social organizations (Pfeffer, 1972, 1973).

Evaluating the contribution of women directors to the board's institutional function is complex. On the one hand, women often provide needed links. For example, Burke (1993) reported that the women in Mitchell's (1984) study of Canadian women directors named "having a community profile" as the top reason why they believed they were selected as directors. On the other hand, the presence of women directors may provide the appearance of legitimacy without further purpose. This is because to acquire legitimacy, organizations often imitate the forms or practices of other organizations. For example, a firm might mimic a particular organization structure (division, matrix) for legitimacy purposes, even if it is not ideal for efficiency or strategic purposes. This means that as long as most companies have only token numbers of women on their boards, there is no increase in legitimacy by appointing more. There is no opportunity for the number of women on boards to increase further via mimetic isomorphism.

Furthermore, organizations build buffers so external actors will not see what they are doing; i.e., they create the appearance of compliance. Appointing token numbers of women and minorities can accomplish this creation of the appearance of compliance with societal norms of diversity. Institutional investors (such as TIAA/CREFF) and others who have called for boards to increase their diversity may not be recognizing this subtle organizational tactic deployed by business firms. The executives quoted at the beginning of this chapter are notable in that they crossed the buffer. They did not care to alter their boards' composition only to create an appearance of compliance. They preferred to remind people of their fiduciary, profit maximization responsibility and hope that would be persuasive.

This perspective on the board's institutional function and its relationship to the role of women directors is supported by a recent study by Catalyst (1995). The top two motives given by chief executives for appointing women directors were (1) image in the community and/or with a constituency, and (2) image with shareholders of the company's commitment to diversity. The first motive supports the linking aspect of an organization's institutional function (e.g., Pampers-buyers, who are predominantly women, are more likely to feel women directors are representative of their viewpoints). The second motive underscores the goal of enhancing legitimacy—creating the appearance of compliance with society's desire to have diversity in organizations.

4. Strategic Function

The third function of the board is its strategic function. It involves making critical strategic decisions, particularly strategic change, so the organization can adapt to environmental changes. Examples of strategic decisions include mergers and acquisitions, divestitures, altering the product or service mix, entrance into or exit from markets and lines of business, and major capital expenditures. Little empirical or theoretical research has been conducted on the board's role in strategic decisions and strategic outcomes (Johnson, Daily and Ellstrand, 1996), but there is consensus that the board's strategic function is relatively more important when the organization is experiencing either poor performance or environmental turbulence or both (Boulton, 1978; Goodstein, Gautman and Boeker, 1994; Mintzberg, 1983; Zald, 1969). This is when the board has the potential to exercise its power. Even the most activist boards rarely get involved in a firm's daily decision-making (Mace, 1971; Johnson, Daily and Ellstrand, 1996).

Existing research gives some indication of the importance of women's presence on boards to the execution of the strategic function. A Korn/Ferry (1995) survey reports that women outside directors rated themselves equal to men directors in terms of their impact on company policies such as financial results, strategic planning, management succession, and executive compensation. Women gave themselves a slight edge in strategic planning (21%) and gave male directors a small advantage in having an impact on executive compensation (22%). Mattis (1993) and Burke (1995) observed that women directors today are more likely to have corporate, business careers than previous women did (they usually had not-for-profit experience). This suggests that women may exert a larger strategic role than they did previously, because their career experience is more aligned with the company's needs. Burke (1993) reported that Bradshaw, Murray and Wolpin (1992) found the more women serving on the board, the more likely the board was to share a common vision and undertake strategic planning. However, Burke (1993) also reported that women directors in Mitchell's (1984) study reported sources of dissatisfaction with board experiences as including the board's lack of impact on corporate policy. It is possible that women directors, with their higher expectations of board service (as noted above), experience frustration with their lack of influence over what they perceive as strategic issues. One reason for this frustration may be that board influence over strategy is done by way of committee (Henke, 1986; Harrison, 1987), not by direct engagement in strategy formulation. According to a study by Bilimoria and Piderit (1994), women serve predominantly on less important and less strategic board committees (e.g., public affairs), while men tend to serve on committees with a larger strategic role (e.g., executive, compensation, finance).

As noted earlier, when analyzing women's appointments to boards of directors, it is important to remember that the women serving on boards tend to be outsiders, since women often have not reached the top management levels necessary to get appointed as inside directors. Usually when boards are dominated by outsiders, particularly strong outsiders, strategic change is more likely (Goodstein and Boeker, 1991; Mizruchi, 1983). This encouragement or imposition of change by the board is, in effect, a reduction of CEO power. Thus, a latent reason CEOs may resist appointing more women is that doing so increases the number of outsiders on the board, thereby potentially diminishing the CEOs' power.

5. Conclusion

This chapter has provided a framework for thinking about women's impact on boards of directors by examining their role in the board's performance of its governance, institutional, and strategic functions. After reviewing the extant literature on women corporate directors, Bilimoria and Wheeler (1999) concluded that the production of such frameworks is critically needed for research in the field to move forward. Research reviewed in this chapter, using this framework, suggests that the presence of women enhances the execution of the board's governance function and possibly its strategic function. Women's presence also serves the organization's interest to build links to its environment and create the appearance of compliance with diversity norms.

This chapter has also explicated how the issue of women's representation on corporate boards is inextricably linked to the issue of chief executive power. The examination of the board's governance, institutional, and strategic functions revealed that the number and percentage of women on boards may be remaining small because chief executive power is diluted when independent and/or outside directors are appointed. Their appointment augurs more strategic change, more power-sharing, more monitoring, less rubber-stamping, and less CEO domination of proceedings. Thus, this likely diminution of power explains chief executives' reticence to appoint large numbers of women--who are usually highly qualified, well-prepared, objective, independent outsiders--to their boards. It is not discrimination against women *per se*; it is a bias against independents and outsiders.

This conclusion may not be welcome news to those of us who would like to see more women serving on corporate boards for equity, economic, and social justice reasons. But in order for progress to continue, it is important to go beyond the conventional thinking about why women are represented on boards in small numbers and begin to acknowledge the importance of power dynamics. One solution is to appoint more women directors who are insiders, that is, managers of the firm; but that raises other power issues, because inside directors are subordinates of the chief executive in the firm's management hierarchy. Whether the women are inside or outside directors, we must no longer talk solely about the number and percentage of them we would like to see serving on boards. We must begin to talk explicitly about how the appointment of women directors affects chief executives' power and their motivation, therefore, to include or exclude additional women.

References

Bilimoria, D. and Piderit, S.K. (1994) Board committee membership: Effects of sex-based bias, *Academy of Management Journal* 37 (6), 1453-1477.
Bilimoria, D. and Wheeler, J.V. (1999) Women corporate directors: Current research issues and future directions, *Women in Management: Current Research Issues*, Volume 2, M. Davidson and R.J. Burke (Eds.), London, Paul Chapman Publishers, in press.
Boulton, W.R. (1978) The evolving board: A look at the board's changing roles and information needs, *Academy of Management Review* 4, 827-836.
Bradshaw, P., Murray, V.V. and Wolpin, J. (1992) Women on boards of nonprofit organizations: What difference do they make? Paper presented at ARNOVA Conference, October.
Burke, R. J. (1993) Women on corporate boards of directors, *Equal Opportunities International* 12 (6), 5-13.

Burke, R. J. (1994) Women on corporate boards of directors. Views of Canadian chief executive officers, *Women in Management Review* 9 (5), 3-10.

Burke, R. J. (1995) Personal, educational and career characteristics of Canadian women directors, *Equal Opportunities International* 14 (8), 1-10.

Catalyst (1995) *The CEO View: Women on Corporate Boards,* Catalyst, New York.

Fama, E. (1980) Agency problems and the theory of the firm, *Journal of Political Economy*, 88: 288-307.

Fondas, N. and Sassalos, S. (1999) A different voice in the boardroom: How the presence of women directors affects board influence over management, *Business and the Contemporary World*, in press.

Goodstein, J. and Boeker, W. (1991) Turbulence at the top: A new perspective on governance structure changes and strategic change, *Academy of Management Journal 34*, 306-330.

Goodstein, J., Gautam, K. and Boeker, W. (1994) The effects of board size and diversity on strategic change, *Strategic Management Journal* 15, 241-50.

Harrison, J.R. (1987) The strategic use of corporate board committees, *California Management Review* 30, 109-125.

Henke, J.W. (1986) Involving the directors in strategic planning, *Journal of Business Strategy* 7 (2), 87-95.

Johnson, J.L., Daily C.M., and Ellstrand, A.E. (1996) Boards of directors: A review and research agenda, *Journal of Management* 22 (3), 409-438.

Korn/Ferry International (1995) *22nd Annual Board of Directors Study,* Korn/Ferry International, New York.

Kosnik, R.D. (1987) Greenmail: A study of board performance and corporate governance. *Administrative Science Quarterly* 32, 163-185.

Mace, M.L. (1971) *Directors: Myth and Reality*, Harvard Business School Press, Boston, MA.

Mattis, M.C. (1993) Women directors: Progress and opportunities for the future, *Business and the Contemporary World* 5 (Summer), 140-156.

McMenamin, B. (1995) Diversity hucksters, *Forbes*, May 22, 174-176.

Mintzberg, H. (1983) *Power in and Around Organizations*, Prentice-Hall, Englewood Cliffs, NJ.

Mitchell, M. (1984) A profile of the Canadian woman director, *Business Quarterly* 51, 121-127.

Mizruchi, M.S. (1983) Who controls whom? An examination of the relation between management and boards of directors in large American corporations, *Academy of Management Review* 8, 426-435.

Pfeffer, J. (1972) Size and composition of corporate boards of directors: The organization and its environment, *Administrative Science Quarterly* 17, 218-228.

Pfeffer J. (1973) Size, composition and function of hospital boards of directors: A study of organization-environment linkage, *Administrative Science Quarterly* 18, 349-364.

Pfeffer, J and Salancik, G.R. (1978) *The External Control of Organizations: A Resource Dependence Perspective.* Harper & Row, New York.

Pollock, E.J. (1996) CEO takes on a nun in a crusade against 'political correctness,' *Wall Street Journal*, July 15, A1, A7.

Singh, H. and Harianto, F. (1989) Management-board relationships, takeover risk, and the adoption of golden parachutes, *Academy of Management Journal* 32, 7-24.

Zald, M.N. (1969) The power and function of boards of directors: A theoretical synthesis, *American Journal of Sociology* 75, 97-111.

WOMEN ON CORPORATE BOARDS OF DIRECTORS: UNDERSTANDING THE CONTEXT[1]

RONALD J. BURKE
York University
School of Business
4700 Keele Street
North York, Ontario CANADA
M3J 1P3

This chapter outlines the evolution of my thinking and research journey regarding women serving on corporate boards of directors. It addresses the following topics:

- Board composition
- Board responsibilities
- Board and board member effectiveness
- Evaluating boards and board members
- Women on corporate boards research
- Board composition and board effectiveness
- The broader board context
- Future research needs

1. Board Composition

Through the 1970s, boards of directors were almost exclusively composed of white males. Although a few token women were appointed, boards were singularly homogenous consisting of white male CEOs over 55 years of age (see Lorsch & MacIver, 1989). Most US Fortune 500 companies now have female directors but it is rare to have more than one. Thus, despite the fact that women have been moving into management over the past few years, their representation on corporate boards of directors still remains low. In Fortune 500 companies, women hold about ten percent of seats (Catalyst 1995, 1997).

---

[1] Preparation of this manuscript was supported in part by the School of Business, York University. Shelley Peterson assisted in tracking down relevant literature; Louise Coutu prepared the manuscript.

R.J. Burke and M.C. Mattis (eds.), Women on Corporate Boards of Directors, 179-196.

Several factors have highlighted concerns about board composition. First, there is increased belief that diverse groups are likely to be more effective since varied perspectives will improve discussion, creativity and decision-making (Forbes & Milliken, 1998). Second, there is increased concern that boards of directors have not had enough influence on management decisions (Mace, 1986). As a result too many problematic management decisions have occurred (Byrne, 1996, 1997). This has led to calls for boards to change their composition to include fewer inside directors, more outside independent directors, more women and minority members, and more representatives from important stakeholder groups (e.g., institutional investors, unions). Boards with a more diverse composition will be less of an "old boy's club", engage in less rubber-stamping of management decisions and be more active in influencing management decisions.

Boards of directors serve as a link between the shareholders of a firm and the managers responsible for the day-to-day functioning of the firm (Monks & Minow, 1995). Boards are responsible for monitoring and influencing strategic decisions; they are not responsible for the implementation of these strategic decisions nor for the day-to-day administration of the firm. Boards also have the legal responsibility to monitor management as representatives of shareholders and to provide advice and guidance to the CEO (Leighton & Thain, 1997).

Board members must work cooperatively if the board is to perform effectively (Charan, 1998). Boards are created on the belief that collective knowledge, experience and dialogue exceeds that of any single member. Boards include outsiders, who, working in a part-time capacity have limited direct contact with the firm's operations. Boards also meet only a few times per year. In addition, the size of corporate boards, typically about eleven individuals, also is a factor in the success of board deliberations.

The nature of corporate boards (large, meet infrequently, cooperative) makes them particularly vulnerable to interaction or group process difficulties that interfere with them reaching their full potential (Forbes & Milliken, 1998). Groups process variables such as participation and interaction, the exchange of information and perspectives, and critical inquiry and debate seem central to board effectiveness (Charan, 1998).

Forbes and Milliken (1998) include two criteria of board effectiveness: the ability to perform its control and service functions (task) and the ability to continue to work together (maintenance) Both criteria contribute to firm performance but in different ways. Task performance is hypothesized to have a direct influence, while board cohesiveness has an indirect effect by influencing present and future levels of task performance.

2. Board Responsibilities

What do boards do? Conger, Finegold and Lawler (1998b) identify the most important activities and responsibilities of corporate boards as follows.

1. Boards are responsible for business strategy development - ensuring that a strategic planning process is in place, is used, and produces sound choices. The board must also monitor the current strategic initiatives to ensure they are on schedule, on budget and producing results.

2. Boards are responsible for seeing that the company has the highest caliber CEO and executive team and that senior managers are being developed to become the next CEO.

3. Boards ensure that adequate information, control and audit systems are in place to inform the board and senior management whether the company is meeting business goals. The company must also conform with external legal and ethical standards and its own values.

4. Boards are engaged in preventing and managing crises.

3. Determinants of Board Effectiveness

What does a corporate board need to be effective? Conger, Finegold and Lawler (1998a) suggest that an effective board needs to have five attributes to be effective. These are:

3.1 KNOWLEDGE

The combined knowledge and experience of the board members must match the strategic demands facing the corporation. This suggests the importance of constructing a board around complimentary skills and backgrounds. The right mix of skills is critical. They suggest that boards create a matrix of director capabilities and strategic tasks to assess the composition of both the board and individual committees. These capabilities might

include: the understanding of company customers, government relations, international markets, and means ofcreating shareholder value.

3.2 INFORMATION

The quality, quantity and timeliness of data that a board receives on its business issues. Boards need information from multiple sources: CEO, outside stakeholders, directors themselves (customers, employees).

3.3 POWER

An effective board needs the power to make important decisions and to hold the CEO accountable for his/her performance. Board power is influenced by the number of independent directors, (no business or family ties to the CEO, no long-term friends, not sit on one another's boards). Directors who are independent of the CEO should be in charge of determining CEO pay and selection of board members, including the next CEO. Board power is also likely to be greater when the chair is not the CEO.

3.4 MOTIVATION

This includes director compensation. It is also sensible to require directors to have an ownership stake (e.g., stocks) in the company, preferably with a long-term orientation.

3.5 TIME

It takes time for directors, as a group, to become well informed, to make effective decisions, and to contribute at a high level.

4. Evaluating Corporate Boards and Directors

Conger, Finegold and Lawler (1998) focus on CEO evaluation. They identify three forces leading to interest in CEO appraisals. First, there is increasing recognition of the key roles CEOs play in corporations reflected in part in their high compensation levels. Second, increased interest by the investment community in corporate performance. Third, increasing use of performance management and evaluation systems in management generally are making it more difficult to not include the CEO.

Conger, Lawler and Finegold (1998), while noting difficulties, advocate individual director appraisal as part of the overall board evaluation process. Appraisals of board performance are becoming more common. Korn/Ferry reports that seventy percent of the largest American companies evaluate the CEO and about twenty-five percent undertake a general board appraisal. About fifteen percent of large corporations evaluated individual directors performance. Individual and institutional investors are supportive of evaluating individual directors and replacing underperforming directors; most individual directors are not in favor of this practice.

Some common concerns are raised about individual board member evaluations. These include: negative effect on collegiality among directors, reducing board consensus and team work, alienating board members who had a demonstrated track record, making board membership less attractive, who should do the evaluations, use of common criteria for all directors may miss unique contributions and competencies, and board performance rather than individual director performance is more consequential.

There are some advantages to some form of individual director appraisal as an element in overall board evaluation. Board members are currently replaced only in extreme cases. Instead, the most common response to poor performance is to not renominate the person when their term expires. It should be noted that underperforming directors are probably few. With the demands and rewards for board membership increasing, organizations can legitimately demand more from their directors. Evaluating individual directors is a good way to clarify performance expectations and help directors sharpen their skills and improve their contributions.

Conger, et.al. (1998a) cite the results of a Korn/Ferry survey of over 1000 directors of the US's largest companies which showed that in companies where individual directors were evaluated, directors rated the boards overall effectiveness more favorably than in boards that do not conduct individual director appraisals. Interestingly, both CEO and whole board evaluations had greater effects on ratings of overall board effectiveness.

Conger, et. al. (1998a) advocate that the board first meet (subcommittee such as the governance or nominating committee) to create a first draft of areas to assess. This list is then circulated to board members before having a total board meeting to finalize the evaluation criteria. They recommend the board's initial effort involve self-assessments, not shared with anyone. Then board leadership (Chairman, CEO, Human Resources committee chair) should use these criteria to evaluate each board member with one of these individuals meeting with individual directors to share the evaluations. A further step, if acceptable to the organization, would involve peer evaluations. Combining these three assessments provides the most balanced perspective.

Conger, et al (1998, p. 53) suggest the following factors be used in board member evaluations: knowledge of the business; knowledge of senior management; initiative; preparation; time; judgement and candor; integrity; motivation, represented by ownership stake; and good ambassadorship for the company.

Conducting effective CEO evaluations requires a solid commitment from the CEO and board members. Evaluating CEO performance was found to have positive effects on strengthening performance accountability and the link between performance and reward, clarifying strategic direction, promoting more effective CEO-board relations and aiding the development of the CEO.

5. My research journey

I first became interested in the subject of women serving on corporate boards of directors about ten years ago. Prior to that time I was actively involved in conducting research in the broader topic of women in management (Burke & McKeen, 1992). A visit to Catalyst peaked my curiosity on the subject of women on corporate boards; Catalyst had both conducted research in this area and had been helping corporations identify qualified women for board membership. I then conducted a few pieces of research using Catalyst – created survey instruments as well as attempted to determine the percentages of board memberships held by women on Canadian boards of directors (Burke, 1997, 1995, 1994a, 1994b, 1994c).

Exhibit 1
Dear Professor Burke,

In response to your letter and your questionnaire regarding women directors I would like to record that the questionnaire reflects an attitude which I regard as unhealthy and unhelpful in the business world.

In well run corporations today women have been directors for many years. Women are selected based on the same criteria as men and are expected to perform the same functions as men - that is - they are supposed to protect the interests of the stakeholders.

A well managed nominating committee pays no attention to personal friendships but examines the idea Board configuration by training, by experience, by age, by personal characteristics and many other criteria, and uses a combination of sourcing techniques to develop short lists of candidates for consideration by the Board.

Each director should bring individual skills to bear on the challenges faced by management as well as have a collective impact on the management of the company. It is rather obvious therefore that women should play an important role on Boards, but not as "women directors" simply as "DIRECTORS".

Good nominating committees have not had a great deal of difficulty in identifying qualified women candidates.

Your questionnaire presupposes there are differences in directors and directors duties. I do not share this view.

Sincerely,

Chairman - Executive Committee

My implicit mission was to raise these percentages. A letter that I received from the CEO of a major financial institution in response to study of CEO's views on women on corporate boards (see Exhibit 1) was initially perceived by me as part of the problem. Why don't the men leading Canada's major corporations see the situation the same way as I do? Corporate governance was becoming a hot topic in business writing, yet most books on this subject did not even mention gender at all (e.g., Fleischer, Hazzard & Klipper, 1998; Gillies, 1992; Leighton & Thain, 1997; Lorsch & MacIver, 1989).

Interestingly, some women directors saw the situation in ways similar to this male CEO. That is, they saw themselves as directors first and women second (Burke, 1994a). They saw their jobs as doing what was best for the shareholders and the company. Championing women's interest was, for many women directors, a lower priority – if a priority at all. This got me thinking over the past year about why should we be interested in increasing women's membership on corporate boards of directors.

It should be stated at the outset that the intention should be the appointment of qualified women and men to corporate boards. With this caveat, I identified several potential reasons for increasing women's numbers on corporate boards of directors. These included the following. There are now a number of qualified women available to serve on corporate boards. There may not be enough qualified men available to serve on corporate boards given their increasing time demands. Women board members may bring a different and valuable perspective to board deliberations.

Initial research was primarily descriptive emphasizing the number and type of directorships held by women and their membership on various board committees (Bilimoria, 1995; 1994; Harrigan, 1981). Early research also detailed demographic characteristics readily available from public records including such things as age, education, occupation, career-history, length of board service and number of boards (business, non-profit) on which they serve (Mitchell, 1984; Mattis, 1993; Kesner, 1988). While a few studies have considered ways women have influenced board deliberations, almost no work on how women might influence (or improve) board functions of monitoring senior management activities and advising management on important decisions has been undertaken.

Most of the early research efforts had focussed on the numbers and percentages of board seats held by women (Mattis, 1997). This research was undertaken in several different countries (Canada, Catalyst, 1998;US, Catalyst, 1997; UK, Holton, 1995a, 1996b; Israel, Izraeli & Talmud, 1997; Australia, Burgess & Tharenou, 1997; New Zealand, McGregor, 1997; Shilton, McGregor & Tremaine, 1996; Pajo, McGregor & Cleland, 1997) with fairly similar results (see Burke & Mattis, 1997). That is, women held about five percent of the board seats in most of these countries; recent figures in the US seemed to be higher than the other countries at almost eleven percent (Catalyst, 1997).

Why are so few corporate directors women? Elgart (1983) reported results from 126 companies to the question "In your opinion, what are the reasons that there are not any (more) female board members". The survey allowed nine choices, plus an open ("other") category. Of the 126 companies responding to this question, 76 offered a single answer, 32 offered two and 17 offered three or more. Forty-three percent of the companies endorsed "already filled with qualified candidates". This seemed to be at odds with resignations, expired terms and board turnover. The second most common reason, cited by 35 percent of the companies was "difficulty in finding qualified candidates with the right experience". It was hard to specify what the right experience was however. The third most common reason was "company opposition to constituency representation on boards" (25%).

In a similar vein, Leighton and Thain (1993) describe corporate boards of directors as "old boys clubs". Board members were appointed exclusively at the request of the CEO.

6. Increasing Numbers of Women Directors?

Lear (1994) believes that women are now accepted as outside directors in most American board rooms though he acknowledge their numbers are small. He cites a Catalyst study of women serving on Fortune 500/Service 500 boards which showed that women had 6.2 percent of these seats (721 out of 11,715). He suggests that the numbers will double or triple in the next four years (the data have proven him wrong!).

Lear raises two important questions: Why has it taken so long? What is causing the current breakthrough? Several answers address the first question. Not enough women have adequate business and executive experience (Burke, 1994c). Women have chosen career paths not conducive to board selection. Too many women have chosen staff jobs instead of line management (Mattis, 1993). Male CEOs feared women board members would be feminists first and directors second. Some older CEOs and directors simply resisted change.

Why the current breakthrough? The "token" board members have performed well. More women have line experience or have become CEOs of small and medium sized companies (Catalyst, 1997, 1998). Older CEOs and directors are retiring and being replaced by younger directors more in tune with women executives and, in turn, women directors.

In struggling with the issue of why one would be interested in increasing women's representation on corporate boards it seemed important to place this issue in a larger context. That is, issues of women serving on corporate boards are embedded in the broader context of industry sector, firm size, board composition, board member roles, and board functioning and effectiveness. Fortunately, each of these areas has received some attention over the past year.

7. Board Composition

Pettigrew (1992), noting that much board research has considered board composition, suggests that a great leap must be made between board composition and board performance, since almost no attention has been paid to the processes and mechanisms that link the two. Such research would include recent studies by Kesner and Johnson (1990), Daily (1995), Daily and Schwenk (1996), Daily and Dalton (1997), Goodstein, Gautam and Boeher (1994), Pearce and Zahra (1992), Stearns and Mizruchi (1993), Kesner (1987), Mallette and Fowler (1992), Westphal and Zajac (1995), Zahra and Pearce (1989), Ibrahim and Angelides (1994), Siciliano (1996) and Zahra and Stanton (1988). He advocates research on the actual <u>behavior</u> of boards, what boards do. Today, many boards are considering their effectiveness as they assume a more important role in corporate governance (Conger, Finegold & Lawler, 1998a; Leighton & Thain, 1997).

Top management team demography offers a theoretical underpinning for this line of research. This framework suggests that increasing demographic diversity in a top management team offers additional viewpoints, perspectives and alternatives for decision making. Such groups are likely to be more creative and less likely to maintain the status quo. Boards with greater diversity should have more influence over management decisions. One could also make the case that greater diversity interferes with communication and group interaction raising levels of conflict. Thus the presence of women directors will decrease board influence over management decisions under these circumstances. A third possibility is that the presence of women directors would have no effect on board influence over management since there are so few women on corporate boards and these women who do serve are less likely to serve on central board committees.

Few studies have examined the relationship of board composition and board influence over management.   Johnson, Hoskisson and Hitt (1993) and Judge and Zeithaml (1992) reported that outside director representation increased board influence over some strategic outcomes.

Fondas and Sassalos (1999) undertook a study of 115 corporate boards of large US firms to examine effects, if any, of the presence of women directors on board influence over management decisions. In addition, they offer a process model to explain why the presence of women directors would be related to board influence of management. The average board for firms in their sample was eleven; forty-two percent of the firms had at least one woman sitting on their boards. Board influence over managerial decisions was derived from director responses (preferably the chair) to nine important management decisions (e.g., capital expenditures, long range planning, management succession). The board could have no, some or a strong influence on any one management decision.   The average firm reported some influence over the management decisions. The results showed that boards having one or more female directors had significantly more influence over management decisions than did boards without female directors. It may also be that influential boards seek out women directors.

Fondas and Sassalos (1999) offer a process model to explain their findings (Figure 1). Women directors have both more varied personal and professional experience and backgrounds and have higher expectations of board members responsibility resulting in there bringing different perspectives and ideas to board deliberations, the board having more influence on management as a result.

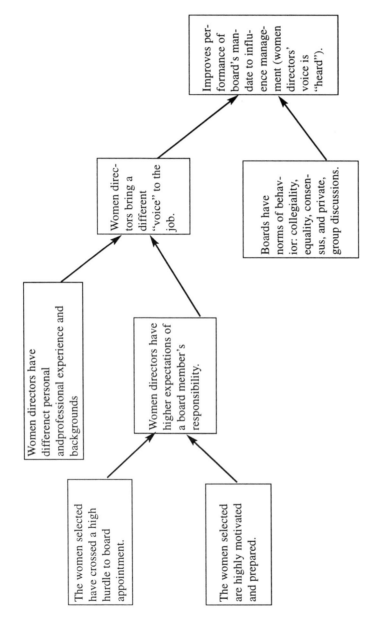

Figure 1: A Process Model of How Women Directors' Different Voice
Affects Board Influence Over Management (Fondas & Sassalos, 1999)

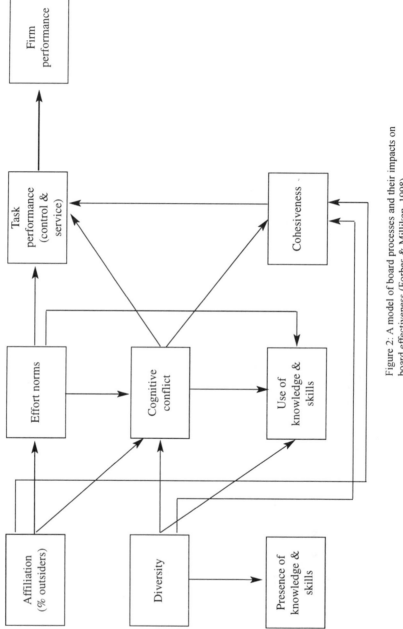

Figure 2: A model of board processes and their impacts on board effectiveness (Forbes & Milliken, 1998)

Forbes and Milliken (1998) integrate the literature on group dynamics and work group effectiveness with the literature on boards of directors to develop a model of board processes with the ultimate goal of understanding what makes boards effective (see Figure 2). Forbes and Milliken identify three board processes (effort norms, cognitive conflict, use of knowledge and skills) that mediate the relationship between three aspects of board demography (% outsiders, diversity, presence of knowledge and skills) and two board-level outcomes (task performance - control and service; cohesiveness). Diversity, which includes gender, is hypothesized to have a positive relationship with both cognitive conflict and presence of knowledge and skills and a negative relationship with use of knowledge and skill; cognitive conflict and use of knowledge and skill enhance task performance while cognitive conflict is hypothesized to have a negative relationship with cohesiveness.

Forbes and Milliken (1998), and others (Pettigrew, 1992), highlight the importance of board processes that intervene between board demographic characteristics and board and firm effectiveness. The incorporation of board process variables into research on board demographics more clearly reflects the complexity of board dynamics.

Baack and Rajagopalan (1998) provide a comprehensive theoretical framework to facilitate research understanding of boards of directors (see Figure 3). Six panels of variables were identified. These included: Environmental factors (e.g., industry type, legal requirements, dynamism), Organizational factors (e.g., size, ownership, structure, prior performance), Board attributes (Composition/Structure; e.g., size, demographics) and Network/linkages (e.g., interlocks, other memberships); Board roles and Processes (e.g., Control/Monitoring, Strategic Decision support, Resource Acquisition, Symbolic), Board Outcomes (Monitoring - CEO selection, compensation; Strategy-change, diversification, restructuring; Resources - financial resources, innovation, Symbolic - legitimizing, lobbying; Organizational outcomes (e.g., financial/growth measures, Strategy). They proposed a number of general hypotheses regarding the relationships between these panels of variables.

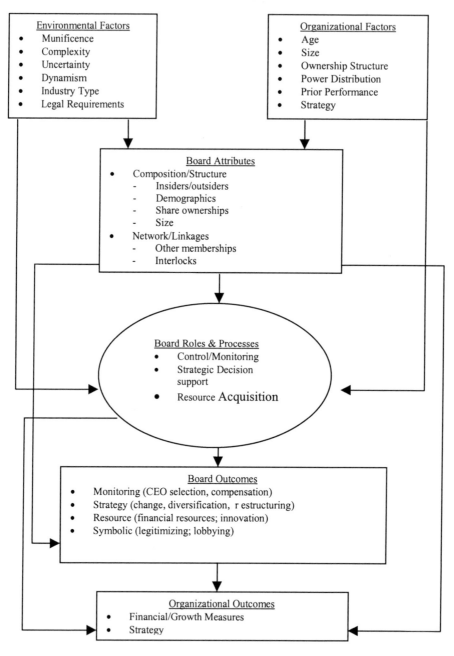

Figure 3 Boards of Directors: A Theoretical Framework
(Baack & Rajogopolan, 1998)

8. Does Board Process Matter?

Charan (1998), more than most writers on corporate boards, devotes much of his attention to group process and dynamics. He believes that leveraging the talents and experiences of board members in a way that proactively creates value, requires that much more attention be paid to group process. The real power of the board lies in its collective wisdom, making group process and dynamics the centrol theme. These include such concepts as open information, open dialogue, trust, joint accountability, learning and improving director and board performance.

Finegold, Benson, Lawler and Conger (1998) empirically examined relationships among variables in three content areas: board practices, effective governance and firm effectiveness. Board practices included measures of the availability of required technical expertise to assess company performance, board had enough time to deal with all its responsibilities, and power of the board. Effective governance, a measure of board effectiveness, was measured by 10 items, falling onto two factors: strategy effectiveness (shaping longterm strategy, monitoring strategy implementation) and networking effectiveness (building network, bolstering company's image). Firm effectiveness was measured by five indicators (ROA, ROI, Market return).

The following general conclusions were reported. First, broad practices were significantly associated with effective governance. Second, effective governance was significantly associated with measures of firm effectiveness. Third, board practices were significantly associated with some of the measures of firm effectiveness. Data were obtained on about 300 firms and all analyses controlled for potentially confounding variables (e.g., industry, number of employees).

9. Conclusions

Interest in corporate governance and the role of corporate boards of directors continues to grow (Johnson, Daily & Ellstrand, 1996). Board demographic and composition factors will remain an area of ongoing research emphasis. It appears, however, that including more of the larger context variables in the next generation of research would not only make our research findings more meaningful, but also support more strongly the case for increasing qualified women's presence on corporate boards of directors. That is, increasing women's board presence enriches board information, perspectives, debate and decision making.

References

Baack, S. and Rajagopolan, N. (1998) Boards of directors: what do we know and where do we go? Paper presented at the Annual meeting of the Academy of Management, San Diego, C.A., August.

Bilimoria, D. & Piderit, S.K. (1994) Board committee membership: Effects of sex-based bias. *Academy of Management Journal*, 37, 1453-1477.

Bilimoria, D. (1995) Women directors: The quiet discrimination. *The Corporate Board*, July/August, 10-14.

Burgess, Z. & Tharenou, P. (1997) Characteristics of Women on Boards of Directors in Australia. *International Review of Women and Leadership*, 3, 46-62.

Burke, R.J. & Mattis, M.C. (1997) Women on corporate boards of directors: International challenges and opportunities. *International Review of Women and Leadership* (Special Issue) 3, 1-84.

Burke, R.J. & McKeen, C.A. (1992) Women in management. In C.L. Cooper & I.T. Robertson (eds.) *International Review of Industrial and Organizational Psychology*, New York: John Wiley, pp. 245-284.

Burke, R.J. (1994a) Women on corporate boards of directors: Forces for change? *Women in Management Review*, 9, 27-31.

Burke, R.J. (1994b) Women on corporate boards of directors. In J. deBruijn & E. Cyba (Eds.) *Gender and organizations – Changing perspectives*. Amsterdam: VU University Press.

Burke, R.J. (1994c) Women on corporate boards of directors: Views of Canadian Chief Executive Officers. *Women in Management Review*, 9, 3-10.

Burke, R.J. (1995) Women corporate boards of directors: Women and men see it differently. *International Review of Women and Leadership*, 1, 55-60.

Burke, R.J. (1997) Women directors: activism on corporate boards of directors: Thriving or surviving? *International Review of Women and Leadership*, 3, 77-84.

Byrne, J. (1996) The best and worst boards: Our new report card on corporate governance. *Business Week*, November 25, 82-106.

Byrne, J. (1997) The best and worst boards: Our report card on corporate governance. *Business Week*, December 8, 90-104.

Catalyst (1997) *Women board directors of the Fortune 500* New York: Catalyst.

Catalyst (1999) *Women board directors of the Fortune 500*. New York: Catalyst.

Charan, R. (1998) *Boards at work: How corporate boards create competitive advantage*. San Francisco: Jossey-Bass.

Conger, J.A., Finegold, D. & Lawler, E.E. (1998a) Appraising boardroom performance. *Harvard Business Review*, , 136-148.

Conger, J.A., Finegold, D., & Lawler, E.E. (1998b) CEO appraisals: Holding corporate leadership accountable. *Organizational Dynamics*, Summer, 7-20.

Conger, J.A., Lawler, E.E. & Finegold, D. (1998) Evaluating individual directors. *Directors & boards*, Winter, 51-54.

Daily, C. & Schwenk, C. (1996) Chief executive officers top management teams and boards of directors: Congruent or countervailing forces? *Journal of*

Daily, C.M. & Dalton, D.R. (1997) Separate, but not independent: board leadership structure in large corporations. *Corporate Governance*, 5, 126-136.

Daily, C.M. (1995) The relationship between board composition and leadership structure and bankruptcy reorganization outcomes. *Journal of Management*, 21, 1041-1056.

Elgart, L.D. (1983) Women on Fortune 500 Boards. *California Management Review*, 25, 121-127.

Finegold, D., Benson, G., Lawler, E.E. & Conger, J.A. (1998) Inside the black box: The factors that lead to effective corporate boards. Paper presented at the Annual meeting of the Academy of management, San Diego, CA., August.

Fleischer, A., Hazzard, G.C. & Klipper, M.Z. (1988) *Board games: The changing shape of corporate power.* New York: Little Brown.

Fondas, N. & Sassalos, S. (1999) A different voice in the boardroom: How the presence of women directors affects board influence over management. *Business and the contemporary world*, in press.

Forbes, D.P. & Milliken, F.J. (1998) Understanding boards of directors as decision making groups. Paper presented at the Annual meeting of the Academy of Management, San Diego, CA., August.

Gillies, J.G. (1992) *Boardroom renaissance.* Toronto: McGraw-Hill Ryerson.

Goodstein, J, Gautam, K. & Boeker, W. (1994) The effects of board size and diversity on strategic change. *Strategic Management Journal,* 15, 241-250.

Harrigan, K.R. (1981) Numbers and positions of women elected to corporate boards. *Academy of Management Journal,* 24, 619-625.

Holton, V. (1995a) Corporate governance report surveying the situation for women directors in the UK. *Corporate Governance*, 3, 102-107.

Holton, V. (1995b) Women on the boards of Britain's Top 200 Companies. *Women in Management Review*, 10, 16-20.

Ibrahim, N.A. & Angelides, J.P. (1994) Effect of board members' gender on corporate social responsiveness orientation. *Journal of Applied Business Research*, 10, 35-40.

Izraeli, D.N. & Talmud, I. (1997) Getting aboard: Mode of recruitment and gender composition: The case of women directors in Israel. *International Review of Women and Leadership_*, 3, 26-450.

Johnson, J., Daily, C., & Ellstrand, A. (1996) Boards of directors: A review and research agenda. *Journal of Management*, 22, 409-438.

Kesner, I. & Johnson, R. (1990) An investigation of the relationship between board composition and stockholder suits. *Strategic Management Journal*, 11, 327-336.

Kesner, I. (1987) Directors' stock ownership and organizational performance: An investigation of Fortune 500 companies. *Journal of Management*, 13, 499-508.

Kesner, I.F. (1988) Directors characteristics and committee membership: An investigation of type, occupation, tenure and gender. *Academy of Management Journal* 31, 66-84.

Lear, R.W. 91994) Here come the women directors. *Chief executive*, April, p. 10.

Leighton, D.S.R. & Thain, D.H. (1993) Selecting new directors. *Business Quarterly,* 57, 16-25.

Leighton, D.S.R. & Thain, D.H. (1997) *Making boards work.* Toronto: McGraw-Hill Ryerson.

Lorsch, J. & MacIver, E. (1989_) Pawns or potentates: The reality of America's corporate board_s_. Boston, M.A.: Harvard Business School Press.

Mace, M. (1986) *Directors: Myth and Reality* Boston: Harvard Business School Press.

Mallette, P. & Fowler, K. (1992) Effects of board composition and stock ownership on the adoption of "poison pills". *Academy of Management Journal*, 35, 1010-1035.

Mattis, M.C. (1997) Women on corporate boards: Two decades of research. *International Review of Women and Leadership*, 3, 11-25.

Mattis, M.C. (1993) Women directors: Progress and opportunities for the future. *Business and the Contemporary World*, 5, 140-156.

McGregor, J. (1997) Making the good woman visible: The issue of profile in New Zealand corporate directorship. *International Review of Women and Leadership*, 3, 1-10.

Mitchell, M. (1984) A profile of the Canadian woman director. *Business Quarterly*, Spring, 121-127.

Monks, R. & Minow, N. (1995) *Corporate governance.* Cambridge: Blackwell Business.

Pajo, K., McGregor, J.& Cleland, J. (1997) Profiling the pioneers: Women directors on New Zealands corporate boards. *Women in Management Review*, 12, 174-181.

Pearce, J. & Zahra, S. (1992) Board composition from a strategic contingency perspective. *Journal of Management Studies*, 29, 411-438.

Pettigrew, A. (1992) On studying managerial elites. *Strategic Management Journal*, 13, 163-182.

Shilton, J., McGregor, J. & Tremaine, M. (1996) Feminizing the boardroom: A study of the effects of corporatization on the number and status of women directors in New Zealand companies. *Women in Management Review*, 11, 20-26.

Siciliano, J. I. (1996) The relationship of board member diversity to organizational performance. *Journal of Business Ethics*, 15, 1313-1320.

Stearns, L. & Mizruchi, M. (1993) Board composition and corporate financing: The impact of financial institution representation on borrowing. *Academy of Management Journal*, 36, 603-618.

Westphal, J.D. & Zajac, E.J. (1995) Who shall govern? CEO/Board power demographic similarity, and new director selection. *Administrative Science Quarterly*, 40, 160-83.

Zahra, S. & Pearce, J. (1989) Boards of directors and corporate financial performance: A review and integrative model. *Journal of Management*, 15, 291-334.

Zahra, S. & Stanton, W. (1988) The implications of board of directors composition for corporate strategy and performance. *International Journal of Management*, 5, 229-236.

THE EXPERIENCES OF WHITE WOMEN ON
CORPORATE BOARDS IN CANADA:

Compliance and Non-Compliance To Hegemonic Masculinity[1]

PATRICIA BRADSHAW
York University
Schulich School of Business
4700 Keele Street, Toronto, Ontario, M3J 1P3

DAVID WICKS
Saint Mary's University
Department of Management
Halifax, Nova Scotia, B3H 3C3

Hegemony: a complex web of conceptual and material arrangements that produce the fabric of everyday life and which work through pervading common sense, consent and by becoming part of the ordinary way of seeing the world, understanding one's self and experiencing needs (Alvesson and Deetz, 1996)

1. Introduction

Increasingly, the extent and perpetuation of, what Connell (1987) originally called hegemonic masculinity is being exposed in the context of the board room of Canadian corporations. As Connell defines hegemonic masculinity, and as we adapt the term in this paper, it is a form of cultural ascendancy achieved in the play of cultural forces which results in non-dominant groups being subordinated but not eliminated. Hegemony is deeply embedded in the structures, policies, doctrines, practices and other cultural artifacts of a society and thus is often rendered largely invisible or taken-for-granted. It is in the play between the everyday and acts of resistance to this form of hegemony that the dynamics of

1 We would like to acknowledge the research assistance of Asaf Zohar and Rhona Berengut in the preparation of this manuscript, and the financial support for this research from the Schulich School of Business at York University, and the Social Sciences and Humanities Research Council of Canada.

R.J. Burke and M.C. Mattis (eds.), Women on Corporate Boards of Directors, 197-212.
© 2000 *Kluwer Academic Publishers. Printed in the Netherlands.*

historical changes in gender and other patterns get played out. The goal of this paper is to explore how women on corporate boards in Canada first experience and then comply with or resist hegemonic masculinity in this context. The paper begins with a brief over view of some of the literature on women on corporate boards and then presents an analysis of interviews with twenty white women who are directors of Canadian corporations and nonprofit organizations.

2. Literature Review

The percentage of women holding board seats on Financial Post 500 Canadian companies appears to have stabilized at 6% (Catalyst Census, 1998). While women remain a small numerical minority on boards, the boardroom is also characterized by a having a strong ideological bias towards unity, stability and harmony (Hill, 1995; Bradshaw, 1996). As Hill says, "Sectional interests are abhorred" and teamwork, collegiality, consent, consensus and agreement informed by informality are reinforced. While we describe this context as characterized by hegemonic masculinity others have called in the "old boys' club". The "boys' club" and its corresponding exclusion of women, according to Leighton, is based on an antiquated systems of director selection which relies on "well-educated, socially homogeneous groups of white males picking people they know and trust, who have similar backgrounds - who are 'like them'" (Leighton, 1993, 1). In the academic literature this process has been called "homo-social reproduction" (Kanter, 1977) and "self-cloning" (Zajac & Westphal, 1996).

The outcome of this reproduction of the existing patterns of dominance and the associated dynamics of conflict avoidance is that women are largely excluded from boardrooms and face consistent patterns of sex-bias in board and board committee membership (Bilimoria & Piderit, 1994; Kesner, 1998). Research shows that women do not lack the experience, credentials or skills to sit on boards but they do lack the demographic similarities that boardroom gate keepers assume will minimize social uncertainty in governance. The importance of personal social ties, trust and social obligations are being explored in the context of governance with Westphal (1999) recently suggesting the positive performance benefits of such social ties for board and CEO relations. Westphal's research conclusions accept and promote the benefits of having directors and managers acting as a "single, cohesive team".

Several authors have speculated about the reasons for this exclusion of women from corporate boardrooms. Reduction of conflict and uncertainty avoidance as described above may be one reason (Hill, 1995; Zajac & Westphal, 1996). Perpetuation of social and business elites and the interlocking nature of established power relations as reflected in complex systems of board interlocks may be another (Pettigrew, 1992). Certainly the social legitimation of class position has been described in the roles of female volunteer directors (Covelli, 1989) and this could be similarly true for corporate directors. Burgess and Tharenou (1997) found the dynamics of social stereotyping and statistical discrimination explain the under representation of women on Australia's boards. The often heard comment that there are not enough qualified women to sit on boards is still repeated in some quarters (Elgart, 1983; McGregor, 1997) and the lack of profile and visibility of women has been suggested as a problem (Mattis, 1993). Final explanations that has been put forward for the dominance of men in the boardroom are the external environmental pressures and social context which reinforce existing demographic patterns (Izraeli & Talmud, 1997; Pettigrew & Whipp, 1991).

Given this male dominance, and what we are suggesting is the operation of a form of hegemonic masculinity, the questions this paper addresses are how women experience being on boards in Canada, how they negotiate their participation, how they define personal success and what strategies they adopt for influencing other directors? While early literature suggested that women on boards can play a unique role, represent the interests of women and act as the social conscience of the organization (Bilimoria & Huse, 1997; Schwartz, 1980; Mitchell, 1984; Harrigan, 1981), Mattis (1993) found a "conspiracy of silence" and female directors not articulating agendas related to women's advancement or women's issues. She suggested that female directors are afraid of being stereotyped and discredited. Similarly, Elgart (1983) suggested that women directors were grateful for their positions and were not prepared to make waves. We wanted to explore these dynamics and determine whether the women we interviewed felt they were at risk of being seen to have a "woman's agenda" (Burke, 1997; Sethi, Swanson & Harrigan, 1981). More recent feminist literature has celebrated the strategies women employ to resist male hegemony and exercise their power (Martin & Meyerson, 1998; Bradshaw & Wicks, 1997). We wanted to assess both the strategies of resistance used in the boardroom as well as the extent to which these women played the game, didn't make waves and complied with the hegemonic masculinity of the boardroom.

3. Research Methodology And Sample

This article presents an interpretive analysis of conversations with twenty white women who sit on corporate boards in Canada. Because of the small number of women on Canadian boards, a few high profile female directors were initially contacted, and a snowball sampling technique was used to contact a wider group of women. Each respondent suggested other potential informants who were then contacted. The data collection method used semi-structured interviews (Fontana & Frey, 1994); each woman was interviewed using a general interview guide approach (Patton, 1990) with a set of issues outlined ahead of time in order to elicit common information from each respondent. The interviews averaged forty-five minutes in length and included questions ranging from basic demographic information to questions about their perceptions of their roles and responsibilities, why they believed they were placed on the board, what attracted them to the position, and what their experiences were as a member of a particular board of directors. Although there was neither one set of questions administered verbatim, nor a rigid sequence of questions posed to all respondents, the interviews focused on understanding the women's experiences of operating on largely male-dominated boards, and how they viewed their contribution to board functioning.

Interpretive researchers typically use interviews of this nature in order to both clarify and extend existing literature. Consistent with the inductive, grounded nature of this study, some observations corroborated our initial expectations of the situation based on the literature reviewed, while others offered different experiences and interpretations that resulted in some emergent themes that could be used to understand white women's experiences on boards.

The sample consisted of white women who were relatively young (41% between 30 and 45, 35% between 46 and 55 and 24% over 56 years of age), highly educated (60% having post graduate or professional degrees), married with children, typically sitting on a number of both profit and non-profit boards. As with Mitchell's (1984) study, almost all respondents had parents who sat on boards or were very active in their community, and tended to grow up in highly enriched and supportive family environments. Women, while relatively small in number in the boardroom, do appear to hold a variety of positions of formal authority on Canadian boards of directors.

The interviews were taped and all the tapes transcribed verbatim. A thematic analysis of the content of the transcribed tapes was performed in order to look for patterns in the data in an inductive or grounded theory fashion (Glaser & Strauss, 1967). The techniques of grounded theory provided suitable tools by which this qualitative data could be monitored, classified and analyzed; helping to organize data through the emergence of broad analytic categories.

4. The Interview Findings

In analysis of the interview transcripts we found a few general themes emerged. We present them below and in tables present some of the quotes from the informants which are illustrative of the issues being discussed. Overall the themes seem to centre on the strategies the women use to influence the boards they sit on, their feelings of effectiveness and definitions of success and their perceptions of gender issues, gender differences and their sense of that despite these issues and differences they play a role that is similar to the role played by men on boards.

4.1. PERSONAL STRATEGIES OF INFLUENCE

From the first conversations with our respondents, strategies for influencing others (frequently male board members) seemed to be an important component of the job, especially if one was to be "successful." The salience of influence as an important aspect of a director's job is hardly surprising given the separation (both physical and symbolic) between directors and the staff/management of the organization, and the strategic nature of the decisions typically made by boards. The personal strategies of influence (summarized in Table 1) existed in a very wide range, from overt conformity by "playing the game" and being like one of the boys, to diplomacy and more aggressive confrontations and ultimatums.

When asked if they felt effective, many respondents said only if and when people listened to them. The particular strategies by which influence was enhanced represent some ways in which these women made sure they were heard, although the range of different types of influence attempts or political strategies they used varied widely. Most respondents indicated that the types of influences used would depend on a variety of factors, including the nature and composition of the board, the issues at hand, and their own individual characteristics including how long they had been on the board and how well trusted they were. One of the more common influence strategies involved building relationships and mobilizing support of other board members (ostensibly their peers) through the formation of alliances, networking or by lobbying. This strategy was used because they perceived that so much of the decision making happened outside the board room and because they didn't want to "embarrass" the other board members. Another of the most frequently espoused influence strategy was being knowledgeable, acting in an expert capacity and over-achieving. Many respondents believed that their success was a direct result of working extremely hard, often times harder than their male counterparts. For example, one board member described visiting every retail store in the chain she was on the board of and actually working in a store for a week when she joined the board. She admitted that her male colleagues would not go to such lengths. From this perspective, the scrutiny that necessarily accompanies women on boards of directors was met with over achievement and technical prowess, justifying that they deserve their place on the board, and that they could demonstrate their commitment. From this basis of knowledge and status, many informants perceived themselves to be more influential.

When asked if they experienced conflict between what they believed should be done and the direction of the board or organization, most women said that at times they had. It appeared, however, that they did not bring all perceived conflict to the attention of the board. The reasons why they remained silent and choose to ignore conflicts and not exercise

Table 1: Personal Strategies of Influence	
Conceptual Distinction	**Illustrative Quotation**
Sexuality	I would definitely flirt. Complementing them on their tie, or how great they look, goes over *very* well.
Knowledge/Legitimacy	Being prepared, understanding the industry and the company. It's a combination of doing your homework and being competent. It takes a bit of time to do that, but then people will begin to listen to you. Being damn sure its on the record, and I'm not shy about demanding that. When you are a legitimate member of the board and you have business experience you can contribute, you have to call it as you see it.
Social Relationship: Centrality/ Alliances/Lobbying	You need to be a person people will talk to, to find out what is going on. Pick up the phone to the chairman of the board and say that I've developed a concern about this or that. Collaborative working relationships with directors is the best way. I was always networking and figuring out who on the board shared my ideas and my vision. So you're always going to luncheon meetings, strategizing, figuring out who's on who's side. That's a constant kind of thing. You have to lobby each and every person on the board, arguing for the good of the company this be done. I've learned that a lot goes on outside the boardroom, and I've learned by asking a lot of questions you can sometimes turn the tide, and have a real discussion on the matter, and other people can begin to see some other issues. That's a technique that is very valuable.

Looking and Acting Like One of Them	I've learned to do what the guys do, because a lot of the work of the boardroom goes on in the corridors. I didn't want to end up as the woman's point of view. I will feed someone else ... I'd rather it came from one of the men. That way I look like one of them.
Diplomacy and Compromising vs. Confrontation and Taking a Stand	On an issue that was mishandled and I wanted to take a stand I would say "This is it guys, take it or I leave." And I could leave and that would be fine. I try to speak at the appropriate time rather than push my way at the beginning without letting other people voice their views. Then I put forward my view in the most convincing way and hope I will convince others. I try to state my case in the best possible way, and frequently you just can't get it across. It happens frequently that when you hear the arguments against you, you realize that another point of view also has some good points and you come to some kind of a compromise solution. I think it is important to try to find a consensus, although its not always possible.

influence included not feeling personally assertive enough (either through disposition or status on the board), fear of being ostracized for pursuing a radical course of action, and the concern for losing political capital and consequently being unable to effect change on issues that are more important or personally significant. Whatever the individual reasons were, many issues appeared to be not worth arguing over, or exerting effort which might increase conflict and tension. Many respondents indicated that they would express their point of view and then live with the outcome of the democratic process of voting and decision making. The effort to look like one of the guys or what Ashforth and Humphrey (1993) call surface acting or pretending to experience emotions that one does not experience was reported by several respondents. For the issues that were important enough to confront, however, a variety of methods for influencing were identified by our respondents, all of which were recounted favourably to the interviewers as behaviours of which they were proud, or courses of action that were successful.

4.2. DEFINITION OF SUCCESS

Perhaps the strongest underlying theme in the conversations with our respondents was the nature of the contribution they felt they made to their boards, and consequently how successful they were in their positions. Not surprisingly, there were a variety of meanings attached to "successful" boardroom behaviours, and a range of feelings with respect to the types of contribution they did make to their boards. On the whole they viewed their contribution as:

1. Expertise and professional experience in areas such as human resources, strategic planning, law or business.
2. Skills, such as analytic and leadership skills, an ability to read financial statements, and negotiation skills.

In addition, many women differentiated between feeling powerful and feeling effective and indicated that while they did not feel powerful they did feel effective. One explained that she was not powerful because as she said; "I do not call the shots" while another said, "I don't care for power particularly, I'm indifferent. It doesn't mean much to me". Another indicated that she was effective as a part of the team but not a leader and another thought of the position as a "wonderful opportunity for growth and it's a great challenge". The types of success women experienced (summarized in Table 2) ranged from gender-neutral functioning in order to be respected for doing a "good job" to fitting in. The local meanings attached to "success" appeared to be very much a personal matter, determined in part by

Table 2: View of Success	
Conceptual Distinction	**Illustrative Quotation**
Technical Effectiveness	If you are performing you have the respect of the people around you. If you have the respect they listen to you, but if you haven't got the respect, you can't make an impact. I'm working with a board now where women are treated just like people. They're expected to do a good job. So you have to be able to stand up to them and you've got to be able to show them that you carried out your duties in a proven fashion and that you've done your homework.

Being Heard and Having a Voice at the Table	I never let anything happen that I didn't have something to say about.
	I just basically provide a perspective and try to engage the people around the table in the same dialogue.
	You have to find your place to be heard, it takes about 2 to 3 years to do that.
	You articulate your point of view as effectively and precisely as you can.
Fitting In	I have to fit into this environment if I don't want to be squashed like a moth . . . you know, dead. That's the reality.
	I think I definitely made some sort of contribution. I remember that one of the first times when someone - this goes way back- when someone asked the chairman of the board about me and he said well she's our conscience - which was sort of an interesting comment. But I purposely didn't want to end up as the women's point of view. I made a point of not doing that.

socialization, education and disposition; their views of success can therefore reveal their deeply-held assumptions about the equality of women and men, their preferred methods for effecting change, and their goars and priorities in this particular social setting.

Examining the local meanings attached to success it became apparent that these repsondents, for the most part, did not see themselves as advocates for other women or change agents for feminist political agendas. In fact, most respondents shunned the feminist label, either because they held negative connotations of the word (usually being something overly radical and/or political), or because they feared backlash from their male counterparts on the board. As one said, "I don't even know what the definition of a feminist is" and another said, "I don't think they (feminists) would include me. Feminist means not only having ideas but promoting them, I don't think I promote them". Another indicated, "To me feminism has a degree of radicalism that I cannot see in me". The meaning of success for these women virtually precluded them engaging in any controversial, political behaviours as success was framed as either behaving like one of the men, or remaining largely invisible so as not to disrupt the efficient functioning and cohesiveness of the board. One of the most frequently repeated patterns in the interview transcripts was the theme of communication or voice. Voice and women's different voice is often discussed in the feminist literature (Gilligan, 1982), and it became an unexpected theme in this data set. For these women, the ability to voice their opinions was a major measure of their success. While not advocating "women's issues" directly, they participated as full members of the board and contributed their point of view to all business issues. One woman reflected on the past and said:

> Women that were on boards in Canada were chosen for the fact that they were women and they would never open their mouth... I think it was wrong and in some ways they have set the cause of women on boards back because they did not contribute, they could not contribute. They were there because companies thought it was important to have a female on the board, but they wanted a female who did not rock the boat. So therefore they wanted women to keep their mouth shut. I'm not one to do that.

4.3. VIEW OF GENDER DIFFERENCES AND WOMEN'S UNIQUE ROLES

The literature review highlighted the debates about the role of women on boards of directors and the potentially unique role that women may play, or be expected to play, on their board. Following on from their definitions of success most of the respondents indicated that if women were on the board to represent women's issues or points of view they were there for the wrong reasons. One women said, "Women on boards should conduct themselves the way men on boards conduct themselves" and another indicated that women would be "foolish to inflict other agendas" on the board. It was also pointed out that representation of any constituency is not how the work of boards of directors is defined. Only one woman indicated that she was a token who was placed on the board because of her gender.

While the women interviewed felt that they were not tokens or representatives of "female concerns," our respondents did hold a range of assumptions or views on the differences between women and men, specifically in terms of how personally they function in their capacity as directors of large commercial organizations. While most women espoused views or beliefs of essential similarities between women and men, all respondents recounted instances when gender made a difference. The differences highlighted included women's sensitivity, their family responsibilities and communications style. Their exclusion from the old boys' club was clearly articulated and other instances of discrimination and stereotyping were described and identified. Gender was seen to be operating in the boardroom and outside it and they did not assume the board was gender-neutral. The types of gender-based differences (summarized in Table 3) represent the range of assumptions of women's and men's essential nature, from virtually identical to fundamentally different.

Table 3: Beliefs of Gender Differences	
Conceptual Distinction	**Illustrative Quotation**
Communication Style	I don't think men want to appear as if they are not knowledgeable about something. Instead of asking a question very openly and directly, they will find a quieter source and get that information. As for me, in some cases I will go that route, but in other cases I will come right out with it.
Sensitivity	I think women are very good at sensing better than men . . . I would be very sensitive to an atmosphere, but the man sitting next me probably wouldn't be.
	I feel that I'm more sensitive . . . it's sort of a body language. I mean we all deal with problems, but you don't want to attack them [men] and damage their ego. You want to build them up, and I feel that I've got a body language where I have a better sensitivity to that.
	In situations where there are a lot of women you often get this group setting where they smile to each other, they are supportive, everyone has the opportunity to speak, you never criticize anyone . . . it was very consensus-building and loving and caring, and talks became very slow, and very difficult to raise opposition.

| Social Networks | I think there is a lot of bonding on boards, and I'm definitely not a part of that.

You know there's an old boy's club, and we girls don't belong. That's always a bit of a barrier, but we are working to try to break that down. We just have not had the same kinds of experience, and we can't belong to the same clubs. So we don't necessarily have the same social circle . . . you just have to live with that. |
|---|---|
| Family Responsibilities | There are more women than men who are wrestling with the balance between home and work, and what pressures that creates, and what trade-offs are fair. There are more women who would be concerned with finding a resolution to that type of problem. |
| Essentially Similar | It's really your performance that counts. Maybe when you join a board a woman can get away with more than a man can, but after the first few meetings it is purely performance.

Women on boards should conduct themselves the way men on boards conduct themselves, and they should being the same kind of judgment to bear. |

5. Discussion and Conclusions

In many ways it is possible to look at the interviewed women's experiences on boards and focus, as they do, on their successes. They achieved access to the top of Canadian organizations in both the corporate and voluntary sectors, broke the glass ceiling (Morrison, White & VanVelsor, 1987), dealt with the old boys' network, had their voices heard in many discussions at the board level, and were models of success or exemplars for other women. From all accounts, these women were real path breakers showing that women can contribute meaningfully in contexts of power and influence, no matter how male-dominated and/or oppressive. Many of these women had done it while simultaneously raising a family.

These women accomplished this success by working extremely hard and proving their worth. They appeared to see themselves as being just like men; their gender was either down played or hidden behind a facade of high performance, strong commitment, and social similarity. They perceived their roles independent of gender-based issues; like any director (female or male), they said it is their primary responsibility to protect the interests of the shareholders.

In general these women felt ambivalent about power, but they did feel effective and articulate. It is an interesting paradox that these women felt influential, yet resisted the idea of being powerful as if it is something they should avoid, or at least not admit. They had expert power, skill, position, visibility and connections and effectively used many influence strategies. Given the ongoing debates about the power of any director (Lorsch, 1989), and criticisms that boards are merely rubber stamps of management (Gillies, 1992), these female directors generally felt as effective as any of their male colleagues. They accomplished this not by stressing their differences as women, rather by fitting in and working within existing institutionalized structures and processes to play the game by the rules.

One of the questions underlying this research was to what extent can or will women, once they reach the top of the organization, effect change in the status quo (Elgart, 1983; Mattis, 1993; Burke, 1994). The women interviewed in this study did not appear to have a feminist change agenda and instead viewed their role as the protector of shareholder rights and wealth, much the same as their male counterparts. The transformation of the existing institutional arrangements was not being facilitated in any way by these women; they viewed their role as a contributor to organizational effectiveness, or as a group to assist management.

Increasingly the literature on women in management is identifying strategies of resistance which women use to undermine existing relations of power. Martin and Meyerson (1998) call the types of disorganized, fragmented, subtle and individualized acts they observed amongst senior women "disorganized coaction". Meyerson and Scully (1995) called such strategies acts of "tempered radicals" and Bradshaw and Wicks (1997) described a range of forms of feminist resistance that varied from subtle to extravagant and private to public. What struck us in this research was how few acts of resistance were described by the women we interviewed. Previous research has focused on senior managers or academics and not on women on corporate boards. Explanations of the compliance of women on boards to date have described the existence of the "old boys club" and the "conspiracy of silence" of female directors. We are dissatisfied with these interpretations and think scholars needs to go further and be more radical (in the sense of questioning deep structures of power, Bradshaw, 1998) in framing the reasons why female directors do not rock the boat. In speculating on why the themes of fitting in, acting like the other directors and not rocking the boat were so dominant we have generated a few possible explanations.

One explanation is the class based structure of Canadian society (Newman, 1975). Many of these women are from the elite of Canadian society, many have husbands, fathers and other family members in business and politics, and some were invited to join the boards primarily because of these family connections. Thus it can be argued that they were colluding and playing a role in the reproduction of the upper class (Covelli, 1989), one which is inherently classist, racist and sexist.

Another explanation for the observed dynamics may be the influence of institutionalized power bases and the network of social power relations, such as the legal system, which influence the way the power relations unfold, and consequently who benefits from (and conversely who is harmed by) the maintenance of these systems and relations. The legal definitions of the roles and responsibilities of the director, for example, act as constraints on what women (or any board member for that matter) can do, and how effectively they can advocate for women's (or other minority) interests. We do not have constituent or representative directors in Canada and the United States, and the legally defined role of the director is to safeguard the interests of the shareholders and the organization. If the women on the board attempt to play an advocacy role and represent interests of women, then they would be legally liable for any deterioration of shareholder wealth, and would not be invited (by the male gatekeepers) to sit on the board again, all in the name of complying with federal legislation. The problem, then, is partly the legal constraints to dialogue on the board about any issues other than maximizing return on investment. Smart (1986) describes the role of law in creating, reproducing and mitigating forms of oppression. In the context of the board of directors, an analysis of the laws and how they constrain change and mitigate against constituent directors lobbying on behalf of other interest groups (for example women) is important. In the current critiques of boards and their functioning, the issue of constituent directors does not seem to be raised (Bradshaw, 1996). If some women were sitting in the boardroom with the legal mandate of advocating for women's interests, then the stories told by female directors might be very different.

We have come to believe that the inherently gendered nature of organizations (Witz & Savage, 1992) and in particular of boardrooms has to be discussed in the literature on women on boards. In this paper we are suggesting that it is this operation of masculinity and its hegemonic nature which limits resistance by female directors. The striving for harmony and unity described by writer such as Hill (1995) is a powerful and under questioned dynamic in the boardroom. Until we begin to deconstruct this form of hegemonic masculinity and understand how it traps women and men and restricts resistance real change in the boardroom is likely to take longer. As Connell (1987) says hegemony does not mean total cultural domination and the obliteration of alternatives. There is still a balance and a play of forces. At the present time, however, we are convinced that the balance is in favour of the status quo and the opportunity for women to contribute to and help address their own subordination and the subordination of femininities and other masculinities will remain very limited. We specifically used the term hegemonic masculinity to describe the boardroom in order to highlight the pervasive, deep and unconscious nature of the constraints on change. We need to go beyond understanding the operation of the "old boys' club" to see how constraints on resistance are also embedded in the actual discourses, policies, structures, rituals and interpersonal dynamics of the board. Foucault describes the micro practices of power and how they subordinate certain knowledge claims. We need to expose the operation of such micro practices and the reveal the implicit assumptions about the board. For example, challenging Westphal's (1999) conclusion that we need to accept and promote the benefits of having directors and managers acting as a "single, cohesive team" would be a good place to start. We wonder who this "team" benefits, who is allowed to play and how the hegemonic masculinity of the board is sustained in the operation of a "team"?

More research from critical and feminist perspectives and more in-depth qualitative studies which can reveal the dynamics of both compliance and non-compliance or resistance are needed. Observational studies will give us more rich understandings. The research reported here is limited by the small sample size and its reliance on interviews. We call on researchers to continue to explore women on boards and to also explore alternative interpretive perspectives from which to understand the observed behaviours.

References

Alvesson, M. and Deetz, S. (1996) Critical Theory and Postmodern Approaches to Organizational Studies, in S. Clegg, C. Hardy & W. Nord (eds.), *Handbook of Organization Studies*, London: Sage Publications, pp.191- 217.
Ashforth, B. E. and Humphrey, R.H. (1993) Emotional Labor in Service Roles: The Influence of Identity, *Academy of Management Review* Vol. 18 (1), pp. 88-115.
Bilimoria, D. and Piderit, S. (1994) Board Committee Membership: Effects of Sex-Based Bias, *Academy of Management Journal* 37, (6), pp.1453-1477.
Bilimoria, D. and Huse, R. (1997) The Qualitative Comparison of the Boardroom Experiences of U.S. and Norwegian Women Corporate Directors, *International Review of Women and Leadership* 3, (2), pp. 63-76.
Bradshaw, P. (1996) Women as Constituent Directors: Rereading Current Texts Using a Feminist-Postmodernist Approach, in D. Boje, R. Gephart and T.J. Thatchenkery (eds.), *Postmodern Management and Organization Theory*, Thousand Oaks, CA: Sage Publications.
Bradshaw, P. (1998) Power and Dynamic Tension and its Implications for Radical Organizational Change, *European Journal of Work and Organizational Psychology* 7, (2), pp 121-143.
Bradshaw, P. and Wicks, D. (1997) Women in the Academy: Cycles of Resistance and Compliance, in P. Prassad, A. Mills, M. Elmes and A. Prassad (eds.), *Managing the Organizational Melting Pot: Dilemmas of Workplace Diversity*, Sage Publications, pp. 199-255.
Burgess, Z. and Tharenou, P. (1997) Characteristics of Women on Boards of Directors in Australia, *International Review of Women and Leadership* 3 (2), pp. 46-62.
Burke, R. (1994) Women on Corporate Boards: Forces for Change?, *Women in Management Review* l9 (1), pp. 191-222.
Burke, R. (1997) Women Directors' Activism on Corporate Boards of Directors: Thriving or Surviving?, *International Review of Women and Leadership* 3, (2), pp. 77-84.
Catalyst Census (1999) Women Board Directors of Canada, 120 Wall Street, New York, 10005-3904.
Connell, R. (1987) *Gender and Power: Society, the Person and Sexual Politics,* Stanford, California: Stanford University Press.
Covelli, L. (1989) Dominant Class Culture and Legitimation: Female Volunteer Directors, in R. Herman and J. Van Til (eds.), *Nonprofit Boards of Directors: Analyses and Applications*, New Brunswick, NJ: Transaction Publishers.
Elgart, L. (1983) Women on Fortune 500 Boards, *California Management Review* 25(4).
Fontana, A. and J. Frey (1994) Interviewing: The Art of Science, in N.Denzin and Y. Lincoln (eds.) *Handbook of Qualitative Research*, Thousand Oaks, CA: Sage Publications.
Gillies, J. (1992) *Boardroom Renaissance: Power, Morality, and Performance in the Modern Corporation*, Toronto: McGraw Hill Ryerson.
Gilligan, C. (1982) *In a Different Voice: Psychological Theory and Women's Development*. Cambridge, MA: Harvard University Press.
Glaser, B. and A. Strauss (1967) *The Discovery of Grounded Theory: Strategies for Qualitative Research*, Chicago, IL: Aldine Publishing.
Harrigan, K. (1981) Numbers and Positions of Women Elected to Corporate Boards, *Academy of Management Journal* 24 (3), pp. 619-623.
Hill, S. (1995) The Social Organization of Boards of Directors, *British Journal of Sociology*, 46 (2), pp. 245 - 278.

Izraeli, D. and Talmud, I. (1997) Getting Aboard: Mode of Recruitment and Gender Composition, The Case of Women Directors In Israel, *International Review of Women and Leadership* 3 (2), pp. 26-44.

Kanter, R.M. (1977) *Men and Women of the Corporation*, New York: Basic Books.

Kesner, I. (1998) Directors' Characteristics and Committee Membership: An Investigation of Type, Occupation, Tenure and Gender, *Academy of Management Journal* 31 (1), pp. 66-84.

Leighton, D. (1993) How Can Women Access Boards?, *Women in Management*. Nov/Dec, 4 (2). Published by the National Centre for Management Research's Women in Management Program, Western School of Business.

Lorsch, J. (1989) *Pawns or Potentates: The Reality of America's Corporate Boards*, Cambridge, MA: Harvard Business School Press.

Martin, J. & Meyerson, D. (1998), Women and Power: Conformity, Resistance and Disorganized Coaction, in R. Kramer, M.Neale (eds.) *Power and Influence in Organizations*, Thousand Oaks, C.A.: Sage Publications.

Mattis, M. (1993) Women Directors: Progress and Opportunities for the Future, *Business and the Contemporary World*, V (3), pp. 140-156.

McGregor, J. (1997) Making Good Women Visible: The Issues of Profile in New Zealand Corporate Directorships, *International Review of Women in Leadership*, 3 (2), pp. 1-10.

Meyerson, D. and Scully, M. (1995) Tempered Radicalism and the Politics of Ambivalence and Change, *Organization Science* 6, pp 585-600.

Mills, A. J. (1989) Organization, Gender, and Culture, *Organization Studies*, 9, pp. 351-369.

Mitchell, M. (1984) A Profile of the Canadian Women Director, *Western Business Quarterly*, Spring, pp. 121-127.

Morrison, A., White, R. and Van Velsor, E. (1987) Executive Women: Substance Plus Style, *Psychology Today*, August, pp. 18-26.

Newman, P. (1975) *The Canadian Establishment*, Toronto, Ontario: McCelland and Stewart Ltd.

Patton, M. (1990) *Qualitative Evaluation and Research Methods* 2nd edition, Newbury Park, CA: Sage Publications.

Pettigrew, A. and Whipp, R. (1991) *Managing Change for Competitive Success*, Oxford: Basil Blackwell.

Pettigrew, A. (1992) On Studying Managerial Elites, *Strategic Management Journal* 13, pp. 163-182.

Sethi, S., Swanson, C. and Harrigan, K. (1981) *Women on Corporate Boards*. Working Paper, Centre for Research in Business and Social Policy, School of Management and Administration, The University of Texas at Dallas.

Schwartz, F. (1980) Invisible Resource: Women for Boards, *Harvard Business Review*, March-April.

Smart, C. (1986) Feminism and Law: Some Problems of Analysis and Strategy, *International Journal of the Sociology of Law* 14, pp. 109-123.

Westphal, J. (1999) Collaboration in the Board Room: Behavioral and Performance Consequences of CEO-Board Social Ties, *Academy of Management Journal*, 42, (1), pp. 7-24.

Witz, A. and Savage, M. (1992) The gender of organizations, in M. Savage and A. Witz (eds.) *Gender and Bureaucracy*. Oxford: Blackwell, pp. 3-62.

Zajac, E. and Westphal, J. (1996) Who Shall Succeed? How CEO Board Preferences and Power Affect the Choice of New CEOs, *Academy of Management Journal*, 39 (1), p. 64-90.

PUBLIC SECTOR BOARD COMPOSITION IN AUSTRALIA: LEADING THE WAY

DENISE K. CONROY
Faculty of Business
Queensland University of Technology
GPO Box 2434
Brisbane, Qld, 4001, Australia

1. Introduction

The position of women on the boards of public sector authorities, corporations and committees in Australia can best be understood by placing contemporary board membership data into a social, economic and political context. The major impetus for the appointment of women onto public sector boards has resulted both from a recognition of the advantages of membership diversity and a thirty-five year period of women's policy development accompanied by women's increased participation rates in employment and education.

However, as a brief overview of women's policy development indicates, the major gains made as a result of legal advances and employment and educational opportunities, have not resulted in significant women's advancement into the upper echelons of decision-making in either the public or private sectors of the economy.

This chapter provides data on public sector board membership and draws some comparisons with private sector boards in Australia as well as some overseas data.

2. Women's policy development - a background.

There is a great deal of literature on women's policy development in Australia and much of it relates to the period from 1972 when, under a Labor government, an adviser on Women's Affairs to the Prime Minister was first appointed. It has been argued that a resurgence of feminism co-incided with the Labor Party coming into office after a period of twenty-three years (Curthoys 1994; Dowse 1983; 1984; Draper, 1991; Encel and Campbell, 1991; Eisenstein 1985; 1991; 1996; Farrer, 1993; 1997; Franzway, 1986; Franzway et. al., 1989; Kaplan, 1996; Mercer, 1975; Reid, 1987; Sawer, 1989; 1993; Simms, 1981; Simms and Stone, 1990; Summers, 1975; 1979; 1991; Yeatman, 1990) and

R.J. Burke and M.C. Mattis (eds.), Women on Corporate Boards of Directors, 213-235.
© 2000 *Kluwer Academic Publishers. Printed in the Netherlands.*

that, at least in the 1970s and early 1980s, women's policy development was facilitated by reformist governments in each of the States and by the ratification of international covenants such as the ILO Convention 111 (1973), ILO Convention 103 (1973), ILO Convention 100 (1974), and the United Nations Convention on the Elimination of All Forms of Discrimination Against Women (1983). (Conroy, 1989a; Sawer in Stetson and Mazur, 1995).

In 1963 the Women's Bureau was established within the federal Department of Labour and National Service to advise on the needs of women in the workforce; in 1966 the marriage bar was removed for women in the federal public service, and in 1969 the concept of equal pay for equal work was handed down by the Australian Conciliation and Arbitration Commission. In 1972 the decision was extended to include equal pay for work of equal value and in 1974 equal minimum award wages were legalised. (Conroy, 1989a; Farrer, 1997)

Other milestones which are significant to women's policy development and progress are included in Appendix 1. However, against these are the problems which seem to mitigate against women's progress. The 1972 equal pay decision has never been fully implemented as women's jobs have not been systematically re-evaluated; there is still the assumption that the male life course is the norm; particular legislation aimed at redressing inequalities has been found to be ineffective necessitating protracted reviews; and patriarchal ideology still pervades in the major decision-making bodies such as parliaments, corporations (public and private), trade and industry associations, and boardrooms (Farrer, 1997; Hartmann and Spalter-Roth, 1996).

At the State level of government, women's advisors were appointed in Victoria, South Australia and Tasmania in 1976; in New South Wales in 1977; in the Northern Territory in 1982; in Western Australia in 1983; the Australian Capital Territory in 1985; and in Queensland in 1990. Women's policy units were established within the Premier's or Chief Minister's departments and consultative/advisory councils were appointed soon after. (Mason, 1994; Sawer, 1990a, 1990b).

Some States have their own anti-discrimination and equal opportunity legislation and most provide information centres and have set up departmental women's advisors. Each women's policy unit produces annual reports on their activities and most provide women's budgets and action plans. (Jordan 1992; Mills, 1981; Sullivan, 1993a; 1993b; Warhurst, 1981).

The most significant 'machinery' used apart from specific legislation and adoption of international covenants has been the women's advisors, women's policy units, advisory councils and information centres as well as women's budgets, national conferences and a network of women inside departments. This Australian model (also referred to as the 'wheel of women's affairs' or 'centreperiphery model') was developed by the Women's Electoral Lobby (WEL) and the first femocrats. Analysis of the women's movement and its influence on federal and State governments since 1972 has been well documented by Sawer (1984; 1989; 1990a; 1990b; 1991; and 1998; and Sawer and Groves 1994a; 1994b).

Apart from this 'second-wave' feminism, there were a variety of other policy 'devices' which have led to an improvement of the status of women. These might be grouped as responses to emerging social issues (from the 1960s) and to economic issues (from the 1980s).

Inequality of pay was addressed in the 1969 and 1972 equal pay judgements but there has been, and remains, an inequality in employment in both occupational and industry categories. At the 1971 census, around 21 per cent of the female labour force was concentrated in a small number of occupations where they represented over 80 per cent of total employment (Riach, 1975). Compared to other OECD countries, Australia has one of the most highly segregated labour forces and this has implications for level of earnings, employment opportunity and access to decision-making. In 1998 over one half of all female employees (54%) worked in clerical, sales and service occupations. In the professional category there were similar numbers of men and women but over half the numbers of women were nurses and teachers and they represented 91 per cent and 69 per cent respectively of all persons in those categories (ABS, 1998a: 114). The labour force participation rate for married women aged 15 to 64 years increased from 34 per cent in 1968 to 63 per cent in 1998, while that for other women increased from 65 to 67 per cent (ABS, 1998a: 112), and part-time employment has risen for women over the last ten years (1988 - 1997) from 13 to 18.3 per cent, with a fall in full-time employment from 59.8 to 50 per cent over the same period (ABS, 1998a: 113).

Baum and McColl (1985; 1990) note that despite major legal advances towards giving women and men equal opportunity and power in society, an analysis of their social, economic and political situation reveals that the majority of women remain in a position of subordination in relation to men. This assessment is supported by Kaplan (1996) in an insightful analysis of Australia's social indicators. She notes that from studies on women in management and data on their participation rates in management, that managerial equality would not be achieved until the end of the next century (Kaplan, 1996: 174).

An analysis of 1996 census data suggests whilst women are well represented in management positions, they are not at chief executive officer, senior executive service or partner level - the 'traditional' qualification route for board appointment. There is some evidence that women are not remaining in, or proceeding to, senior positions in companies but are exiting earlier than men to become self-employed. It would appear that the pipeline theory is not going to eventuate. (Conroy, 1998: 7-8).

Equal opportunity and affirmative action policies have been used as both women-specific and gender-normative measures to achieve change. However, as Eveline points out, these strategies used the 'discourse of disadvantage' (Eveline, 1994: 140). The material benefits which men gain when women perform most of the domestic and caring responsibilities is harder to tackle. Sawer has pointed out that:

'the first rule of democratic politics is never to be seen taking
anything away from anyone... equal opportunity policies are
sold because they give opportunities to women and benefit
everyone, rather than because they take away male advantages.'
(Sawer quoted in Eveline, 1994: 141-142).

The passage of the Sex Discrimination Act in 1984 and the Affirmative Action
(Equal Employment Opportunity for Women) Act in 1986 and concomitant changes in
human resource management practices have expanded opportunities for women to work
and to combine work with traditional family responsibilities but, as evidenced above,
mostly in part-time or casual jobs.

The participation rate of young women (15-19 years) in part-time work
increased from 46 to 74 per cent between 1988 and 1998 (compared to an increase from
29 to 51 per cent for young men). In 1998, 46 per cent of female teenagers attending
tertiary education and 43 per cent of female attendees 20-24 years old were working part-
time. In 1997, 46 per cent of married mothers and 32 per cent of lone mothers with a
child aged 0-4 were employed, mostly in part-time jobs. (ABS, 1998a:112-113). The
participation rates of women in tertiary education continues to rise, reflecting, since 1989,
a trend of higher rates of university entrance by females as well as graduations. (ABS
1998a:85).

Like the occupational data, at May 1998 women are concentrated in five
industry groups – health and community services (77.2%), education (66.5%), finance
and insurance (57.4%), accommodation, cafes and restaurants (54.4%) and retail trade
(51.1%). Two other industry groups nearing equal representation (50%) are personal and
other services (48.7%) and cultural and recreational services (48%). (ABS, 1998b).

In 1997, half (52%) of all public sector employees were female compared to 43
per cent of private sector employees, and 73 per cent of the public sector employees
worked in three industry groups – education (29%), government administration and
defence (23%) and health and community services (21%). (ABS, 1998a:117).

What is evident from the foregoing analysis is that women-specific and gender-
normative policies have resulted in increased numbers of women and qualified women in
the labour force, but they have not resulted in a broader representation of women across
industries, occupations or employment status or category.

From the 1980s, economic rationalism has dominated the political and economic
spectrum and there has also been a tendency towards 'mainstreaming' by liberal-
democratic governments at the state and federal level. This has been seen by some
feminists as an erosion of 'equality' measures or at least an incompatibility of EEO/AA
measures with a drive for economic efficiency, and a 'threat to the achievement of a
woman-friendly polity'. (Sawer, 1993:21). David Conway, in a provocative essay on
free-market feminism, suggests that feminists should support competitive markets instead
of attacking them as a liberal market order maximises the opportunities of women to
participate in the labour force whilst retaining an option of caring for a family. (Conway,
1998). His objections are that practical measures such as anti-discrimination laws,

affirmative action, comparable worth (equal pay for work of equal value) and state-provided or subsidised childcare are both ineffective in delivering equal opportunity and not in women's best interests.

Essentially, the difference is a philosophical one based on the extent to which the state should intervene and western feminism has defined itself, according to Almond, by division into 'theoretical' classifications: conservative, liberal, social, separatist and

post-modern feminism. As Almond points out, there is a different need between women who are in occupations where they can control their time, working hours and energies and/or in a committed relationship where the division of labour is compatible with work, and those women who need to work for basic financial reasons and who cannot afford child care (or elder care) in order to do so. (Almond in Conway, 1998:65).
In Australia, the development of women's policy has followed political party line. Although both social-democratic and liberal-democratic governments have left the legislative measures in place, there has been a different emphasis between 'separatist' and 'mainstream' developments and a reduction in women's policy structures federally. (Goward, 1997).

Currently, the emphasis is on diversity, opportunity and choice but what has been removed are some of the mechanisms for policy audit such as the women's budget (1998), the women's year book (1997) and report to CEDAW every four years 1984, 1988, 1992 and 1996. Australia reported in 1986, 1992 and 1994 – a supplementary report to the second report prepared in 1993 – and submitted as Australia's third periodic report in 1995. The fourth periodic report due in August 1996 was not submitted – there was a change of government in March 1996. (CEDAW, 1997: para. 18; Commonwealth of Australia, 1986; 1992; 1997; Federal Labor Caucus, 1997).

At the State level, women's policy co-ordination units have been moved outside the central agency (Premier's departments) and thus, Ministers responsible for women's affairs now come from less senior portfolios which are generally outside Cabinet.

It is against this social, economic and political context of women's policy development, especially since the mid 1980s, that public sector board profiles should be examined. In 1988 the then Labor government set a target of 'half by 2000' for Commonwealth public sector board appointments. (House of Representatives Standing Committee on Legal and Constitutional Affairs, 1992).

3. Public sector boards

Data on public sector boards is available at the federal level and for all States except New South Wales and the Northern Territory which are presently reviewing their databases. Registers are kept of women seeking board appointment, but the nature of the registers varies. South Australia has conducted executive searches to identify top level women; Victoria is considering outsourcing its register; the Federal government has appointed an executive search organisation to find suitable women for boards in portfolio areas where vacancies have been hard to fill with women candidates.   Western Australia has 'mainstreamed' its register and there is now only a Register of Interested Persons; and Queensland has recently advertised a 'central' register but still maintains a separate women's register. This self-nomination process to registers results in an uneven quality of candidates and any requests for nominations can result in unreasonable expectations of appointment.   In more recent times most registration forms carry a 'disclaimer' that lodgement of a form does not guarantee appointment. (Northern Territory 1998; n.d.; Office of Women's Affairs, 1998; Queensland Government, 1995; 1997; 1998).

Data on gender representation on boards has been available for several years but, disappointingly, has not been published in such places as The Australian Women's Year Books (ABS 1994; 1995; 1997) nor in Women in Australia - Australia's Third Progress Report to CEDAW. (Women in Australia, 1997).   Instead, data from Korn Ferry surveys of directors has been used regrettably, uncritically, and this data (as for Cullen Egan Dell) distorts the 'real' situation of women on boards (Burton, 1997: 4-5; Conroy, 1996a: 26; 1998:3).

In 1992 the percentage of women on Commonwealth public enterprise boards (statutory marketing authorities and government business enterprises) was 10.9 per cent. (Beckett, 1994: 204). In 1997 the figure is 28.5 per cent of all appointments to boards (boards, councils, commissions, tribunals, consultative committees, statutory authorities and government business enterprises). It should be noted, however, that data from year to year is not strictly comparable because of changes to portfolio composition and privatisation.   Despite the National Agenda for Women (1988) goal of equal representation of women on boards and committees by the year 2000, there has not been a marked increase in the representation of women as the following tables illustrate.

Table 1:   Percentage of Women on Boards - Appointments Within Commonwealth Discretion: Commonwealth Government

Department	31/12/97		31/12/96		31/12/95	
	Total	% Women	Total	% Women	Total	% Women
Administrative Services	-	-	102	18.6	168	23.2
Attorney General's	406	28.8	439	30.8	501	29.9
Communication & Arts	292	37.0	162	38.3	127	39.4
Defence	65	6.2	51	23.5	51	25.5
Employment, Education, Training & Youth Affairs	1198	27.9	1161	26.3	294	26.5
Environment	117	30.8	143	34.3	183	35.0
Finance	-	-	23	4.4	27	7.4
Finance and Administration	41	2.4	-	-	-	-
Foreign Affairs & Trade	220	25.9	216	25.9	243	23.9
Health & Family Services	764	35.6	789	42.2	648	44.4
Housing & Regional Development	-	-	-	-	62	24.2
Immigration & Multicultural Affairs	145	43.4	124	41.1	237	42.2
Industry, Science & Tourism	507	22.1	521	24.0	609	16.9
Primary Industries & Energy	130	26.2	114	25.4	89	18.0
Prime Minister & Cabinet	92	38.0	64	35.9	121	36.4
Social Security	467	58.2	409	59.9	424	58.3
Tourism	-	-	-	-	26	19.2
Transport	-	-	-	-	62	17.7
Transport & Regional Development	50	16.0	55	18.2	-	-
Treasury	156	16.7	127	15.8	130	14.6
Veteran's Affairs	333	25.8	244	20.9	112	18.8
Workplace Relations & Small Business	272	17.3	201	16.9	193	11.9
TOTAL	5255	30.7	4945	31.6	4307	31.30

Source: Appoint Database 1995, 1996, 1997

When compared with Table 2 (below), it is obvious that the government strategy is easier to implement where the Commonwealth has discretion over the process. For those departments 'targetted' for the executive search process - Finance and Administration, Foreign Affairs and Trade, Primary Industries and Energy and Workplace Relations and Small Business, two show an increase in Table 1 (Primary Industries and Energy and Workplace Relations and Small Business). 'Appoint' data has been available since 1994 and there has been a steady increase in appointments of women over the period 1994 to 1997, with the government making a special effort to stem the decrease in appointments to boards where there is only partial, or no, Commonwealth control.

What is noticeable from Table 2 is that women are concentrated in 'soft' areas such as social security, immigration and multi-cultural affairs, education, health and family services and not in finance, defence, transport or agriculture. The same pattern is reflected in the States where women comprise over 40 per cent of appointments in education, arts, family/children's services, human services, disability services and health and fewer than 10 per cent of appointments in primary industries, mining, state development, energy, local and regional development, transport and emergency services. The exception is South Australia, where women comprise a minimum of 20 per cent in all portfolios (see Table 7).

Table 2: Percentage of Women on Boards - All Appointments: Commonwealth Government

Department	1997 Total	% Women	1996 Total	% Women	1995 Total	% Women
Attorney General's	419	28.2	455	29.9	507	30.0
Communication & Arts	390	37.2	381	39.1	328	36.3
Employment, Education, Training & Youth Affairs	91	16.5	129	21.7	141	22.0
Defence	1271	28.8	1328	28.2	531	32.4
Environment	350	26.6	321	29.3	353	29.2
Finance Administration	58	13.8	-	-	-	-
Foreign Affairs & Trade	252	25.8	241	26.1	275	23.6
Health & Family Services	1415	37.8	1495	41.0	1781	41.3
Immigration & Multicultural Affairs	151	43.0	141	39.7	257	41.2
Industry, Science & Tourism	920	17.2	937	17.9	887	13.6
Primary Industries & Energy	382	17.0	406	16.5	510	12.4
Prime Minister & Cabinet	533	25.7	150	29.3	177	35.6
Social Security	472	58.1	417	59.7	430	57.7
Transport & Regional Development	61	16.4	80	15.0	-	-
Treasury	197	15.2	151	14.6	162	14.8
Veteran's Affairs	339	25.4	316	22.2	278	18.3
Workplace Relations & Small Business	551	12.7	464	12.5	451	9.3
Administrative Services	-	-	173	13.9	230	18.3
Finance	-	-	27	14.8	48	14.6
Housing & Regional Development	-	-	-	-	79	20.3
Tourism	-	-	-	-	50	18.0
Transport	-	-	-	-	79	16.5
TOTAL	7852	28.5	7612	29.3	7554	28.9

Source: Appoint Database 1995, 1996, 1997

Table 3 depicts the method of appointment and shows a decrease in the influence of Cabinet and Ministerial appointments, and more appointments resulting from departmental efforts both directly and by ex-officio nomination. To some extent this indicates the degree of influence of the Minister responsible for Status of Women in providing a 'watching' brief, and the efforts made by departments in putting forward names. A change of government in March 1996 (from Labor to a Liberal-National coalition) is reflected in the 1997 data, where Cabinet appointments are reduced by 17.1 per cent.

Table 3: Percentage of Women on Boards by Method of Appointment: Commonwealth Government

Appointment Method	1997		1996		1995	
	Total	% Women	Total	% Women	Total	% Women
Governor - General	1437	38.8	1125	33.2	1057	29.7
Cabinet	160	28.1	197	45.2	242	40.1
Ministerial	2712	25.7	3082	31.4	3403	32.7
Portfolio	962	33.1	712	28.9	845	23.1
Elected	508	22.4	75	22.7	80	28.8
Ex Officio	676	26.8	263	19.0	266	10.2
Other	1252	22.0	1966	23.5	1333	24.5
Unclassified	145	35.9	192	34.9	328	26.2
TOTAL	**7852**	**28.5**	**7612**	**29.3**	**7554**	**28.9**

Source: Appoint Database 1995, 1996, 1997

Table 4 gives data on the roles played by women on boards (relative to men) but apart from an increase in the ex-officio appointments, there is no discernible trend towards an increased 'share' of leadership roles.

Table 4: Position by Gender: Percentage of Women on Commonwealth Boards

Position	1997		1996	
	Total	% Women	Total	% Women
Chairperson	662	21.6	619	22.8
Deputy Chair	203	17.7	156	17.9
Ex Officio	221	19.9	212	15.1
Member	6370	30.4	6102	31.3
Other	386	20.2	443	22.6
Unclassified	10	20.0	80	30.0
TOTAL	**7852**	**28.5**	**7612**	**29.3**

Source: Appoint Database 1996, 1997. 1995 data not available

Table 5 provides an analysis of the degree of Commonwealth control over appointments and Table 6 reveals the percentage of appointments with total Commonwealth discretion.

Table 5: Percentage of Women on Boards by Degree of Commonwealth Control

Degree of Control	1997		1996		1995	
	Total	% Women	Total	% Women	Total	% Women
Total Commonwealth Control	5255	30.7	4945	31.5	4307	31.3
Commonwealth Influence	1187	30.7	1193	28.1	1472	28.4
No Commonwealth Influence	1240	17.1	1045	15.6	1018	15.4
Unclassified	170	30.0	429	40.6	757	34.5
TOTAL	**7852**	**28.5**	**7612**	**29.3**	**7554**	**28.9**

Source: Appoint Database 1995, 1996, 1997

Table 6: Percentage of Board Appointments with Commonwealth Discretion as a Percentage of Total Appointments

Department	1997 %	1995 %
Attorney General's	96.9	98.8
Communication & Arts	74.9	38.7
Defence	71.4	36.2
Employment, Education, Training & Youth Affairs	94.3	55.4
Environment	33.4	51.8
Finance & Administration	70.7	70.1
Foreign Affairs & Trade	87.3	88.4
Health & Family Services	54.0	36.4
Immigration & Multicultural Affairs	96.0	92.2
Industry, Science & Tourism	55.1	68.7
Primary Industries & Energy	34.0	17.5
Prime Minister & Cabinet	17.3	68.4
Social Security	98.9	98.6
Transport & Regional Development	82.0	78.5
Treasury	79.2	80.2
Veteran's Affairs	98.2	40.3
Workplace Relations & Small Business	49.4	42.8

Source: Tables 1 & 2

As noted previously, a comparison cannot be made between years for departments due to quite significant changes in portfolio composition. For example, between 1995 and 1997, the Department of Employment, Education, Training and Youth Affairs added 48 committees (mostly consultative committees on employment), an increase of 92 per cent; Defence almost halved its number of boards; Primary Industries and Energy lost one third of its boards and the Department of Prime Minister and Cabinet increased from 6 to 52 boards and committees, due mostly to the establishment of 42 Aboriginal and Torres Strait Islander Commission regional councils.

However, what is obvious from the 1997 data is that most departments have significant discretion over appointments - the major exceptions being Prime Minister and Cabinet (where, rightly, Aboriginal and Islander peoples control their own agendas), Environment, and Primary Industries and Energy. In the Environment portfolio, many boards and committees are of a scientific or regional nature, and in Primary Industries, board positions are determined by 'producers' via elections and most women in agricultural and rural pursuits work as 'silent' or unpaid partners. Although there are a few high profile women in the industry (the National Farmers Federation CEO is a woman and, in Queensland, women head grower groups such as the Cattleman's Union and the Beef Industry Development Advisory Council) they tend not to be elected to boards.

The overall picture for women on public sector boards in Australia is encouraging although it has been static for the last three years (1995-1997). The overall percentage of women on public sector boards is (at 30 June):

New South Wales (NSW)	27%	1997
Victoria	25%	1998
Queensland	23%	1998
South Australia (SA)	31%	1998
Western Australia (WA)	22%	1998
Tasmania	27%	1997
Aust. Capital Territory (ACT)	40%	1998
Northern Territory (NT)	24%	1997
Commonwealth	29%	1997

These percentages reflect the number of board positions held by women compared to total board positions.

In Table 7, data is given (where available) for the percentage range of positions held by the number of agencies. As with the data in Tables 1 to 6, comparability (between governments) is limited because of the different numbers of departments and agencies in each State as well as the different number of boards. In the ACT where the percentage is highest, there are only five departments, 129 boards and half of these are in the areas in which women dominate - education, community services, health and cultural activities. There are no primary industry boards. Conversely, Western Australia which has the lowest percentage of women on boards, has 647 boards (including 208 primary industry bodies) and a significant number of departments (57%) with female board representation under 20 per cent.

Table 7: Number of Departments/Agencies by Percentage Female Representation on Australian Government Boards, Committees and Council (Latest Year Available)

Government	Year	Percentage													Total Depts/Agencies
		0	1-5	6-9	10-20	21-30	31-40	41-50	51-60	61-70	71-80	81-90	91-99	100	
Commonwealth #	1997	-	1	1	3	6	4	1	1	-	-	-	-	-	17
N.S.W.		-------------------- not available --------------------													
Victoria	1997	-	-	-	4	2	1	1	-	-	-	-	-	-	8
Queensland	1998	-	1	2	6	3	4	1	-	-	-	-	-	-	17
South Australia	1998	-	-	-	-	13	1	2	1	-	-	-	-	1*	18
Western Australia	1998	-	3	6	12	5	6	2	1	1	-	-	1*	-	37
Tasmania	1997	4	1	2	7	2	2	4	-	-	-	-	-	1*	23
Northern Territory		-------------------- not available --------------------													
Australian Capital Territory	1997	-	-	-	-	1	1	1	2	-	-	-	-	-	5

Source: Conroy, 1998(b).
* Office for Status of Women/Women's Affairs
# Appointments within Commonwealth discretion

As can be seen from the foregoing discussion, the data can be easily misinterpreted when totals or percentages only are given, yet this is the way in which data is frequently reported in the media and in government reports. To understand the nature of the problem as to why there are no overall gains being made by women in board representation, governments need to publish data in its most disaggregated form. In many cases, greater codification or analysis is required to identify direct cause-effect relationships in policies and strategies.

4. Private sector comparison

Data on the gender composition of private sector boards is difficult to assess and, as stated earlier, only misleading information tends to be publicised. However, there are a few studies which provide accurate data. Stapledon and Lawrence in their analysis of the top 100 companies in 1995, ranked by market capitalisation as listed on the Australian Stock Exchange, report 29 non-executive directorships and 3 executive directorships held by women. The number of female directors in these top 100 companies was 27, representing 3.9 per cent of all directors. (Stapledon and Lawrence, 1997: 172). Whilst the list of companies is not given, the top group would include Qantas and Telstra which accounted for 3 women on their boards in 1995.

Boyden Global Executive Search undertook an analysis of the 1996 annual reports of Australia's top 50 listed companies. Companies were grouped into four industry sectors:

- finance - major banks, insurance companies and investment houses;
- services - media groups, major retailers, entertainment, energy supply and property development;
- manufacturing - construction, building, chemicals and food and beverages;
- resources - mining, oil and gas extraction.

Whilst the number of women on boards is low in all sectors (finance, 5% of seats; services, 7% of seats; manufacturing, 4% of seats and resources, 5% of seats) three boards had more than one women director. A total of 24 women held board positions with four holding more than one seat, however, there were five major public sector boards amongst the 50 selected. (Boyden, 1998: 3,7).

Conroy (1996b) reports similar data for 1995-96. Updating this for 1997-98, the representation of women on the top 10 companies (by gross revenue) in each State in Australia is:

	1995-96 (Percentage)	1997-98 (Percentage)
N.S.W.	6.1	6.4
Victoria	7.4	7.1
Queensland	7.5	12.5
S.A.	4.2	12.7
W.A.	6.0	5.9
Tasmania	Nil	2.5
A.C.T.	Nil	Nil
N.T.	33.3	33.3
Australia	6.1	8.3

However, if the data is adjusted to exclude public sector bodies, the situation becomes:

	1995-96 (Percentage)	1997-98 (Percentage)
N.S.W.	5.6	6.1
Victoria	6.7	7.7
Queensland	Nil	Nil
S.A.	1.6	6.1
W.A.	4.3	3.7
Tasmania	Nil	Nil
A.C.T.	Nil	Nil
N.T.	Nil	Nil
Australia	3.9	4.2

For the top 50 mining companies (by gross revenue) the percentage of women is:

	1995-96 (Percentage)	1997-98 (Percentage)
N.S.W.	1.7	1.3
Victoria	2.5	1.9
Queensland	Nil	4.8
S.A.	2.6	4.0
W.A.	Nil	Nil
Tasmania	Nil	Nil
N.T.	Nil	Nil
Australia	1.7	1.8

The representation of women on private sector boards is currently between 4 and 8 per cent; for mining companies it is between zero and 5 per cent.

Yet again caution is required in interpreting this data. Representation of women differs by State reflecting *inter alia* the geographic location of company head offices (approximately 60 per cent of public companies have their head offices in Sydney (NSW) and 26 per cent are located in Melbourne (Victoria); differences by industry sector and by type of company. Of the total private companies, around 42 per cent are family owned. For the data collected on the top ten companies in each State (as depicted above) there are, in 1997-98, a total of 35 positions held by women but 20 of these positions are on public sector boards. (Conroy, 1998).

Although there was a reduction in the size of many company boards between 1995 and 1998, there was an increase in some as well. However, there was no instance of an increase in the number of female directors on boards where the number of directors increased.

The number of women on private sector boards is considerably fewer than on public sector boards, but the explanation is in the different type of board and scale, as well as the particular 'geography' of the major private companies in Australia. What is obvious, though, is that most of the women who have been appointed to the largest publicly listed companies have first served on public sector boards.

5. Leading the Way?

Australia's model of women's policy machinery was developed by feminists, many of whom went on to fill significant, and senior, roles in the federal bureaucracy. The women's budget process, introduced in 1984, was claimed as a 'world first' in educating bureaucrats to analyse the impact of their 'mainstream' programs on women, and was pivotal in revealing who benefitted from government activity. (Sawer, 1993:1). However, as discussed earlier this, and other disaggregated data analysis, has been discontinued.

A comparison between Australia's progress towards the appointment of women to board positions and that of other countries such as Canada, New Zealand, the United Kingdom and the United States is limited due to the lack of data in those countries on public sector boards and committees. New Zealand is probably the closest comparator as state owned enterprises are subject to equal opportunity regulations and are publicly accountable. (Shilton et. al., 1996).

Surveys in the United Kingdom in 1989 and 1993 relate to the top 200 companies (Holton et. al., 1993; Holton, 1995) as do those in Canada in 1984 (Mitchell, 1984) and 1993 (Burke 1994a; 1994b; 1995; 1997a; 1997b), and New Zealand in 1997 (Pajo et. al., 1997), and include mostly private sector companies. The annual census by Catalyst covers the Fortune 500 companies, again private sector companies. (Catalyst, 1998a).

However, what is common amongst these studies and those conducted in Australia by Burgess and Tharenou (1997), and Stapledon and Lawrence (1997) is that the increased incidence of the appointment of women as non-executive directors is linked to an acceptance of diversity in corporate governance as a competitive advantage, as well as work-place reforms such as equal pay, equal opportunity and affirmative action.

The increase in the labour force participation of women coupled with trends in work and family relationships has also had a positive impact, although in Australia, womens' labour force participation in 1998 (50%) is slightly below that for women in the United States in 1976 (57%) and 27 per cent below the U.S. rate in 1996 (77%). (Catalyst, 1998b). This increased labour-force participation is due to an increase in tertiary education participation by women (20.9% compared to 17.3% for males), and these superior qualifications are reflected in womens' public sector appointments (Conroy 1989a; 1989b; 1994) and also in board appointments (Boyden, 1998; Burgess and Tharenou, 1997 and Conroy 1996b). Similar findings are evident in Canada (Burke 1994a; 1994b), New Zealand (Hill, 1994; McGregor, 1997; Pajo et. al. 1997; Shilton et. al., 1996 and Tapsell, 1998), the United Kingdom (Holton et. al., 1993; Marshall, 1995)) and the United States (Bilimoria and Piderit, 1994; Catalyst, 1998a; Hartmann and Spalter-Roth, 1996; Mattis, 1993; 1997; Stephenson and Rakow, 1993; and Valian, 1998).

The major hurdles in Australia to board appointment for women are a dominant male organisational culture, unsupportive board and executive leadership, 'traditional' recruitment practices, a belief that qualified women are not available, and exclusion from informal networks. (Arbouw, 1997; Conroy 1996a; 1996b; Karpin Report, 1995; Sinclair, 1994; 1998). However, in the public sector these are ameliorated by equal opportunity policies and a vigilance over board appointments by Ministers responsible for status of women issues.

The level of representation of women on public sector boards in Australia is high (average 28% over all governments) and is on track to reach 30 per cent by the turn of the century. The target of 'half by 2000' is clearly not attainable without the creation of additional board positions, and this is unlikely given recent trends towards government 'down-sizing'. Improvements could be made to women's representation across functional areas and those departments with the lowest representation are targetted and executive search strategies are being used with some success.

The state still plays an active role in public sector board appointments for, if left to the 'market', women would not maintain their level of representation. The major contributions of the social and liberal democratic feminist strategies over the period 1963 to 1998 are an increase in the diversity of decision-making on public sector boards, especially over the last five years, and an opportunity for women on the larger public sector boards to achieve appointment to the boards of significant private sector corporations.

The test of women's policy development in Australia will be to see that the representation of women on public sector boards does not regress, and that successes in the public sector are mirrored by increasing appointments of women to private sector boards. Progress will not be rapid for, as mentioned, the pipeline theory is not evident and the public sector is constantly 'downsizing'. However, if all States and the

Commonwealth Government can achieve a representation rate of 25-30 per cent for each board, then the advantages of 'critical mass' will start to emerge.

Milestones in Women's Policy Development, Australia, 1963-1998.   **Appendix I**
Federal Government

1963	Women's Bureau established within the Department of Labour and National Service
1966	marriage bar removed for women in the public service
1969	equal pay for equal work
1972	equal pay for work of equal value
1973	ILO Convention 111 ratified
1973	ILO Convention 103 ratified
1974	Prime Minister appointed Elizabeth Reid as special advisor on women's affairs
1974	Women's Affairs Section created in the Department of Prime Minister and Cabinet.
1974	Ratification of ILO Convention 100, Equal Remuneration
(1975	United Nations International Women's Year)
1976	Office of Women's Affairs set up in the Department of Prime Minister and Cabinet.
1977	women's units established in some federal departments
1978	National Women's Advisory Council established
1980	Australia signed UN Convention on the Elimination of All Forms of Discrimination Against Women
(1980	UN World Conference on the Decade for Women)
1981	Human Rights Commission Act passed
1981	Federal Sex Discrimination Bill introduced as a Private Member's Bill by Senator Susan Ryan
1983	Ratification of UN Convention on the Elimination of all Forms of Discrimination Against Women.
1984	Sex Discrimination Act passed
1984	Women's Budget Program introduced (assessment of impact of budget on women)
(1985	UN World Conference on Achievements of the UN Decade for Women)
1986	Human Rights and Equal Opportunity Commission Act passed
1986	Affirmative Action (Equal Opportunity for Women) Act passed
1988	National Agenda for Women launched
1988	Australian Women's Employment Strategy launched
1989	Half Way to Equal - Report of Inquiry into Equal Opportunity and Equal Status for Women in Australia
1990	Ratification of ILO Convention 156 on Workers with Family Responsibilities
1992	Government Response to Half Way to Equal
1993	The New National Agenda for Women released

1993	Review of Affirmative Action (Equal Opportunity for Women) Act
1993	Amendment to Sex Discrimination Act, 1984.
1994	Production of Women's Year Books (joint OSW and ABS publication).

Sources: ABS 1993: (x)-(xiv); ABS 1997: (vi)-(vii); Conroy, 1989: 43-45

References

(ABS) Australian Bureau of Statistics, (1993), *Women in Australia*, ABS Catalogue No. 4113.0, Canberra.

(ABS) Australian Bureau of Statistics, (1995), *Australian Women's Yearbook 1995*, Office of the Status of Women and ABS, ABS Catalogue No. 4124.0, Canberra.

(ABS) Australian Bureau of Statistics, (1997), *Australian Women's Year Book 1997*, ABS Catalogue No. 4124.0, Canberra.

(ABS) Australian Bureau of Statistics, (1998a), *Australian Social Trends*, ABS Catalogue No. 4102.0, Canberra.

(ABS) Australian Bureau of Statistics (1998b), *Labour Force Australia*, ABS Catalogue 6203.0, Canberra.

Alexander, Malcolm, (1998), 'Big Business and Directorship Networks: the Centralisation of Economic Power in Australia,' *Journal of Sociology*, Vol. 34(2), August, pp. 107-122.

Arbouw, John, (1997), 'Government Boards: Where To Now?", *Company Director*, Vol. 13(7), August, pp. 8-15.

Baum, Frances and McColl, Margaret, (1985), 'Women', in Woodward, Dennis, Parkin, Andrew and Summers, John, (eds.), *Government, Politics and Power in Australia*, Third edition, Longman Cheshire Pty. Ltd., Melbourne.

Baum, Frances and McColl, Margaret, (1990), 'Women', in Summers, John, Woodward, Dennis and Parkin, Andrew (eds.), *Government, Politics and Power in Australia*, Fourth edition, Longman Cheshire Pty. Ltd., Melbourne.

Beckett, Ian, (1994), 'Public Enterprise Boards in Australia' in Corkery, Joan, O Nuallain, Colm, and Wettenhall, Roger, (eds.), *Public Enterprise Boards: What They Are and What They Do – Reports from an International Study*, Australian Journal of Public Administration in collaboration with IASIA, Hong Kong.

Bilimoria, Diana, (1995), 'Women Directors: The Quiet Discrimination,' *The Corporate Board*, July-August, pp. 10-14.

Bilimoria, Diana and Piderit, Sandy, (1994), 'Qualifications of Corporate Board Committee Members', Group and Organization Management, Vol. 19(3), September, pp. 334-362.

Boyden, (1998), *Board of Directors Survey - The Balance of the Board*, January.

Burgess, Zena and Tharenou, Phyllis, (1997), 'Characteristics of Women on Boards of Directors in Australia', *International Review of Women and Leadership*, Vol. 3(2), pp. 46-62.

Burke, Ronald J., (1994a), 'Women on Corporate Boards of Directors: Forces for Change?' *Women in Management Review*, Vol. 9(1), pp. 27-31.

Burke, Ronald J., (1994b), 'Women on Corporate Boards of Directors: Views of Canadian Chief Executive Officers', *Women in Management Review*, Vol. 9(5), pp. 3-10.

Burke, Ronald J., (1995), 'Personal , Educational and Career Characteristics of Canadian Women Directors', *Equal Opportunities International*, Vol. 14(8), pp. 1-10.

Burke, Ronald J., (1997a), 'Women Directors' Activism on Corporate Boards of Directors: Thriving or Surviving?', *International Review of Women and Leadership*, Vol. 3(2), December, pp. 77-84.

Burke, Ronald J., (1997b), 'Women on Corporate Boards of Directors: A Needed Resource', *Journal of Business Ethics*, Vol. 16, pp. 909-915.

Burton, Clare, (1997), *Women's Representation on Commonwealth and Private Sector Boards*. A Research Paper for the Office of the Status of Women, Department of the Prime Minister and Cabinet, Canberra, August.

Catalyst, (1998a), *The Catalyst Census of Women Board Directors of the Fortune 500*, http://www.catalystwomen.org/press/infobrief3.html (accessed October, 1998).

Catalyst, (1998b), *Women in the Labour Force*, http://www.catalystwomen.org/press/infobrief3.html (accessed October, 1998).

(CEDAW) Committee on the Elimination of Discrimination Against Women, (1997), *CEDAW/C/1997/II/L.1/Add. 8.Consideration of Reports – Third Periodic Report. Australia*, United Nations, New York.

Commonwealth of Australia, (1986), *Convention on the Elimination of All Forms of Discrimination Against Women. Report of Australia*, June. AGPS, Canberra.

Commonwealth of Australia, (1992), *Women in Australia*. Australia's Second Progress Report on Implementing the United Nations Convention on the Elimination of All Forms of Discrimination Against Women. AGPS, Canberra.

Commonwealth of Australia, (1997). *Women in Australia*. Australia's Third Progress Report on Implementing the United Nations Convention on the Elimination of all Forms of Discrimination Against Women. AGPS, Canberra.

Conroy, Denise K., (1989a), *Opportunities and Barriers to Career Development in Management. The Senior Executive Service in the Australian Public Service*. Paper presented at the International Association of Schools and Institutes of Administration Annual Conference, 18-21 July, Marrakesh.

Conroy, Denise K., (1989b*)*, *The Global and Regional Situation of Women Top Civil Servants*. Paper presented to Expert Group Meeting on Equality in Political Decision-Making. United Nations Office, Vienna, 18-22 September.

Conroy, Denise K., (1994), 'The Glass Ceiling: Illusory or Real?, *Canberra Bulletin of Public Administration*, No. 76, April, pp. 91-103.

Conroy, Denise K. (1996a), *Boardroom Renaissance*. Paper presented to Women in the Public Sector Conference, Sydney, 26-27 March.

Conroy, Denise K., (1996b), *Challenges Faced by Women on Decision-Making Bodies*. Paper presented to Board Directorship Forum, Brisbane, 22 August.

Conroy, Denise K., (1998), ACOB *National Women in Leadership Project - A Formative Evaluation*. Paper presented to the 7th International Women in Leadership Conference, Perth, W.A., 2-4 December.

Conway, David, (1998), *Free-Market Feminism*, The Institute of Economic Affairs, London.

Curthoys, Ann, (1994), 'Australian Feminism Since 1970', in Grieve, Norma and Burns, Ailsa (eds), *Australian Women: Contemporary Feminist Thought*, Oxford University Press, Melbourne.

Dowse, Sara, (1983), 'The Women's Movement's Fandango with the State: The Movement's Role in Public Policy Since 1972', in Baldock, Cora V. & Cass, Bettina, (eds.), *Women, Social Welfare and the State in Australia*, George Allen and Unwin Australia Pty. Ltd., North Sydney.

Dowse, Sara, (1984), 'The Bureaucrat as Usurer', in Broom, Dorothy (ed.), *Unfinished Business: Social Justice for Women in Australia*, Allen and Unwin Australia Pty. Ltd., Sydney.

Draper, Mary, (1991), 'Theoretical Frameworks for Women's Policy Development', *The Australian Quarterly*, Vol. 63(3), Spring, pp. 321-335.

Eisenstein, Hester, (1985), 'The Gender of Bureaucracy: Reflections on Feminism and the State', in Goodnow, Jacqueline and Pateman, Carol (eds.*)*, *Women, Social Science and Public Policy*, George Allen & Unwin Australia Pty. Ltd., Sydney.

Eisenstein, Hester, (1991), 'Speaking for Women', Voices from the Australian Femocrat Experiment, *Australian Feminist Studies*, Vol. 14, Summer, pp. 29-42.

Eisenstein, Hester, (1996), *Inside Agitators: Australian Femocrats and the State*, Allen and Unwin, St. Leonards NSW.

Encel, Sol and Campbell, Dorothy, (1991*)*, *Out of the Doll's House: Women in the Public Sphere*, Longman Cheshire Pty. Ltd., Melbourne.

Eveline, Joan, (1994), 'The Politics of Advantage', *Australian Feminist Studies*, Vol. 19, Autumn, pp. 129-154.

Farrer, Vanessa, (1993), 'Gender and Patriarchy', in R. Smith (ed.), *Politics in Australia*, Second edition, Allen and Unwin Pty. Ltd., St. Leonards, NSW.

Farrer, Vanessa, (1997), 'Gender and Patriarchy', in R. Smith (ed.), *Politics in Australia*, Third edition, Allen and Unwin Pty. Ltd., St. Leonards, NSW.

Federal Labor Caucus Status of Women Policy Committee, (1997), *Back to the 60s? Progress Report on the Australian Government's CEDAW Obligations and Beijing Platform for Action Implementation Report*, July 18, New York.

Franzway, Suzanne, (1986), 'With Problems of their Own: Femocrats and the Welfare State', *Australian Feminist Studies*, Vol. 3, Summer, pp. 45-57.

Franzway, Suzanne, Court, Dianne and Connell, R.W., (1989*), Staking a Claim. Feminism, Bureaucracy and the State*, Allen and Unwin Australia Pty. Ltd., North Sydney.

Goward, Pru, (1997), 'Diversity, Opportunity and Choice', *Canberra Bulletin of Public Administration*, No. 85, August, pp. 56-58.

Hartmann, Heidi and Spalter-Roth, Roberta, (1996), 'A Feminist Approach to Public Policy Making for Women and Families', *Current Perspectives in Social Theory*, Vol. 16, pp. 33-51.

Hill, Linda, (1994), 'Feminism and Unionism in New Zealand', *Hecate*, Vol. 20(2), pp. 124-139.

Holton, Vicki (1995), 'Women on the Boards of Britain's Top 200 Companies', *Women in Management Review*, Vol. 10(3), pp. 16-20.

Holton, Vicki, Rabbetts, Jan and Scrivener, Sean, (1993*), Women on the Boards of Britain's Top 200 Companies: A Progress Report*. Ashridge Management Research Group, Ashridge, Herts.

House of Representatives Standing Committee on Legal and Constitutional Affairs, (1992), *Government Response to 'Half Way to Equal'*, A.G.P.S., Canberra.

Jordan, Deborah, (1992), 'Women's Policy', in Parkin, Andrew and Patience, Allan (eds.), *The Bannon Decade*, Allen and Unwin Pty. Ltd., Sydney

Kaplan, Gisela, (1996), *The Meagre Harvest: The Australian Women's Movement 1950s - 1990s*, Allen and Unwin Pty. Ltd., Sydney.

(Karpin Report) Commonwealth of Australia, (1995), *Enterprising Nation: Renewing Australia's Managers to Meet the Challenges of the Asia-Pacific Century*, Report of the Industry Taskforce on Leadership and Management Skills, AGPS, Canberra, April.

Marshall, Judi, (1995), 'Working at Senior Management and Board Levels: Some of the Issues for Women', *Women in Management Review,* Vol. 10(3), pp. 21-25.

Mason, Carolyn, (1994), 'Women's Policy in Queensland', *Social Alternatives*, Vol. 12(4), January, pp. 13-16.

Mattis, Mary C., (1993), 'Women Directors: Progress and Opportunities for the Future,' *Business and the Contemporary World*, Summer, pp. 140-156.

Mattis, Mary C., (1997), 'Women on Corporate Boards: Two Decades of Research', *International Review of Women in Leadership*, Vol. 3(2), December, pp. 11-25.

McGregor, Judy, (1997), 'Making the Good Women Visible: The Issue of Profile in New Zealand Corporate Directorship', *International Review of Women in Leadership*, Vol. 3(2), December, pp. 1-10.

Mercer, Jan, (1975), 'The Women's Electoral Lobby and the Women's Movement. The History of the Women's Electoral Lobby', in Mercer, Jan (ed.), *The Other Half: Women in Australian Society*, Penguin Books Australia Ltd., Ringwood, Vic.

Mills, Helen, (1981), 'Equal Opportunities', in Parkin, Andrew and Patience, Allan (eds.), *The Dunstan Decade*, Longman Cheshire Pty. Ltd., Melbourne.

Mitchell, Meg, (1984), 'A Profile of the Canadian Woman Director,' *Business Quarterly*, Vol. 49, Spring, pp. 121-127.

Northern Territory, (1998), *Women in the Budget 1998-99*, Northern Territory Government Publications, Darwin.

Northern Territory Government (n.d.), *Looking Ahead. Plan of Action for Women in the Northern Territory to the Year 2000.* Government Printer, Darwin.

Office of Women's Affairs, (1998), *Draft 2 Year Action Plan for Women: 1998-2000*, Office of Women's Affairs, Victoria.

Pajo, Karl, McGregor, Judy and Cleland, Jacquie (1997), 'Profiling the Pioneers: Women Directors on New Zealand's Corporate Boards,' *Women in Management Review*, Vol. 12(5), pp. 174-181.

Queensland Government, (1995), *A Social and Economic Profile of Women in Queensland*, Women's Policy Unit, Brisbane.

Queensland Government, (1997), *State Budget 1997-98. Women's Affairs Budget Outlook*, Office of Women's Affairs, Queensland Treasury.

Queensland Government (1998), *State Budget 1998-99. Women's Affairs Budget Outlook*, Office of Women's Affairs, Queensland Treasury.

Reid, Elizabeth, (1987), 'The Child of Our Movement: A Movement of Women,' in Scott, Jocelyn A. (ed.), *Different Lives*, Penguin Books Australia Ltd., Ringwood, Victoria.

Riach, Peter, (1975), 'Women and the Australian Labour Market: Problems and Policies', in Mercer, Jan, (ed.), *The Other Half: Women in Australian Society*, Penguin Books Australia Ltd., Ringwood, Vic.

Sawer, Marian, (1984), 'Women and Women's Issues in the 1980 Federal Elections,' in Simms, Marian (ed.), *Australian Women and the Political System*, Longman Cheshire Pty. Ltd., Melbourne.

Sawer, Marian, (1989), 'Women: The Long March Through the Institutions', in Head, Brian and Patience, Allan (eds.), *From Fraser to Hawke*, Longman Cheshire Pty. Ltd., Melbourne.

Sawer, Marian, (1990a), 'Governments and Women', in Power, John (ed.), *Public Administration in Australia: A Watershed*, Hale and Iremonger Pty. Ltd., Sydney.

Sawer, Marian, (1990b), *Sisters in Suits. Women and Public Policy in Australia*, Allen and Unwin Australia Pty. Ltd., Sydney.

Sawer, Marian, (1991), 'Why Has the Women's Movement Had More Influence on Government in Australia Than Elsewhere?', in F. Castles (ed.), *Australia Compared: People, Policies and Politics*, Allen and Unwin Pty. Ltd., North Sydney.

Sawer, Marian, (1993), 'Reclaiming Social Liberalism: The Women's Movement and the State', *Journal of Australian Studies*, June, pp. 1-21.

Sawer, Marian (1998), Where Are We Now? Gender Audit in Australian Government. Background Paper for Tasmanian Women's Policy Workshop, 2 October.
http://www.utas.edu.au/docs/humsoc/cpmp/ES1.html (accessed 23 November).

Sawer, Marian and Groves, Abigail, (1994a), 'The Women's Lobby': Networks, Coalition Building and the Women of Middle Australia,' *Australian Journal of Political Science*, Vol. 29, pp. 435-459.

Sawer, Marian and Groves, Abigail, (1994b), *Working from Inside. Twenty Years of the Office of the Status of Women*, AGPS, Canberra.

Shilton, Jacqui, McGregor, Judy and Tremaine, Marianne (1996), 'Feminizing the Boardroom: A Study of the Effects of Corporatization on the Number and Status of Women Directors in New Zealand Companies,' *Women in Management Review*, Vol. 11(3), pp. 20-26.

Simms, Marian, (1981), 'The Australian Feminist Experience', in Grieve, Norma and Grimshaw, Patricia (eds.), *Australian Women*, Oxford University Press, Oxford.

Simms, Marian and Stone, Diane, (1990), 'Womens Policy', in Jennet, Christine and Stewart, Randal, (eds.), *Hawke and Australian Public Policy*, The Macmillan Company of Australia Pty. Ltd., Melbourne.

Sinclair, Amanda (1994), *Trials at the Top*, The Australian Centre, University of Melbourne, Parkville, Vic.

Sinclair, Amanda (1998), *Doing Leadership Differently*, Melbourne University Press, Carlton South, Vic.

Stapledon, G.P., and Lawrence, Jeffrey (1997), 'Board Composition, Structure and Independence in Australia's Largest Listed Companies,' *Melbourne University Law Review*, Vol. 21(1), pp. 150-186.

Stephenson, Kurt and Rakow, Steve, (1993), 'Female Representation in U.S. Centralised Private Sector Planning: The Case of Overlapping Directorships', *Journal of Economic Issues*, Vol. 27(2), June, pp. 459-470.

Stetson, Dorothy McBride and Mazur, Amy, (1995), *Comparative State Feminism*, Sage Publications, Thousand Oaks, California.

Sullivan, Barbara, (1993a), 'Women and the Current Queensland State Government', *Hecate*, Vol. 19(1), pp. 8-26.

Sullivan, Barbara, (1993b), 'Women and the Goss Government', in Stevens, Bron and Wanna, John (eds.), *The Goss Government*, Centre for Australian Public Sector Management, Macmillan Education Australia Pty. Ltd., Melbourne.

Summers, Anne, (1975), 'The Women's Electoral Lobby and the Women's Liberation Movement. Where's the Women's Movement Moving To?' in Mercer, Jan (ed.), *The Other Half: Women in Australian Society*, Penguin Books Australia Ltd, Ringwood, Vic.

Summers, Anne, (1979), 'Women', in Patience, Allan and Head, Brian (eds.), *From Whitlam to Fraser*, Oxford University Press, Melbourne.

Summers, Anne, (1991), 'Speaking for Women?' Comments on Paper by Hester Eisenstein', *Australian Feminist Studies*, Vol. 14, Summer, pp. 43-46.

Tapsell, Sherrill, (1998), 'Leading Ladies', *Management*, February, pp. 24-37.

Valian, Virginia, (1998), *Why So Slow? The Advancement of Women*, Massachusetts Institute of Technology, Cambridge, Massachusetts.

Warhurst, John (1981), 'The Public Service' in Parkin, Andrew and Patience, Allen (eds.), *The Dunstan Decade*, Longman Cheshire Pty. Ltd., Melbourne.

Yetman, Anna (1990), *Bureaucrats, Technocrats, Femocrats: Essays on the Contemporary Australian State*, Allen and Unwin Australia Pty. Ltd., North Sydney.

PART FOUR

Views of Corporate Directors

FROM MALE LOCKER ROOM TO CO-ED BOARD ROOM:
A TWENTY-FIVE YEAR PERSPECTIVE

CECILY CANNAN SELBY
Independent Scholar

1. Introduction

In 1973, after my first meeting as a member of the RCA Board of Directors, I asked a fellow director, a banker, if he had observed changes in corporate board operations since recent public attention to the diversity and accountability of corporate directors. I remember his answer well. "Cecily", he said, " the decisions that used to be made in the locker room are now being made in the boardroom." Over my next twenty-five years of experience with several corporate boards, I observed, again and again, the significance of this observation. When strategies, properly within the responsibility of directors, are initiated outside the boardroom, they usually serve the interests of those initiating the strategies rather than those of all shareholders. One definition of a well-functioning and responsible board of directors could be one that will not let such behaviors succeed! But this requires directors with unselfish, not vested, interests and comprehensive, not parochial, vision.

My own experience has included work with boards and chief executives exhibiting such broad vision and responsible judgement. It has also included unhappy experiences with selfish interests and narrow vision: experiences where locker room deals successfully by-passed or directed board action. In these cases, all shareholders were not well served. To protect shareholders against such behavior, *and* to provide added value to the work of management, directors are needed who will ask the hard questions and seek the best answers. And, the culture of the boardroom must support such integrity and diversity of view. This paper will argue the case that directors with diverse skills, experiences and backgrounds are more likely to raise questions that add, rather than simply echo, the voice of management. They can, thereby, provide additional dimensions of wisdom for corporate leadership and help transform boardroom culture, when and if needed. The best CEO's I have worked with relish the interaction and advice they can access through such directors. There is a loneliness in being #1 in any organization that makes good confidential dialogue with peers invaluable. Corporate directors are a group of peers with whom the CEO should be able to be fully confidential. But peers with similar backgrounds and experiences will tend to ask similar questions.

R.J. Burke and M.C. Mattis (eds.), Women on Corporate Boards of Directors, 239-251.
© 2000 *Kluwer Academic Publishers. Printed in the Netherlands.*

Peers in the same "club" are unlikely to want to disturb the club. The wiser and broader the questions asked, the more useful the dialogue and judgements derived, --and the better the interests of all shareholders will be served. I hope that my personal tales will illuminate how diversity, --- gender, ethnic, professional ---- contributes to such an outcome.

As someone obviously different in gender and profession from most corporate directors, I am asked more often about the impact of these differences, this diversity, than about my experiences in general. Questions frequently asked are: "How and why did they choose you?" "How does it feel to be the only woman on the board?" "Were you able to make a difference? ", " What about the woman's point of view?" And, finally, "How can I get on a board?" I will, therefore, address these questions first before turning to more general thoughts about diversity and board form and function.

2. How and why was I elected to board memberships?

My invitations to serve on boards started at the time (1973) when legal, social and political pressures were forcing nominating committees to "find women". My job then was as National Executive Director of Girl Scouts USA. The annual budget (including magazines) of this organization was about $30 million. At that time, few women were operating an organization of that size, profit or non-profit, so I became a likely candidate for executive search firms seeking potential female corporate board members. I was also the right age (45) and had a respectable resume in science and education, including a Ph.D. from the Massachusetts Institute of Technology (M.I.T).

RCA had elected its first woman, Mildred McAfee Horton in 1951. At that time she was President of Wellesley College. Previously she had had an outstanding career in the Navy, during World War II. She was the first woman commissioned a captain in the U.S. Navy and rose to be commander of the WVAVES . When Mrs. Horton retired from the RCA board in 1962, Mrs. Everett Case succeeded her as the lone woman director. After her retirement in 1972 it became my turn. Reviewing RCA Annual Reports of 1951 and thereafter, I am reminded of the heavy influence of Wilma Soss on board nominating committees. She was the founder and president of the Federation of Women Shareholders in American Business and regularly spoke up at the Annual Meetings of major corporations to lobby for female representation on their boards. In the early 70's, when I was attending annual meetings, her voice in the discussion period was loud and strong and often reported in the press. I do not recall a more influential voice in this cause at that time----although that voice was often called unwelcome or unattractive by corporate leaders. Many of us women probably owe our nominations as corporate directors to her public lobbying of companies and shareholders on our behalf. I regret not having more information to share here about the history and impact of her interventions.

Avon Products, a company dependent upon women as salespersons and as customers, was beginning to address their need to represent women at both Board and top management levels. They had, not yet, any women officers or board members. An

Executive Search firm "found" me for Avon Products, while Robert Sarnoff, then Chairman of RCA, heard of me through his work as a member of the board of Boy Scouts

of America. He approached me directly. Following my election to these two boards, I was approached by one or two other large corporations, but decided, under good advice of the board of Girl Scouts USA, that I should not commit to more than two major outside corporate responsibilities. After I left Girl Scouts, I was elected to the boards of two smaller companies: Loehmanns Inc. and the National Education Corporation. I resigned from NEC after a short period and lost my seat on the Loehmanns board when it was sold to AEA, an investment conglomerate. My term as a RCA director ended in 1986, when the company merged with General Electric. At the mandatory retirement age of 70, (in 1997) I retired from the Avon board, after 25 years.

My impression was that the corporate leaders who approached me were looking for a woman who had run an organization successfully, had a title that would appear appropriate in a nominating committee report and proxy statement and who would fit into the sociology of board formal and informal work. Given the shortage of women then in top corporate management positions, they (and other board nominating committees) had to turn to the non-profit world to find a woman with these characteristics. That I brought along credentials in science, technology and education, in addition to management experience, did not appear interesting to nominating committees at the time. In retrospect, I believe it should have been. Their focus may have been to add the "woman's point of view" to board deliberations, as Wilma Soss was demanding. But, in my case at least, what they were adding was a person who could and would bring different questions, skills and values to the board table. By including gender diversity, boards (inadvertently?) were including diversity in other values and experiences.

3. What was it like to be the only woman on a board?

For me, and for other women board members I knew, it was not a new experience to be the only woman present at a committee or business meeting. I had 25 years experience in being the only or the rare woman in class or at meetings. In science and mathematics classes as an undergraduate at Harvard, and as a graduate student at M.I.T., there were seldom more than one or two other women around. The same was also true in the laboratories at the Sloan-Kettering Institute and at Cornell Medical School where I spent my late 20's and early 30's as a researcher in cell biology. Even in education, although of course the cohort of teachers was largely female, males still predominated in positions as heads of schools, so we women school heads were usually in the minority at meetings.

The new experience was, rather, being the only one in the room whose full-time job was not finance, or law or business. And, usually, the only democrat! Where I felt different was in business background and, sometimes, in political values. Of course, I could understand a balance sheet or a profit-and-loss statement, as I had been responsible for about 13 years, for the management of a small and then a very large not-for-profit institution. But I could not touch the long experience with hundreds of P/L statements, balance sheets and audit reports of those with whom I shared the board table.

This minority position also made it virtually impossible to share in the gossip about other business leaders and companies. I learned plenty by listening but missed the advantage of seeing financial issues, acquisitions, and the nomination of new directors in the context of other corporate situations. Often boards are criticized for interlocking corporate relationships of their members. When confidences are not kept, from one boardroom to another, company business can be hurt. With ethical directors, however, experiences in one business situation can add entirely legal and appropriate value to board deliberations about other situations. While Avon was dealing with difficult challenges from outsiders who wished to acquire and then break up the company, individual and collective counsel and support of board members, particularly those who had experienced similar situations, added real value to management.

Despite all the areas in which I was "different", the men I was working with did show consistent personal and professional respect to me. Their accepting me as a peer was probably helped by scientific and management credentials that the men could respect. It would have been more difficult for them to treat me as a peer if I had held an inferior position in their professional world. In the early seventies, there was a veteran Avon director who could not help making remarks such as, "O Cecily, you and your feminist ideas." But I have few memories of such comments. Few men will speak badly to or about Girl Scouts or science! My behavior as a minority was also influenced by the responsibility I assumed I should carry for helping the older generation of men adjust to their increasingly co-ed workplace. I was determined to help them *enjoy and value* working with a woman, for the sake of all the women who would follow me. It was important to me that the men grew to like me, as I felt that helped the chances of more women being invited in. I believed that part of my job was to open the door wider for those that followed. Perhaps my living with three sons and a husband at home increased my confidence in working with men!

It has always been difficult for me to deal with questions about being the only woman at the board table. I have always believed that it should be taken for granted that anyone who is qualified to serve on a board, no matter how different in background and skin color, has the experience and the know-how necessary to function in a new professional situation. I expected people to feel that way about me, too. There was much adjustment to be made, however, on both sides. I do remember well my first evening dinner with the Avon Board in 1973. Clearly most men there had never had to share such a dinner with a middle-aged professional woman and mother, and I could feel a certain discomfort. I broke the ice, however, when after-dinner cigars were being passed around. I took one. My husband was a devoted cigar smoker and, in happy self-defense I had learned to smoke one properly. I knew how not to inhale—and really enjoyed the flavor! That I smoked a cigar with the boys became a press story and is now part of the annals of Avon. So often, small gestures and a sense of humor make the difference.

4. Was I able to make a difference?

When Avon settled for a director who was a manager of a non-profit girls and women's organization, they got, in addition, a woman who had studied the biology of skin. In the late 1950's I had presented a paper on the submicroscopic structure of skin to the Society of Cosmetic Chemists—as well to the Society of Investigative Dermatologists. I had received my Ph.D. in Physical Biology in 1950 (at the age of 23) in a department teaching new strategies for looking at biological tissues with sophisticated physical instruments, such as the electron microscope and x-ray diffraction. In those days, virtually everything we looked at with this new microscope was being seen for the first time. At the Memorial Center for Cancer Research, where I worked in the 50's, I became interested in skin, and published its first extensive electron microscopic study in 1958-59. My photos were in textbooks for many years. My point here is that by looking for someone different (i.e. female) for board service, this company got someone who also had other characteristics not shared by any other board members—i.e. a certain understanding of skin and biological processes and, thus, of the form and function of cosmetic products. Avon had hundreds of experienced research chemists and other scientists on its staff, and consulted with academic dermatologists and related scientists. Management did not need any more professional expertise in this area. But, at the board level, would it not provide the CEO some check and balance on technical decisions to have someone who can at least ask technically informed questions?

My sci-tech experience was also both unexpected and relevant to RCA. Through seeking a woman, RCA got someone who was experienced in one RCA technology and with some elementary understanding of their major product, electronics. Robert Hillier, then Director of the justly famous RCA Sarnoff Laboratory, had earned his Ph.D. in Toronto, Canada in 1946 with his design for an electron microscope. His design was then turned into the RCA electron microscope, an instrument I had been using. Dr. Hillier had also visited my Sloan-Kettering laboratory to try some techniques for biological specimens. Since RCA could hire all the electron microscope specialists they needed, they had no particular interest in my scientific background, and gave no indication of thinking it would have any value at the board level.

In this, I believe they were mistaken. The lack of scientific and technological literacy among board members became, in my judgement, a detriment to RCA's business. New products were explained and research budgets justified at board meetings. But, apart from my own comments, I can remember no questions about these products or these budgets that addressed technical issues subsequently critical to the future of the company. The prevailing attitude in most companies at that time was to leave the technical details to technical staff and let the Board focus on financial and legal issues. Management of technology was considered for technologists only. Indeed, this was the answer given to me in the late 70's when I asked the president of the Harvard Business School why there were no courses (beyond an elective) in management of technology at his school. Nor were there any required such courses at the MIT Sloan School of Business at that time. The only professorship in the management of technology at either school was a Sarnoff (endowed) professorship! Some up-and-coming companies of that time (notably Intel and Xerox) did believe and work differently. Their cutting-edge success was often credited to their superior management of innovation and technology.

Leadership of Research and Development at RCA welcomed opportunities to make product presentations to the board and to show board members around laboratories and manufacturing operations. Some spoke openly and responsibly with me about the company's need for top management and board involvement in their sci-tech issues. During board presentations on technical products, it was difficult for me, as only a generalist not a specialist in these fields, to be the only one to raise technical questions. For example, I can remember when we were shown a model for the first VCR. It was a large machine, as microprocessors were not yet incorporated. The staff person showing us the model explained carefully how the VCR could not become any smaller because of all the complex electronics inside. No director asked whether new emerging microprocessors might not facilitate a smaller instrument. RCA subsequently lost business in this technology. In defense of the quality of RCA work itself, I should mention that I still use that first VCR model and that it operates with finer resolution than current small, inexpensive models!

In the last year of RCA's independent operation, before the GE merger, a prime technical disappointment was the inability of the RCA Compact Disk to compete with other designs in the market place. The RCA design incorporated techniques of electron microscopy, the specialty of Dr. Hillier, their research director. It is tempting to speculate on whether management could have promoted alternative designs and whether objective informed questions from knowledgeable people outside the company, such as directors, could have helped reverse the laboratory's dependence on one strategy. Of course, it is not appropriate or wise for boards to micromanage operations. However, for a company like RCA, driven by research and development, more informed deliberation of R & D issues in the boardroom would have better served the shareholders-----and the nation's competitive position in electronic enterprises.

As an RCA director, I was also elected to the board of NBC. In the 70's these board meetings were wonderful. David Adams and Julian Goodman, the company's chairman and president, at that time, cared deeply about the news operations and initiated extensive presentations and discussion of news issues at every meeting. Both RCA and NBC were doing well financially and there was interest in expanding the budget for news operations, rather than in cutting news budgets, as today. Company leadership was committed to producing news for the sake of news rather than for entertainment and profit. We, the board, learned much about news and entertainment, as well as about company finances. And with a son then working as a television news reporter, I had another source of questions and answers. Questions from directors were encouraged. I had many opportunities to ask about issues close to my interests: children, education, and science. Later, I sought an opportunity to meet privately with Fred Silverman, then the Head of NBC's Entertainment Division, to ask his advice about enhancing public awareness of certain social issues (such as scientific and technological literacy). I remember his answer well, because it has been helpful to me in so many ways.

"Cecily, the best way to attract public attention to issues is to find a Prime Time star who cares about your issue and persuade her/him to influence the show's writer to include it in the script. " There is nothing better than having a prime source for advice!

At RCA and Avon, there was no difference between how the other directors and I were treated in committee assignments. I served on a number of RCA committees and, for many years, chaired the Corporate Responsibility Committee. This committee was responsible for reviewing and approving corporate contributions, as well as some related matters. My particular professional background was well used in this capacity. The staff person, Todd Reboul, in charge of this work kept his staff and the committee fully informed about educational issues and educational institutions to support decisions about allocation of RCA's contributions to colleges, schools, universities and student scholarships and fellowships. This included the matching gift plan for employees and directors. All of us serving on this committee became more informed through the background material Dr. Reboul gave us for each committee meeting. I recall this committee work as an outstanding example of functioning corporate social responsibility. Committee members and staff did their homework and were conscientious and informed in their judgements. The Board and the CEO supported our work and recommendations.

At Avon, I recall serving on the Audit Committee, the Compensation Committee and the Nominating Committee, chairing this committee for a while. Audit committee work included environmental audits. These were always particularly interesting to me and included matters about which I could sometimes provide particular experience. For Compensation Committee work, experience with such matters on other boards was helpful. Avon Board work was facilitated in a thoroughly responsible way through committees, enabling directors to make informed judgements on matters brought to committees.

In the early years at Avon, there were so few women in top management that consumer/ product/ female questions were needed and helpful. For example, I recall a presentation, at one of my first meetings, about opening Avon business in Japan. My query about how the Avon sales approach was being adapted to the sociology of women in Japan was considered a very valuable intervention! Also, in the 70's, I asked for a meeting with the CEO to talk about how Avon could adapt its strategies to the changing sociology of women in the U.S. At that time (1970's) they had not, and the then CEO was not impressed with my questions! Others in top management were thinking along the same lines, and were happy that my attempt at intervention supported their work. Apparently, I did see it as part of my role as a company director to identify a need and try to fill it by communicating to the head of the company.

I think the shareholders would have approved! In later years, with more women leading in management and a thoroughly competent marketing staff in hand, there was little need for such queries on women's issues. With all the female talent that Jim Preston (CEO) brought into his management team, it was only appropriate that comparable quality and quantity of female talent was also present in the boardroom. That I understood what creams could and could not do, and found manufacturing technologies fascinating certainly enriched my personal and professional growth, and led to some useful input. I believe this sci-tech literacy also came to be of some comfort and interest to staff and management, although, as at RCA, boardroom culture emphasized financial, not product issues.

5. What about the woman's point of view?

There certainly were times when I felt it relevant and important to represent "the woman's point of view". At NBC, these questions were related to television programming, and, at Avon, in relation to consumer products. In another context, with much different management than that directing the company now, I felt compelled to challenge some recruitment material that called on women to join Avon's sales force "to provide good things for you and your family". I suggested that a more contemporary motivation would be to provide personal and professional development for oneself as well as things for one's family. This was considered a new thought then, but is the central theme of Avon's recruitment message now.

For the last ten years, Avon has been my only board responsibility, so I do not feel qualified to comment upon needs for " a woman's point of view" on other boards now. Through the leadership of James Preston as CEO, Avon has developed a deeply "co-ed" company. Through its complement of women among the company's officers and top earners, and through management policies and attitudes throughout the company, the company now reflects the needs and interests of women employees as well as consumers. And, I know that it is not a coincidence that Avon's performance has improved significantly during this period. There are now outstanding female role models and mentors for all staff members throughout this company now, together with an evident commitment to diversity. That six of the current thirteen directors are now women reinforces this commitment. Women directors may well have served current top management women as role models and mentors. I know many of us have become good friends.

So many women in their forties and early fifties now hold leadership business positions that the candidate pool for women directors is entirely different from when I was chosen. The women on the Avon board now are all presidents of for-profit enterprises. All are successful businesswomen who would compete with men in qualification in any line-up. Each of the four women members of the board when I retired had a different background. I am confident that none of us believe that we are representing only the "woman's point of view". Each of us grew up in a different profession but, as is true for all professional women, we do have a special bonding through our shared experiences— as wives, mothers, daughters, aunts, housekeepers, clothes shoppers and professional minorities. Rather than representing women, I believe we feel we are representing women *being in power*. During my time, each one of us contributed primarily from our personal professional background rather than from a gender identity. The one with top-level corporate management experience contributed outstanding business perspectives. The one with deep knowledge of the Latin American market contributed from this experience, so relevant to Avon's market. The president of a pre-eminent magazine contributed her journalistic and public relations perspective plus her direct professional knowledge of many industries and businesses. Another provided perspectives from business leadership in the Afro-American community. In addition to some perspectives I have mentioned, I was able to also speak from my long history with Avon, having worked with several CEO's. At my retirement dinner, Jim Preston gave me credit, also, for contributing my social conscience. That was rewarding to hear. I hope it was true.

6. How can I get on a board?

I have been asked this question often by both men and women, and usually find it embarrassing to answer. For the reasons reviewed here, I still believe that any candidate for a corporate board position must hold a position of professional responsibility and status that is comparable to that of other members of the board. I start with the assumption that women selected for corporate directorships are respected and accomplished professionals. Since the overriding responsibility of a director is to vote on hiring or firing the CEO, personal and professional judgement and experience in accountability, is the most relevant experience. As long as this defines board function, chief executives, chief operating officers of profit or non-profits or senior partners in partnerships are the most appropriate candidates. To be effective in today's climate for board operations, there are few substitutes for experience in being a good boss.

Another valuable qualification is experience in how to behave in committee meetings. I have enjoyed watching the style of some eminent business leaders. My favorite was the expert financier who would graciously ask, after a complex finance report, "Please refresh my memory. Did you say...?" and then he would pick up on some financial point in a way that immediately revealed the weakness inherent in a presentation, or the point on which he would recommend more analysis, and a reconsideration of action. And another effective director who would shift position, lean back in his chair (I sat next to him and could tell when this was coming!), make some light remark and then zero in with a suggestion that would go to the heart of the matter under discussion. I did not have such consummate committee skills, but I had a lot of experience in analyzing situations in ways that gave me a framework on which to build my recommendations. I had worked long enough with men to also be able to fit my way of thinking and acting into their style of conference Questions and Answers (Q & A). In the professional world of that time, I believed this essential for effective participation.

Significant groups of people and organizations have come together and grown over the past generation to work on increasing the numbers of women on corporate boards. Services are provided, such as building files of eligible and interested women and providing some training in finances. Women interested in corporate board nominations are urged to expand and enrich their network of professional relationships through professional meetings and not-for-profit board work and social contacts. Such advice is wonderful for building any career, and for enlisting business talent for not-for-profit boards. "Who you know" helps define any career path.

I urge, however, that ambition for board service be coupled with informed and aggressive interest in improving board function---profit and not-for-profit. They and their prospective companies will move ahead if board candidates inform themselves of current board practices, both good and bad. I hope they will study the recent history of effective and ineffective boards, and use this information to advocate best practices, from within and without the boardroom. What a group of comprehensively informed corporate directors this would bring us! What a giant step this would be toward demonstrating, for all time, that increasing the quantity of women on boards can increase the quality of boards!

7. How will increasing the diversity of board members improve the form and function of boards?

There are abundant legal, financial, international, and political reasons to improve the form and function of boards of trustees and corporate directors. Media business reports remind us daily of how imprudent board actions can damage and even destroy institutions, while prudent boards can strengthen and even save them. The following comments will focus only on issues that relate to the subject of this essay: moving board membership from a homogeneous population of business leaders to a diverse population of women and men leaders skilled and experienced in non-corporate as well as corporate work.

How can diversity assist board function? The tales I have told of my experiences makes clear that *the culture* of the boardroom is a defining issue. The "culture" of meetings influences which questions are asked, and which ones are not. Looking back on my experiences as a corporate director and as a non-profit trustee, I am sad to remember important questions that I was qualified to ask but did not, and questions others were qualified to ask, but did not. For example, when the companies I knew were caught up in acquisition fever, there was a resounding silence from board members who might have alerted management to pitfalls ahead. Boardroom culture was a determinant of my reticence, and also of others, I believe.

The culture of both RCA and Avon boards was to talk about and question *corporate performance,* seldom *corporate product.* Quality of product influences quality of performance, as Wall Street analysts know so well, but these boards concentrated mostly on performance. I found the relative neglect of product issues in board level discussions puzzling. Now I wonder whether the cause was in the homogeneity of most board members background: finance and management, not product development and/or not marketing. And when directors did raise product questions, they were not as searching as their financial questions. In effect, the culture of the finance-oriented boards did not encourage my product-related questions. Another dimension of culture was born of the professional and social homogeneity of board members. There were unwritten rules about what was to be mentioned at a meeting, and what was not. Some rules related to minutes and legal issues. Others were culture. The two much smaller companies for which I was briefly a director, had less complicated finances and spent more time in board general conversation about product. But, in these cases, finances should have been a greater focus! The culture of these boards did not include rigorous financial analysis---to the detriment of shareholders.

If the culture of boardroom work influences what questions are asked, and how they are answered, then changing some board cultures may be necessary to improve their function. The initial motivation for adding women to boards was structural—creating a diverse board---but the beneficial outcomes are functional. Perhaps compositions of board should be designed by starting first with the culture that is desired. In my experience, the Avon Nominating Committee did just this. It targeted its search for candidates when the committee decided that more international, more marketing or more ethnic representation was needed. Diversity can improve boards by diversifying the culture, adding values and discourse that better reflect diverse consumers and shareholders.   As a structural biologist, I am always reminded that *form follows function!*

Lately I have been working with practitioners and researchers concerned about the recruitment and retention of talented and successful women scientists and engineers. We have found[1] that work and workplace cultures are defining factors in women's choices of where to work and what to work on. Research is revealing significant differences between established male styles of professional discourse, conduct and organization and styles women may prefer or be more adept in. Such observations are certainly applicable to business, the law, and--- to corporate boardrooms. Gender and ethnic diversity can now be found in all workplaces, from boardrooms to assembly lines. But, particularly at high levels in the hierarchy, this workplace is usually still governed by attitudes, rewards and evaluative criteria designed for a formerly homogenous male population. When the attitudes and practices anyone finds in the workplace are discongruent with those one believes in or enjoys, the worker, the work and the workplace suffer. That men can suffer such discordant situations as much as women is highlighted by recent news of graduate student suicides at Harvard University[2].

To ensure the productive participation of people of diverse cultural (considering gender as a culture) backgrounds in the practice of science and engineering, we have learned that the evaluative criteria, rewards and incentives, and styles and behavior governing the workplace must reflect and reward diversity. Rather than assuming that women and "others" must adapt to established work environments, we are now suggesting that policies and practices that govern laboratories and offices, backrooms and boardrooms, reflect the values of women and all the other diverse talent in these workplaces.   And,   here,   we   could   add,   shareholders.

---

[2] "After suicide, Harvard alters policies on graduate students", New York Times, p.20, October 21, 1998

This is today's thinking. But twenty-five years ago I was of the generation of women that were, mostly, just happy to be doing what the boys were doing. I was happy and proud to be at an Avon, RCA and NBC board meeting, I considered that part of my job was to adapt to the board's established ways of speaking and doing. A generation ago, I simply felt fortunate to have the opportunity to learn about and contribute to a sector of our society in which I had no experience. If I was 45 years old now and taking on new responsibilities as a corporate director, I would be less committed to fitting into existing styles, and more secure in helping boards change styles to better serve the company.

Another secondary benefit of diversifying board membership is to increase understanding and interaction between business, academe and government. Learning about corporate enterprises has greatly broadened my vision and my knowledge base, and, thereby, vastly improved my work in the not-for-profit sector. These wider horizons of experience have certainly made me a more informed professor and manager. Until 1973, my life's experience had been almost entirely academic. My father was an academic, with several generations of physicians preceding his work as a chemistry professor, researcher and, later, leader in science policy. I doubt that I ever met a businessperson in my home, let alone an engineer! The elite schools and colleges I attended taught about ideas: about literature, history, language, science and mathematics in relation mostly to ideas, not action. The actions we learned about in history or in Latin were about wars—not about technologies or trade or marketplaces. After my first experience working in Washington D.C., coupled with my corporate board meetings, I wrote an article announcing that there was a big world out there interested not so much in ideas as in strategies. Why, I asked then, do we not include more talk about strategies and strategic thinking in our school and college curriculum? Through the companies I served as a Director, I learned of real people, real ideas and real strategies in business enterprises. I learned how interesting and valuable the work could be and of all the fine people so involved. From this for-profit experience I was able to develop recommendations for not-for-profit management enterprises[3].

My scientific-technical background drew me to concern about the management and development of technology, and the application of these ideas to education. In the late 70's and early 80's I was also serving as a Member of the MIT Corporation, and thus had the opportunity to discuss these issues with many CEO's' of sci-tech companies, who also served as MIT Corporation Members. My eldest son was also starting at McKinsey & Co, and getting involved with comparable issues at a "hands on" level. And my late husband shared these interests through his presidency of Research Corporation; a non-profit organization devoted to promoting the advancement of science through assisting scientists with technology transfer. The coincidence of all these connections helped me promote technology education through writing[4] and national and state education commissions for which I was then responsible.

---

[3] "Better Profit from Non-Profits", Cecily Cannan Selby, Harvard Business Review, Sept/Oct 1978
[4] "Technology: From Myths to Realities, Cecily Cannan Selby, Phi Delta Kappan, May 1993, 684-689

Would it not be valuable to our society to provide more opportunities for academics like me to learn, first-hand, of other ways of work and organization? Experience in government enterprises was available to me through jobs and committees in Washington D.C., and Albany, N.Y. But, absent was my opportunities to serve as a corporate director, I would have remained critically ignorant of how, why and with whom business enterprises work. With two sons and one daughter-in-law now importantly involved in finance and management, I would be far less able to communicate with them!

Finally, there is the question of political diversity. Will diversification of board membership have an impact on the political make-up of this leadership? An analysis of the past, current and future political composition of boards would be illuminating! I can recall recognizing only one or two other democrats among the directors I worked with in four boardrooms. Democrats may be even less well represented on corporate boards than women or minorities! Should this be so? Does such a situation provide either the corporate world or shareholders the breadth of judgment they need and deserve? From my side, exposure to discussion and conversation with so many leading and responsible republicans enriched and informed my political thinking. It certainly made me a more informed voter and citizen. I know it enriched my teaching, in increasing my understanding of other points of view.

The pool of women and minorities now qualified for corporate board membership through their business credentials must now be large enough to make all corporate boards "co-ed". I dearly hope that those women who are now "in the club" of business leadership will not allow boards to fall back onto old habits of restricting board memberships to people in this club. I hope all corporate leaders will consider helping the form and function of boards evolve to include diverse outlooks and questions, the better to guard corporate interests. As biology informs us, the organism that adapts internally to external change, is the organism that survives.

MAKING BOARDS WORK

Recruiting for Balance, Competence and Results

DAVID S.R. LEIGHTON
Professor Emeritus
Ivey School of Business
University of Western Ontario
London, Ontario

1.   Introduction

One of the more notable features of recent business history has been the spotlight placed on the governance of our corporations. There has been a virtual explosion of conferences and writing on the subject, of the committees and commissions publishing best practice guidelines, of legal actions against delinquent boards and directors, and calls for increased regulation by stock exchanges and securities commissions.

The trend has been international in scope, and annual statistical studies, backed by personal observation, have reflected considerable improvement as boards have become smaller in size, more independent, better organized and better managed. Yet at the same time they have been curiously resistant to change in a number of aspects, notably in their diversity (or, more correctly, lack thereof). A particular example of the lack of diversity is the relative absence and glacial pace of change in the number of women on U.S. and Canadian corporate boards of directors.

Recent statistics show that only six per cent of the directors of Canada's 300 largest corporations are women. The equivalent number among the largest U.S. companies is 11 percent, dropping to eight percent for mid-cap companies (Table 1), which is probably a better comparator with the 300 largest Canadian companies. Over half of Canada's largest companies have no women directors at all! This in the face of the fact that between one-third and one-half of graduating M.B.A.s today are women.

Why? What are the causes of this anomaly? A number of commentators have studied this situation, and an equal number of diagnoses have been suggested, ranging from overt and covert discrimination, to lack of qualified women, to a lack of aggressiveness on the part of women.

R.J. Burke and M.C. Mattis (eds.), Women on Corporate Boards of Directors, 253-261.
© 2000 *Kluwer Academic Publishers. Printed in the Netherlands.*

TABLE 1

Structural Characteristics of Canadian and U.S. Boards of Directors

	Canada (n=303)	United States (n=1500)
Average Size	11	11.7a 9.8b 8.6c
Average Age	59	59-60
% with Nominating Committee	31	80a 66b 50c
% with at least 1 female director	46	87.4a 58.4b 38.2c
% with 2 or more female directors	15	36a 18b 8c
% with 3 or more female directors	3	5a 4b 1c
Overall % female directors	6	11.1a 8.1b 5.5c

a.   Standard and Poor's 500 large capitalization
b.   "   " 400 mid-capitalization
c.   "   " 600 small capitalization

While there may be elements of these factors in individual cases, research and first hand observation by my colleague, Donald Thain, and myself have led me to two conclusions:

The slow rate of acceptance of women as directors is largely due to demographic factors, and will change rapidly as the female cohort with business experience ages;

The problem has been aggravated by the selection process followed by most boards, and this in turn has been rooted in a board culture that has led them to stubbornly resist pressures for change.

2.   **The Demographic Factor**

The participation of women in management has been a relatively recent phenomenon. When I did my M.B.A. at Harvard in the years 1951 to 1953, there were no women in a class of approximately 600 men, a few hardy females were banished to an offshoot, non-degree program at Radcliffe College taught in part by Harvard professors. (Incidentally, there were almost no Blacks or Hispanics in that all-male group either). During the 1950's and 1960s, when I was teaching in Canada, there was seldom a woman in my M.B.A. classes, and the same was true of numerous M.B.A. programs that began to sprout up at universities all over North America. By 1974, when I returned to teach at Harvard, about one quarter of my M.B.A. class was female.

Women and most minority groups did not participate in business schools in significant numbers until the 1970's, and the full tide did not appear until the last two decades. The history of women in management, and indeed in the related professions of law and accountancy, is really less than 20 years old. Only now are these pioneers, now approaching 50, beginning to reach the heights of their professions.

The significance of this fact becomes apparent when we look at the age distribution of corporate directors in Canada and the U.S. today. The average age of directors in both countries is 59. The average rises in the larger companies; in Canada's largest companies, (those with assets over $5 billion), 56% of directors are over 60, and another one-third are aged 51 to 60. A similar pattern is evident in the U.S. and there has been relatively little change in this picture during the years for which there are statistics.

This age pattern may be due in part to the nature of the self-perpetuating selection process of directors, but it is hard to avoid the conclusion that age and experience are considered to be critical qualifications for being a corporate director, and this makes some sense when one considers what directors do, or are supposed to do. The job is no sinecure: to be done well, it requires a high level of financial literacy, only part of which comes from the textbook. It requires judgement of people, a skill enhanced by years of observation and interaction in a business setting. It requires time, commitment and reflection, features more often found towards the end of a career, and it requires the ability to think broadly and strategically, and not to micro-manage. In short, a good director must exhibit wisdom built on business and life experience. While the correlation of these qualities with age is far from perfect, it is not surprising that they should be found more frequently in older individuals.

What this suggests is that there is still a relatively small core of women who are qualified to be directors, and that the demographic wave has yet to hit the directorial world.

The revolution represented by women in management is still working its way through the system, and if my diagnosis is correct, it will result in rapid change in the next decade as the women M.B.A.s of the 1970s and especially of the 1980s match or exceed their male competitors in the qualities required for directorships. Competence will, eventually, prevail and the proportion of women directors in both Canada and the U.S. should show substantial growth in the years to come.

While I believe this is true, it must be conceded by any knowledgeable observer that the selection process for directors, as currently practiced, is strongly stacked against women and, indeed, others who are outside today's main stream of business ownership and management. Although director selection has become more professional in recent years, mainly in the larger public companies, the process remains largely informal, unplanned, and lacking in rigor. Worse, it results in reinforcing and perpetuating the "closed shop" character of boards that has been the main target of criticism by qualified outside observers. Homogeneity begets more homogeneity. This too must change.

3.   **How are Directo:s Chosen? The "Ideal" Model.**

In response to the growing discussion about corporate governance, a small number of boards now review and replenish themselves by creating a committee of existing directors called a Corporate Governance or Nominating Committee. Ideally, these committees consist entirely of "outside" directors, so as to ensure the independence of the director nominating process; most of the corporate guidelines that have been published in various countries in recent years, including in Canada by the Toronto Stock Exchange (Dey) Committee and in the U.S. by the Business Round Table, among others, have recommended this type of structure to implement the process of director selection.

Under this system, the committee develops a set of specifications for new director candidates, preferably part of a long-range plan for board composition that is built in large part on an analysis of the present board structure, and the structure best suited for the future based on the company's strategic plan. A list of candidates meeting these specifications is then developed, often using the services of a professional search firm which works with the committee in sounding out and evaluating the candidates and making a selection. The candidate's name is then placed on a nomination list of directors for approval at the next Annual Meeting of Shareholders, where it is almost always routinely approved.

The board chairman then is given responsibility for designing and implementing a program for briefing or indoctrinating the new director, introducing him (seldom her) to the board and management, and the process continues. There may or may not be periodic evaluation of the individual directors' performance, and occasionally a director's name may be left off the nominating list, either for reasons health or poor performance. But essentially, given reasonable attendance and performance, the director has a tenured job until he or she reaches the mandatory retirement age, if there is one.

The above represents a very idealized model of how directors are selected and appointed (or "elected", as the fiction has it). The process is controlled by independent (i.e. outside) directors and is designed to result in a board with maximum independence and sufficiently diversified composition to provide strategic direction and oversight on behalf of the shareholders. The fact is that it seldom works out this way.

4.   **How are Directors Chosen? The Real World**.

Some years ago, when I was a member of the board of a major company in the hospitality industry, I was asked to head a committee of the board to develop a plan for selecting board members. After a number of sessions, the committee came up with a long-range plan which identified the number of vacancies that would occur over a five year period, developed an ideal future model of desired board composition, and a set of specifications for director candidates as each vacancy occurred. The plan was taken to the full board and approved; the committee was given the responsibility for implementing the plan.

About a year later, when the first three vacancies occurred due to several board retirements, the committee met to begin considering the nomination of new director candidates. After a brief introductory discussion, the son of the controlling shareholder (who was one of those retiring) put forward the names of three individuals he had met through his membership in the Young Presidents Organization and informed the committee that he had already asked the three individuals involved to serve. He stated that he felt it was his prerogative as controlling shareholder to appoint board members.

I objected strenuously to this, pointing out that the board had approved an entirely different procedure. One thing led to another, and the next annual meeting my name was not on the list of those put forward by the company for re-election. So much for corporate governance!

The reality is that the independence of directors in any absolute sense is a myth. The moment an outsider is appointed to a board and accepts his or her first director's fee, a director becomes part of a social group, subject to a host of pressures, obligations, rewards and liabilities, many of them subtle and unstated. "Independence" becomes a relative concept, to be used sparingly by the director depending on a number of factors, most notably the locus of power in the organization.

In the widely-held corporation, the predominant pattern among the Fortune 500 in the U.S., the locus of power has rested in management, due in part to the failure of many institutional shareholders to exercise their voting rights, coupled with the wide diffusion of shareholders and relative impotence of individual shareholders. The result in many cases has been a vicious circle; boards have had little power, and the selection process has been controlled by management, who have little incentive to select strong and independent individuals as directors. By the same token, such strong and independent individuals have had little incentive to serve on weak and ineffectual boards.

In companies where there is a majority shareholder, or a shareholder effectively controlling the company (the dominant Canadian pattern), no director is going to be elected without the approval of the controlling shareholder. There is at least an effective veto over the process, whether or not the controlling shareholder is part of the nominating committee. The same is true in companies where the Chairman of the Board is also the Chief Executive Officer. In such cases, the Chairman/C.E.O. must be part of the selection process. It would be an unusually brave (or foolish) major shareholder or Chairman/C.E.O. who agreed to the appointment of a director who has different values, and is likely to be a disturbing influence by challenging the owner or management. The result is a process that results in the appointment of a director who is usually "one of us."

As their shareholdings have increased, and with growing pressure on them for performance, many institutional shareholders have become more active in exercising their shareholders rights. Indeed, a number of institutions have become quite vocal in insisting that they have the right to elect or designate a number of directors roughly in proportion to their holdings of the company's shares - that is, if the institution holds 20 percent of the shares, it may seek roughly 20 percent representation on the board.

With all these complications, it is small wonder that the board selection process deviates significantly from the model. It is much easier and hassle-free to operate on an ad hoc process built on an old boys' network, where the board has at most a kind of veto over candidates put forward by the chairman or major shareholder. Names submitted for board approval usually represent an individual who is a friend or close acquaintance of the chairman or major shareholder, someone who will not "rock the boat". One of the unwritten rules governing this process is that an individual has to be invited to join a board.

Under these circumstances, it takes a bold and secure director or search firm to put forward the name of a woman, a labor sympathizer, socialist, environmentalist or other outspoken advocate to any board selection committee, and if someone is suggested from "outside the box", that name usually just disappears in the process and the sponsoring director is made to feel he or she is a disturbing influence, not one of the team, for making such an outlandish suggestion.

5.   Does Diversity Matter?

Studies of the composition of Canadian corporate boards demonstrate clearly the result: the preponderance of large company directors are white, male, Anglo-Saxon businessmen, 55 and over, married, wealthy, university educated, politically conservative, belonging to the same clubs, and participate in the same sports (notably golf). In Canada, most directors come from four centers; Toronto, Montreal, Vancouver and Calgary. They have limited experience with other countries, mainly as tourists or on business trips, where they travel first class, stay in five star hotels, and eat at the finest restaurants. The corporate director universe in Canada is relatively small, so that most directors know each other, either personally or by reputation. It is a comfortable pew!

This is not, as conspiracy theorists might suggest, some sort of male plot to deny women or other members of society their rightful participation in this key element in governing our corporations. Most leading businessmen would be surprised to think they might be systematically excluding worthwhile candidates from corporate boards, and would, upon reflection, likely reject vigorously the notion that the existing order might have serious flaws. Viewed pragmatically, it seems to work more or less satisfactorily, there is little pressure for change, it "ain't broke", and so they just don't think about it.

Directors have serious and demanding responsibilities, and liabilities for failing to perform. Boards are not intended to be democracies, reflecting the makeup of the society in which they operate. If corporate performance is at least in significant measure dependent on board performance, directorship is an important job, requiring a high degree of training, skill, judgement, commitment and intelligence. Possession of these qualities is, or should be, the sine qua non of every director.

Moreover, a certain amount of homogeneity of backgrounds on a board is not necessarily a bad thing. Homogeneity does not preclude a board from being effective; there can be enough independent free thinkers among today's directorship social group that it is quite possible to put together a dynamic and challenging board without consciously looking for social diversity. Properly led, homogeneity on the board can eliminate a great deal of painful and fractious discussion at meetings, speeding and simplifying the process of working together towards a consensus. Diversity is no guarantee of better performance. So director searches tend to lead, thus far at least, into the considerably larger and more accessible pool of known executives.

The fact remains that competence as a director is not the exclusive preserve of this group. In my experience, boards that can rise above the social and cultural pressures of groups made up of "people like us" are the exception, not the rule. Group pressures tend often to result in a "group think" mentality, where critical assumptions are not challenged or examined and where sensitivity to the consequences of board decisions (for example on communities or employees) is lacking. These blind spots in board thinking can and do have serious, indeed sometimes fatal, consequences. This is particularly true when major investment decisions are made in foreign countries without an adequate understanding of the politics or culture of the recipient country. The same is true when decisions are made to diversify into fields in which the board and management have little experience or expertise.

John H. Bryan, Chairman and C.E.O. of Sara Lee Corp., wrote on *Allegiance to a Diverse Board* (Directors & Boards, Spring, 1995:

"It is clear to me that a group of generally older, white male executives of the same nationality- men who have usually reached the same status in various companies- represents a dangerously narrow profile of exposure for a board in a world changing as rapidly and dramatically as ours is today. It is a world demanding aggressively creative approaches to business, and it is through diversity that much of that creativity can be found. Diversity is a major source, if not an imperative, for creativity in the future."

6.   **The Road Ahead**

There is considerable evidence to suggest that diversity on boards is a matter of sound corporate strategy, not a bow to political correctness. This is not, however, fully appreciated as yet, and the performance of boards in developing greater diversity has lagged badly, a dangerous situation.

To the extent that the relatively low participation of women on Canadian and U.S. Boards of directors is a consequence of demographic factors that are changing, the percentage of women directors should begin to increase in the next decade, and should be at significant levels by the years following 2010. By then, there should be a large pool of highly qualified women, aged mainly 50-60, with substantial business experience and expertise, and with sufficient seniority that they can dedicate the time required to be an effective director.

The acceptance of women as directors will not happen smoothly and to the full extent warranted by the availability of qualified candidates unless and until changes are made to the process of managing boards, particularly in the identification and selection of prospective directors. In this respect, the prospects.are less sanguine. The board selection process now in widespread use is deeply rooted in a board culture that is highly resistant to change. The resistance is at least as much unconscious as it is conscious, which makes it even more difficult to overcome. The fact of its existence (ie. resistance to change) must first be identified, acknowledged, and the need for change accepted before any real movement can be expected from existing boards. This will be slow, but should accelerate as the larger, high profile boards appoint more women. And this, in turn, will happen as research, articles, papers, and conferences on governance address the issue and receive publicity in the business press.

Some will advocate affirmative action mandated by governments, regulatory bodies, securities commissions, and stock exchanges. This, in my view, would be a step backward. It would seriously underestimate the issues of director qualifications and the necessity for effective teamwork on the part of corporate boards. Internally-generated change, while often frustratingly slow, is infinitely to be preferred to externally-mandated change. While many corporate leaders may still be oblivious to the issue, one should not conclude that they lack either intelligence or conscience; once aware and convinced, they will move. Indeed, it will be seen as a bad mark against the business not to move, and the herd instinct will take over.

The trick is to heighten awareness of the issue among business leaders and institutional shareholders, something best accomplished by presenting solidly-researched facts, examples and making available names of qualified women candidates, i.e. to help make the selection process easy. In some cases this might include making nominations at Annual Shareholder meetings. Working with placement firms to make sure that qualified candidate lists include a strong female representation offers a real opportunity, as such firms are increasingly being called upon to assist in the selection process, and maintaining strong data bases of prospective candidates is their life blood.

"There is no secret formula for the 'optimum' diversity of membership in a board of directors, whether diversity means including people with a range of finance, marketing, law, and government experience, or including women and minorities. The goal is directors who are the best qualified, by virtue of knowledge and temperament, to provide the overall guidance and monitoring to keep management responsive to change." (Robert A.G. Monks, *Shareholders and Director Selection*, Directors & Boards, Spring, 1995, p.11.)

References

Making Boards Work: What Directors Must Do To Make Canadian Boards Effective, D.S.R. Leighton and D.H. Thain, (McGraw-Hill Ryerson, Toronto, 1997), ch 13. The authors develop a six-factor model of effective boards; one factor is board selection and   training, dealt with in chapter 13.

There are a number of sources of statistical information on boards in Canada and the United States. Data in Table 1 are taken from *Corporate Board Governance and Director Compensation in Canada: A Review of 1997*, Patrick O'Callaghan & Associates/Caldwell Partners Amrop International; and *1997-98 Board Practices Survey: The Structure and Compensation of Boards of Directors at S & P 1500 Companies,* Russell Reynolds Associates/the Investor Responsibility Research Center, March, 1998. Spencer Stuart, Korn Ferry and the Conference Board of Canada also publish regular statistical analyses of Canadian and U.S. boards.

The National Center for Management Research and Development, Ivey Business School, University of Western Ontario, London, Ontario has for a number of years sponsored research on Women in Management, and has published the *Women in Management Newsletter* containing a wide range of articles, including several on the subject of women on boards. See particularly *Women on Corporate Boards of Directors: A Needed Resource,* by Ronald J. Burke; and *How can Women Access Boards?* By D.S.R. Leighton, Nov-Dec. 1993. The Center has also published demographic studies of Canadian directors.

The Spring, 1995 issue of *Directors and Boards* was dedicated to *The Power of Diversity on the Board,* and included a number of excellent articles on the topic, including the two which have been quoted.

CATALYST CORPORATE BOARD PLACEMENT:
NEW SEATS AT THE TABLE

MERLE POLLAK
Catalyst
120 Wall Street, Fifth Floor
New York, New York 10005, USA

1. Overview

To serve as a director on the board of a leading American corporation is to hold a position of exceptional power and influence. Indeed, the decisions made in corporate boardrooms affect the lives of millions of employees and consumers as well as the performance and policies of other corporations, the ebb and flow of economic activity, the dealings of the global marketplace and international business strategies. Yet, up to now, the players at the highest level of corporate governance have been and are for the most part just one segment of the population - a homogeneous group of men, many of whom are active or retired chief executive officers.

Women on boards disrupt "business as usual". It is a disturbance that can be good for both women and for the bottom line as new ideas, new points of view, surface and are evaluated. Women on boards also send a message to employees in the company that there is a commitment to women. For the female board member it is an unparalleled learning experience and admission to a network of overlapping circles of access rarely equaled in potential.

The number of women on corporate boards has been steadily increasing over the last twenty years. Yet clearly much more remains to be done to expand the presence of women in the boardroom. Catalyst knows this because we know women represent at least half of the talent pool for leadership positions in our country. We know this because we know board diversity makes business sense. By drawing on the experience of women, decisions that affect the increasingly diverse populations of shareholders, employees, consumers, and other corporate stakeholders will be better-and more profitable-decisions.

In order for change to occur at a faster pace, companies need to be educated to the fact that a number of talented women hold significant titles below CEO and COO in U.S. corporations of various sizes. And that there is an ever-growing number of executive and senior vice presidents, presidents of major divisions and CEO's of smaller companies who

R.J. Burke and M.C. Mattis (eds.), Women on Corporate Boards of Directors, 263-269.
© 2000 *Kluwer Academic Publishers. Printed in the Netherlands.*

are women. A fact is that inside directors of corporate boards, most of whom are men, as well as other male directors, hold titles below that of CEO or COO. The CEO and his nominating committee must keep this in mind when a decision is made to recruit new members who are female.

How does a company achieve diversity on its board? Approximately half of the CEOs surveyed in one Catalyst study agreed that female candidates are "difficult to identify." This was the third most often cited reason by CEOs for the low representation of women on corporate boards. With this in mind, it makes sense to look outside of the board, and beyond personal contacts, letting an objective and experienced third party like Catalyst Corporate Board Placement do the leg work. Armed with a vast database of qualified, high-level women, CBP can put together a slate of candidates that are tailor- made to meet the needs of a company board.

2. Who We Are

Catalyst Corporate Board Placement, CBP, has been helping corporate chairmen and chief executives identify female candidates for their boards of directors for over twenty years. Catalyst, the nonprofit research and advisory organization that works with business to advance women, has as its dual mission the enabling of women to achieve their full professional potential and helping employers capitalize on women's talents and abilities. A pragmatic and solutions-oriented approach has earned the confidence of business leaders who count on Catalyst to address women's workplace issues and develop cost-effective responses. These leaders of corporate America who help support Catalyst understand the bottom-line business motivation for tapping women's talents.

Corporate Board Placement (originally Corporate Board Service), was first established at the request of corporate leaders. The earliest Corporate Board Placement searches were more informal. Many were obtained by word of mouth. CEOs knew that Catalyst's extensive research on women in business put us in contact with highly qualified women on a daily basis. They called Felice Schwartz, Catalyst's founder, to ask about women who might be good board candidates. Felice was the contact between Catalyst and the company or CEO and was always directly engaged with each search. Recognizing that Catalyst's unique and extensive knowledge base of high-level women should be put to best use, Felice worked this into the organization. CBP evolved, along with research, advisory services, the Catalyst Award and public education, as one of five ways in which Catalyst pursues its mission. It is one of Catalyst's most tangible methods of making change in corporate America.

3. What We Do

Corporate Board Placement is now retained by corporations ranging from those long established Fortune 50 to smaller companies, to find top-notch women for what is the highest echelon of corporate governance. It is the other side of the glass ceiling. Among our clients are organizations in such industries as consumer products, finance, health care, insurance, manufacturing, mutual funds, petroleum, retail, technology, telecommunications, transportation and utilities.

CBP is unique in that it engages in searches only for women and exclusively for board members. Unlike larger search firms performing searches for male board members and for executives of corporations, CBP can focus on those women across the country who are eligible and available for service on corporate boards. There are other ways in which CBP offers special advantages:

- Because Catalyst Corporate Placement has been in existence since the 1970's it has the experience of having helped hundreds of companies place talented women on their boards.

- Catalyst brings to the table the strength of our mission which gives us credibility.

- Through our research, we understand what it takes for women to advance in business and on to boards. And through our links with corporate members, we have direct insight into what corporate governance issues they face in the constantly evolving business environment of today.

- Because of Catalyst research into various companies and industries, CBP has a wide-angle lens perspective on where women fit into the boardroom portrait.

- Because it is part of Catalyst, there is special access to the best, brightest, and most diverse women in business. We learn of them from members of Catalyst as well as from our board members, from executives we meet through our advisory services, and from women themselves who know of Catalyst and want to be considered as board candidates.

- A vital synergy between the various arms of Catalyst and CBP enables us to develop close working relationships with high-level women. They tell us when they are ready for another board, when they are not taking on any more boards, and what types of boards they want to be on. This enables us to make sure they are available and interested in a board before we present them to a company.

- With more than 2500 high-level women, CBP has the only women-only director-ready database in America.

- Because of our concentration on women and corporate boards, CBP is able to deliver a slate of potential women in less than two months.

4. How We Do It

Once CBP is retained and a contract is signed, we begin by learning as much as possible about the company and its board. In order to better understand the profile of who they might want, we need to know the current board makeup. We need to learn about the future of the company, who the company's competition is, and when the board aims to fill a board seat or, in some situations, to create a new one. We also want to know which industries might provide a perspective that current board members do not have and what professional functions might add depth to the board. The more CBP knows up front, the happier the client will be with the slate of potential candidates.

An integral part of the discussion is, of course, learning just what qualifications the board is seeking in a potential candidate. This, fortunately, has been changing to some extent.

CEOs and nominating committees have begun to reach beyond the short list of male CEOs - some because they have to, and some because they want to. In either case, there is some willingness to expand the definition of "top level" to include executive and senior vice presidents, division presidents, chief financial officers, entrepreneurs, and other candidates with strong managerial and operational skills. This development is encouraging.

5. What Corporations Look For

- People in line management positions who have profit and loss responsibility.

- The CEO is looking for people who understand the problems he faces every day.

- Experience in marketing, sales and distribution.

- International experience. Even if a company doesn't sell its products abroad, it is safe to assume it is touched by international commerce.

- Entrepreneurs; owners of small to mid-size businesses.

- Financial expertise.

- Less traditional backgrounds in hi-tech, science, engineering, manufacturing, heavy industry.

- Strategic planning and the ability to translate and adapt ideas and methodologies of one industry to that of the board they are joining.

- Commitment to attend all board meetings and to being an active participant in decisions affecting the company.

When we know just what qualifications are being sought after, we go to the drawing board, querying our data base, to look for such candidates. CBP can run queries in almost 50 different ways; including by industry, by function, by geography, and/or by race. A list of sources is also generated. Any person or group who might know about a strong candidate matching the company's description is contacted. Industry groups, friends of Catalyst and Catalyst's Information Center are all good sources. In fact, this is a valuable way for Catalyst Corporate Board Placement to keep up its contacts. Once, when doing a search for a real estate investment trust, we contacted a friend of Catalyst at the National Women in Real Estate Organization. In that case, we were able to use some of their contacts and sources to add to our database.

After determining a number of potential candidates, CBP contacts these women before narrowing the list to six to ten candidates. We provide as many details as possible about the company involved in order to determine whether or not a potential candidate is interested in serving on the client's board and whether they have the time to serve before we give their names to the company. This up-front interaction with potential candidates is important because: 1) Companies often complain that they have worked with search firms who give them names to consider of women who are not available, i.e. those women who are the most qualified have often already been spoken for; 2) Women are extremely careful about choosing a board. They don't want to sit on too many boards, spreading themselves too thin. Many boards prefer the search to remain confidential until they have decided which candidates they want to pursue. We do, however, reveal the size of the company, the industry and a general location as well as frequency and times of board meetings. This cuts down on time and avoids dashed hopes, benefiting both the woman and the company should she not be interested.

CBP promises to deliver a slate of qualified women to the client company within two months of signing a contract. They then determine the pace of the search. Each is different and there is no usual time for closure. Some boards agree on what they are looking for and are ready to move immediately. Sometimes circumstances may alter the criteria and we may be asked to present a different slate. And, too, there are many factors such as mergers, changing CEOs or other particular problems that emerge during the process that can slow it down or place a search on hold.

As there is no set time from the day we are asked to find a woman for a board to the day she takes her seat at the table, there is no typical search. A "dream" search, however, is one that was recently completed for a Fortune 500 financial services corporation in the Midwest. Key players, the decision-makers, were accessible and responsive. The CEO himself called. He knew of Catalyst and appreciated our work. His board already had two women but they wanted another, maybe two, and hopefully the slate would include women of color. I flew out to meet with him and the chair of the nominating committee, first having lunch with the SVP of human resources which enabled me to get a flavor of the culture of the corporation. A slate of eight candidates was presented in six weeks, including three women of color. A diverse number of candidates is a mandate for CBP, whether or not it is specifically asked for.

In four weeks, the CEO called to inform me of his positive reaction to the slate which, he said, he would review with the board nominating committee the following month. Two days after that meeting he phoned to say that of the many good candidates they had picked two. Four months later these two women, one of whom is African-American, happily took their seats at the table.

It is yet another positive development in board search that more and more companies are moving beyond the "quota of one" and adding more than one woman to their board.

It is difficult for a woman to be the only voice. With two, women find it easier to express their opinions. Three or more women on a board they can really make an impact. Companies benefit from the pull multiple women directors bring to the boardroom and from the value of true diversification by adding women of color.

As seats open up, women are asking where they fit in. Are they a potential candidate? And, if not, how can they position themselves to serve on a corporate board? We give the following advice:

6.   What Women Can Do

- Obtain leadership experience. As mentioned, CEOs and nominating committees want directors with senior management credentials, especially profit and loss responsibility.

- Make a strategic plan for yourself that points toward line positions. Operating experience and financial knowledge are becoming key. It could mean making a lateral move. It may mean taking risks.

- Think globally. Any company can benefit from international experience.

- Entrepreneurs are "in". If you are running your own business, you are in a good position. Companies are looking for women with midsize company leadership where they are making all the profit and loss decisions.

- Be visible. Seek out committees or projects that will give you a chance to interact with top management. Get involved in professional organizations.

- Serve on not-for-profit boards, especially boards of hospitals or local chapters of national organizations. It could be a way of meeting those who are already on boards. And you get valuable lessons in board dynamics.

- Prepare a good resume specific to boards. Emphasize what boards are looking for; be clear about responsibilities and in describing your company; use dates for education and positions; list all not-for-profit boards and other organizations you belong to as well as awards and honors you may have received.

7.   A Changing Business Culture

The types of women that corporate boards are seeking continues to change. CBP is glad to note that we no longer gets calls for the "token" woman. Boards want women who will make significant contributions. There are women ready and able to fill the need. More will become available as pipelines open up for coveted positions in top management.

There is pressure on all fronts. The all white male board is no longer acceptable. Naming friends to the company board raises questions about how effectively a company will perform. New technology means expectations are immediate and that there is no longer time for complacency. Today's global economy has changed the face and tastes of the average consumer. Diversity is a major issue. To make the best business decisions, *everyone* must understand what the consumer needs and wants. What better way to do that, than by starting at the top?

Boards feel more and more of a need for accountability. Company shareholders know that adding women to a board helps the bottom line. Many board members do see the value, as do female employees in upper management and women's networks. Wives and daughters point out the inequities; so does the media. What's happening in the boardroom has become the topic of the popular press and not just the business journals.

Slowly, but surely. The more multiple women on boards the more women will be folded into the mix and fears and barriers will be gently beaten down. Women are now better prepared than ever before to effectively fill directorship positions as they open up. When boards become comfortable with women, more and more places will open up for women on those boards. Between the success of women at these new seats at the table and these external pressures, hopefully, the process will accelerate.

INDEX

Issues in Business Ethics

KLUWER ACADEMIC PUBLISHERS – DORDRECHT / BOSTON / LONDON